International Organization in Time

D1562269

International Organization in Time

Fragmentation and Reform

Tine Hanrieder

OXFORD
UNIVERSITY PRESS

OXFORD
UNIVERSITY PRESS

Great Clarendon Street, Oxford, OX2 6DP,
United Kingdom

Oxford University Press is a department of the University of Oxford.
It furthers the University's objective of excellence in research, scholarship,
and education by publishing worldwide. Oxford is a registered trade mark of
Oxford University Press in the UK and in certain other countries

© Tine Hanrieder 2015

The moral rights of the author have been asserted

First Edition published in 2015
Impression: 1

Published in the United States of America by Oxford University Press
198 Madison Avenue, New York, NY 10016, United States of America

British Library Cataloguing in Publication Data
Data available

Library of Congress Control Number: 2014957919

ISBN 978-0-19-870583-3

Printed and bound by
CPI Group (UK) Ltd, Croydon, CR0 4YY

Links to third party websites are provided by Oxford in good faith and
for information only. Oxford disclaims any responsibility for the materials
contained in any third party website referenced in this work.

For Rosina Grimm

Preface and Acknowledgments

In summer 2014, while I was completing the manuscript for this book, the West African Ebola outbreak turned into the most severe Ebola epidemic in human history. The spread of the virus had gotten out of control in Liberia, Guinea, and Sierra Leone, infecting and killing thousands of people, and leaving health and social infrastructures devastated. Critiques were voiced that the WHO had intervened far too late and missed the point when the catastrophe might still have been averted. The ensuing analyses of the outbreak painfully exposed the defects of global health governance in general, and of the World Health Organization (WHO) in particular.

Like many times before, the crisis struck the WHO in the midst of an ongoing organizational reform (this one launched and declared "historical" by Director-General Margaret Chan in 2011). And like in previous times, the WHO of 2014 was criticized for its internal fragmentation and for its unsustainable financing. Analysts bemoaned that the organization's heavy reliance on earmarked, voluntary contributions had hollowed out its core functions—including the domain of emergency preparedness that had most suffered from budget cuts in the wake of the global financial crisis. The internal fragmentation of the WHO was also blamed for having slowed down its reaction to Ebola. In particular, the regionalized structure of the WHO came under renewed attack, as the perception gained ground that the regional office for Africa was unduly politicized (see Sack et al. 2014).

This book goes back to the historical origins of these organizational problems, and provides an explanation as to why they have survived all WHO reforms. It investigates the peculiar mix of grand internationalist ideals and petty bureaucratic problems that have marked the WHO's history since 1946, showing that this is a history of organizational fragmentation. It started from the halfway integration of the Pan American Sanitary Bureau during the organization's founding moment, which made the WHO the most regionalized of all United Nations (UN) organizations. Later on, the grand reform designs of Primary Health Care in the 1970s and of One WHO in the late 1990s had to confront this legacy and well-nigh reinforced the fragmentation pathway—by granting more authorities to the regional offices, or by circumventing them through the creation of separate thematic programs. Hence,

I will argue in this book that WHO reforms have been consequential even when they did not attain their declared goal. They reinforced an organizational fragmentation process even where centralization was the aim of reform. This process is ongoing, as the WHO is torn between incantations of corporate agency and organizational power struggles.

This analysis of the WHO's "fragmentation trap" highlights the path dependent determinants of international organization (IO) design and reform. It contributes to an emerging debate on how history matters in the relatively young project of global governance, combining historical institutionalist concepts with organization theoretical tools. As the UN system grows older and increasingly complex, the organizational patterns reconstructed in this book should become increasingly relevant as well, both for individual IOs and for organizational complexes in world politics. Hence, looking beyond the WHO case, I will argue that the fragmentation trap not only explains the WHO's reform dilemmas, but that it sheds light on organizational dynamics that are at work throughout the UN system. The family of UN organizations is itself marked by complexity and overlaps, and we will see that IOs such as the United Nations Educational, Scientific and Cultural Organization are embarked on their own fragmentation pathways. As the shadow of history is growing longer by the day, historical dynamics will further gain in relevance for students and practitioners of global governance.

Many people and institutions have made this book possible. Most importantly, Bernhard Zangl has supported this research ever since it started as a dissertation project at the Bremen International Graduate School of Social Sciences (BIGSSS). I am deeply grateful for Bernhard's advice, his confidence, and engaging feedback. I completed most parts of the book as a member of his Global Governance and Public Policy research team at LMU Munich, accompanied by fantastic colleagues: Rainer Hülsse, Alex Spencer, and especially Andreas Kruck, whom I thank for his feedback on many ideas and chapter drafts, and for the WTO beer (and that it was only one). I also thank the participants of the Global Governance/IR research colloquium at LMU Munich (among others) Julia Hagn, Eva Herschinger, Michel-André Horelt, Johannes Jüde, Judith Renner, Berthold Rittberger, Frank Sauer, and Moritz Weiss. The final strides to the manuscript were made at the WZB Berlin Social Science Center, with valuable input from Benjamin Faude, and from Christian Kreuder-Sonnen, who provided important comments to many chapters since the Munich times.

Philipp Genschel supported the project as a co-supervisor, providing critical advice at critical junctures of the empirical research. Jelena von Achenbach and Monika Sonntag made presenting enjoyable, and Duncan Snidal and Klaus Dingwerth were both sharp and constructive examiners. The Bremen

International Graduate School of Social Sciences provided material and intellectual support, and Werner Dressel's wholehearted encouragement. A special thanks to Werner and Frank Strengel for participating in the defense committee, and to Sebastian Büttner who shared many eureka!s and setbacks. I also received important inputs from the joint BIGSSS/InIIS colloquium, (among others) Rainer Baumann, Heike Brabant, Nicole Deitelhoff, Klaus Dingwerth, Christoph Humrich, Anja Jakobi, Peter Mayer, Luicy Pedroza, Christian Reisinger, Andrea Schapper, Dieter Senghaas, and Silke Weinlich. For their comments at conferences and workshops, I thank in particular Tim Büthe, Dirk de Bièvre, Andreas Dür, Orfeo Fioretos, Thomas Gehring, Alex Grigorescu, Stefano Guzzini, Stephanie Hofmann, Anne Holthoefer, Anna Holzscheiter, Bob Reinalda, Thomas Rixen, Theresa Squatrito, Matthias Staisch, Jonas Tallberg, Alex Thompson, Lora Viola, Michael Zürn, and the TKI colloquium at the WZB that has now become Global Governance (GG). And Heiko Baumgärtner, whom I can no longer thank for his rigor and his generosity.

For research funding, I thank BIGSSS, the German Academic Exchange Service (DAAD) and Mentoring@LMU*excellent*, whose travel grants supported several research stays at the WHO headquarters in Geneva between 2009 and 2010. Above all, I heartily thank the many current and former WHO staff members who were willing to share their views with an outsider from the academy, Norbert Dreesch who established initial contacts, and Thomas Allen and Reynald Erard who were most helpful in navigating me through the WHO Records and Archives. Yves Beigbeder and Socrates Litsios took the time to discuss the WHO's history, and Socco generously shared his personal library with me. Our conversations in and around Baulmes, and his and Susan's humor and hospitality were always highlights of my trips to Geneva.

Some of the arguments presented in Chapters 2 to 5 have been published in the article "The Path Dependent Design of International Organizations: Federalism in the World Health Organization" in the *European Journal of International Relations* (published online on May 30, 2014). I thank SAGE publishers for the reprint permission. Finally, I thank Luisa Braig, Pavel Satra, Jan Tiedemann, and Susanne Wildgruber for their research assistance, and Dominic Byatt and Olivia Wells from Oxford University Press for their great support.

It goes without saying that the author bears responsibility for all errors and for the narrative that is offered in this book. As a narrative about path dependence and the limits to choice, it may seem to confer a fatalistic view of what reforms can and do achieve in international organizations. Yet, if it is in this sense an instance of "tragic" historiography, we can conclude with the historical theorist Hayden White that ultimately, the book has a pragmatic intent. As White has pointed out, human defeat against historical forces is only one aspect of tragedies. The flipside is that unveiling these forces has an empowering effect. For at the end, "[t]here has been a gain in consciousness for the spectators of the contest" (White 1975a, p. 8). This is all the more important when the "contest" described—IO reform in the shadow of path dependence—is still ongoing.

Tine Hanrieder
Berlin, January 2015

Contents

List of Figures and Tables

Figures

Tables

List of Abbreviations

AFRO	African Regional Office (WHO)
AMRO	American Regional Office (WHO)
CAME	Conference of Allied Ministers in Education
CMC	Christian Medical Commission (World Council of Churches)
DALY	disability-adjusted life-year
DDT	dichlorodiphenyltrichloroethane
DG	director-general (WHO)
EB	Executive Board (WHO)
ECJ	European Court of Justice
EMRO	Eastern Mediterranean Regional Office (WHO)
EU	European Union
EURO	European Regional Office (WHO)
FAO	Food and Agriculture Organization (UN)
FCTC	Framework Convention on Tobacco Control (WHO)
GAVI	Global Alliance for Vaccines and Immunization/GAVI Alliance
GHG	global health governance
HFA	Health for All
HI	historical institutionalism
HIV/AIDS	Human Immunodeficiency Virus/Acquired Immunodeficiency Syndrome
IHC	International Health Conference
IHR	International Health Regulations (WHO)
ILC	International Labour Conference (ILO)
ILO	International Labour Organization (UN)
IO	international organization (referring only to inter-governmental organizations)
ITU	International Telecommunication Union (UN)
JIU	Joint Inspection Unit (UN)
LNHO	League of Nations Health Organization
MSU	management support unit (WHO)

NATO	North Atlantic Treaty Organization
NGO	non-governmental organization
NIEO	New International Economic Order
NPM	new public management
NWICO	New World Information and Communication Order (UNESCO)
OAS	Organization of American States
OECD	Organization for Economic Cooperation and Development
OIHP	Office International d'Hygiène Publique
PA	principal-agent (approach)
PAHO	Pan American Health Organization
PASB	Pan American Sanitary Bureau
PASO	Pan American Sanitary Organization
PHC	Primary Health Care
RBM	Roll Back Malaria partnership
SARS	Severe Acute Respiratory Syndrome
SEARO	South-East Asian Regional Office (WHO)
SPHC	Selective Primary Health Care
TPC	Technical Preparatory Committee (for the IHC)
UK	United Kingdom (of Great Britain and Northern Ireland)
UN	United Nations
UNAIDS	Joint United Nations Programme on HIV/AIDS
UNCTAD	United Nations Conference on Trade and Development
UNDP	United Nations Development Programme
UNFPA	United Nations Population Fund
UNHCR	United Nations High Commissioner for Refugees
UNICEF	United Nations Children's Fund
UNIDO	United Nations Industrial Development Organization
UNRRA	United Nations Relief and Rehabilitation Organization
UNSC	United Nations Security Council
US	United States (of America)
USSR	Union of Soviet Socialist Republics
WHA	World Health Assembly (WHO)
WHO	World Health Organization
WHOIC	Interim Commission of the World Health Organization
WPRO	Western Pacific Regional Office (WHO)

1

Reforming International Organizations in the Shadow of Fragmentation

A recently appointed program director at the World Health Organization (WHO) described his initiation to the new job as a curious encounter. Working for the WHO meant, in his words, learning to live with "two elephants in the room." One was the WHO's regionalization and the constant bargaining with regional offices over program formulation and budgeting. The other one was the dependence on extra-budgetary funds, which required program directors to constantly raise funds for their projects and staff.[1] The director seemed puzzled that these obstacles were hardly ever problematized in talks among colleagues, but that everybody appeared to be used to them—and found their way around them in daily business. Though he would have preferred to get them out of the room—and regional directors and private funders would surely have disagreed—the new director had no choice but to follow his colleagues' example.

The director's bewilderment reflects an everyday experience in modern organizations, including international organizations (IOs):[2] Organizational leaders are confronted with intricate and hard-to-change institutional structures when initiating change. Most institutional preconditions go unnoticed and are hardly questioned, while others become central issues in, and targets of, organizational reform. When deliberate organizational change is attempted, reformers have to factor in locked-in constraints and vested interests, and thus tailor reform goals to attainable reform outcomes. They have to accommodate well-positioned players and may in fact have to make further concessions in order to make the reform happen at all. They operate against the backdrop of, and are induced to reinforce, path dependent IO trajectories. Yet at the same

---

[1] Source: Author's interview with WHO officer on September 10, 2010. On methods and data see Section 1.4.

[2] In this book, the term "international organization (IO)" refers only to inter-governmental and not to non-governmental organizations.

time, they have to demonstrate to outside supporters that intentional change and corporate reform is possible, in a world where the capacity to reform is a main currency of organizational legitimacy, and thus central to the process of international organization. Hence, the quest for organizational reform cannot be given up, even if its prospects are closely circumscribed.

The present book is about the implications of this common yet neglected insight: that organizational change never occurs on a clean slate, but feeds into preexisting organizational structures. I focus on one particular organizational pattern that the WHO exemplifies, that is fragmentation. Fragmentation refers to an organizational *outcome* that is marked by the coexistence of powerful subunits—thematic departments or territorial offices that have their say in reform endeavors, and that defend their position with the help of local allies who have a vested interest in these subunits. At the same time, fragmentation becomes a self-reinforcing *process* when subunit support is crucial for the reform but costly for the reformers. Where subunits can formally or informally veto a reform, leaders are induced to buy their support with further political concessions, and thus *deepen* the IO's fragmentation. Where such deals are not feasible, reformers can still opt for creating new agents of IO change and *widen* the IO's fragmentation to additional units with independent powers. In other words: Fragmentation generates a path dependent organizational dynamic whereby it is locked in and reinforced over rounds of reform.

This fragmentation trap is extreme in the WHO with its "two elephants." The WHO is territorially fragmented due to the considerable autonomy of its six regional directors, and it is thematically fragmented due to the exceptional status of WHO special programs that are funded through extra-budgetary contributions. The organizational processes whereby this fragmentation has been reinforced over time are at the center of this study (see Chapters 3–5). Yet local strongholds can be found in many IOs. The World Bank operates a growing number of semi-autonomous "trust funds" (Distler 2012), the European Union operates a host of quasi-independent regulatory agencies (Rittberger and Wonka 2011), and in the United Nations Educational, Cultural and Scientific Organization (UNESCO) organizational activities are monopolized by the theme-specific "sectors." This last example of a sector-driven fragmentation trap will be presented in the final empirical chapter on decentralization dynamics in the UN system (see Chapter 6).

An analysis of path dependent IO fragmentation draws attention to the ways in which IOs generate vested interests over time. It highlights how attempts at engineering change are confronted with local coalitions, coalitions which form around historical bargains in IOs and make these bargains persist. It sheds light on the historical preconditions of organizational reform, and contributes to understanding the long-term outcomes of reform initiatives in IOs. This book thereby develops a distributional and historical perspective on IO change, short, power-driven path dependence (PDPD). PDPD combines insights from historical institutionalism (HI) in political science and resource dependence theory in organization theory to analyze institutional dynamics of IO design and change. PDPD stresses that early winners are favored in these struggles because institutions lock in and reinforce historical advantages. Unlike efficiency-based explanations of "rational design," PDPD highlights that rational design and adaptation can be prevented by local coalitions that are privileged by a given pathway. Organizational change, though triggered by deliberate attempts at reform, is shaped by endogenous organizational dynamics. Unlike socialization-based accounts of IO "cultures" however, PDPD stresses the conflicts and local strategies that drive IO change. IO change is a conflictual process, wherein reform coalitions and status quo coalitions always bargain about policy and organizational changes at the same time. They remake IO policies within institutional constraints, but in parallel seek to manipulate these constraints for future rounds of organizational change. Those who can reap increasing returns from their historical advantages ensure that IO change is path dependent.[3]

This work sheds new light on the dilemmas faced by the reformers of the WHO and the UN system more generally, and it contributes to ongoing attempts to grasp the temporal dynamics of international organization (see Fioretos 2011). At a time when many IOs are older than fifty and therefore are unlikely to be abandoned (see Ingram and Torfason 2010, p. 598), choices about IO creation and change are made in a deeply institutionalized context (Jupille et al. 2013). States and IO leaders have multiple incentives to engage in local deals rather than all-out reform, and thus are complicit in the process whereby IOs take on a life of their own. The model of the fragmentation trap explains this dilemma and deepens our understanding of the historicity of international organization, and offers a dynamic account of how structural determinants and reform choices interact over time.

In the remainder of this chapter, I introduce the book's main empirical and theoretical building blocks. First, I lay out the core puzzle that informs this study, namely the WHO's dual fragmentation pathway, which has been the target of repeated yet futile reforms (see Section 1.1). Next, I present the book's central argument, which is that this development is based on a self-reinforcing fragmentation trap that can be triggered in other IOs as well (see Section 1.2). I then discuss how this argument contributes to and differs from established explanations of IO inertia (see Section 1.3). Finally, I present the book's case design and data and give an outline of the chapters following (see Section 1.4).

---

[3] On the rational design of IOs see Koremenos et al. (2001a), on bureaucratic culture see Barnett and Finnemore (2004). See the discussion of contemporary IO research in Section 1.3.

1.1 The WHO's Fragmentation

For the WHO, the current decade has begun as yet another period of crisis and reform. In a speech given to the 2011 World Health Assembly (WHA, or Assembly),[4] Director-General (DG) Margaret Chan announced a "time of unprecedented reforms at WHO" (WHO 2011a). The DG warned the state delegates that "we are not functioning at the level of top performance that is increasingly needed" and that "we need to undergo some far-reaching reforms" at the "administrative, budgetary and programmatic levels" (WHO 2011c, p. 6). Her announcement followed a year-long consultation with member states and a series of reports which described the WHO as over-extended, underfunded, and incapable of strategic action (Sridhar et al. 2012). Publications released from the WHO's Geneva headquarters empha-sized that the organization could not carry out the policies determined by the WHA because of its dependence on extra-budgetary funds, funds that came in on an erratic basis and were not aligned with the program budget (WHO 2010, p. 6, 2011c, p. 6). Outside observers reiterated the criticism of organizational dysfunction (e.g. Hawkes 2011; Horton 2006; People's Health Movement et al. 2008, p. 228), and the WHO was asked, not for the first time in its history, to "change or die" (Chow 2010; Smith 1995).

Given the WHO's familiarity with recurrent organizational crises (Hawkes 2011), it is unlikely that the UN's specialized agency for health is about to "die." The WHO is still the focal player in international health work and enjoys high esteem for its normative, informational, and technical work. The organization does face more competition from other international and transnational organizations that have entered the field of global health work—ranging from IOs such as the World Bank and the United Nations Children's Fund (UNICEF) to civil society organizations such as Médecins Sans Frontières (MSF) and private philanthropists such as the Bill and Melinda Gates Foundation (Hanrieder forthcoming 2015)—yet it still has a preeminent role as a global standard setter and central advisor to national ministries of health. With more than 7,000 staff members working in its Geneva headquar-ters, its regional, and its country offices, the WHO represents one of the biggest bureaucracies in the UN system.[5] Its technical standards and guide-lines inform public health practices, its technical advice shapes national policy choices, and its recommendations direct global responses to contagious

---

[4] The World Health Assembly (WHA) is the WHO's supreme governing body and meets once per year, usually in May, at the Palais des Nations in Geneva. It is composed of all WHO member states that enjoy formally equal status and voting rights, exerting final authority over the WHO's program and budget, resolutions, and recommendations, and the appointment of the DG (see Section 3.1).

[5] See <http://www.who.int/about/structure/en/> (accessed June 25, 2014).

outbreaks.[6] Its global outbreak alert and response system has especially gained in prominence in recent years (Hanrieder and Kreuder-Sonnen 2014), and the steady influx of extra-budgetary funds also testifies to its continued relevance for state and non-state donors. As activists around the world mobilize for their vision of global health, the WHO continues to be the central rallying point for movements such as the People's Health Movement and initiatives such as WHO Watch, which again underline the organization's authority in contemporary global health governance.[7]

Nevertheless, "change" only goes so far in the WHO. By 2014, Chan's reform initiative had brought varied managerial and procedural changes such as new output indicators, streamlined agendas for the governing bodies, an intensified engagement with non-state actors, and trainings for WHO staff on issues ranging from emergency communication to the use of Twitter (WHO 2014a). To convince skeptics of the value of WHO reform, these changes were tracked in a "Change@WHO" newsletter, and progress was closely monitored by evaluators giving advice on the next reform steps.[8] Yet, among the aspects that the reform has not altered are the two "elephants" mentioned at the beginning of this chapter: the quasi autonomy of the regions (Sridhar and Gostin 2011, pp. E1–E2), and a budgetary imbalance that undermines the implementation of its program (Shashikant 2011; WHO 2010).

These two features are at the core of an organizational design that observers describe as "fragmentation": The WHO is today marked by multiple and overlapping power centers, which escape centralized governance and thereby make the WHO "unfaithful" to its member states, program, and mandate (Graham 2014). First, the WHO has been faced with recurrent criticisms of its regional offices, whose quasi autonomy is blamed for jeopardizing policy coherence and implementation in this IO (Godlee 1994a; see Levine 2006, p. 1017). Second, the rise of semi-autonomous special programs in the WHO with their tendency to focus on isolated and short term goals is criticized as pathological and ineffective (Godlee 1995c). Still, despite repeated efforts at (re-)centralizing the organization, the WHO has grown more and not less fragmented along both these lines.

Hence, the WHO's fragmentation is both an organizational *outcome* and an organizational *process*. As an outcome, fragmentation refers to the extent of autonomy held by the organizations' subunits, which rest on their delegated policy discretion and control of budget and personnel decisions, and on their exclusive ties to external supporters, which allows them to control the access

---

[6] For an introduction to the WHO's mandate, activities, and structure see Lee (2009).

[7] See <http://www.ghwatch.org/who-watch> (accessed June 25, 2014).

[8] See <http://www.who.int/about/who_reform/en/> (accessed June 26, 2014). On the opposition raised against particular reform proposals such as stakeholder assembly called the WHO Forum see Gopakumar and Wanis (2011); Shashikant (2011).

to vital organizational resources and provides them with their own external support base. Fragmentation as an *outcome* is the opposite of hierarchy. As a *process*, fragmentation is the opposite of centralization and refers to the growing authority of subunits, which weaken the directorate's ability to steer the IO and thus implement corporate policies (see Section 2.3). To different extents and in different varieties, fragmentation can be observed in many national and international organizations, and full hierarchy and centralization will hardly ever be met. In the WHO, however, fragmentation is a particularly extreme outcome of two coherent fragmentation processes.

Regionalization Against all Obstacles

The WHO's regionalization is unique in the UN system. While other UN entities also entertain regional offices, only in the WHO can the regional organizations determine their leaders and program budget practically without headquarter oversight. Its six regional organizations in the Eastern Mediterranean, the Western Pacific, the Southeast Asian, the European, the African, and the American regions are governed by self-organized member state assemblies, and administered by the regional offices.[9] The offices are headed by regional directors who are elected by the regional member state assemblies, the so-called regional committees. Due to this system of regional self-governance, the regional directors are on a par with the DG, a source of subunit authority not found in other UN organizations.[10] Hence, although the WHO's policies are formally determined by the Assembly and directed from the headquarters in Geneva, their implementation depends on the consent and collaboration of the regional offices, through which all resources and communication have to pass (Jacobson 1973, p. 201).

The extent to which the WHO is regionalized has increased over the years, even though it goes beyond, if not violates, constitutional provisions.[11] According to the WHO constitution, the regional subunits shall be "integral parts" of the organization, which implement corporate policies at the regional level and formulate policies for "exclusively regional" concerns (Arts. 45 and 50). Yet, over time, ever more administrative authorities over staffing, program formulation,

[9] The delineation and headquarters of the six regional organizations are listed in Appendix 2. Note that different from the WHO regional committees (the regional member state assemblies), the regional conferences of other IOs such as the International Labour Organization (ILO) and the UN Food and Agriculture Organization (FAO) are not self-organized but convened and scheduled by the central governing bodies. See for the ILO <http://www.ilo.org/public/english/bureau/leg/publ/reg/noteintro.htm> and for the FAO <http://www.fao.org/unfao/govbodies/gsbhome/gsb-regconf/en> (both accessed January 4, 2012).
[10] Only the International Telecommunications Union (ITU) has elective managerial positions besides the DG (Daes and Daoudy 1993, p. 24).
[11] The WHO constitution (WHO 2006) was signed in 1946 and entered into force in 1948 (see Chapter 3).

and budgeting have been delegated to the regional offices so that they have become close to autonomous in operational terms (Beigbeder 1997, pp. 56–60; Henderson 2009, pp. 85–6). In the words of former DG Halfdan Mahler, the devolution of managerial capacities to the regional level has pushed regionalization to "the limits of what was constitutionally possible" (Daes and Daoudy 1993, p. 5). Furthermore, the autonomous governance of the regions at least stretches the constitution. Formally, the regional directors shall be appointed by the Executive Board—the WHO's executive council which meets twice per year—"in agreement with" the regional committees (Art. 52). De facto, however, the Board has no say in the selection of the regional directors, although this (un-)constitutional practice has been challenged more than once in the WHO's history (Burci and Vignes 2004, p. 57).

Indeed, the WHO's regionalization has survived a series of centralization initiatives. As depicted in Figure 1.1, attempts to curb the regions' autonomy (here: moves to the left) have consistently failed, while each transfer of further authorities to the regions (here: moves to the right) has dependably stuck with organizational structures. Figure 1.1 sketches that the initial institutionalization of the regional offices was already a further regionalization step when measured against the constitutional baseline. Subsequent moves to further strengthen the regional offices have turned out to be very sustainable, especially when considering the recurrent centralization attempts. Beginning as early

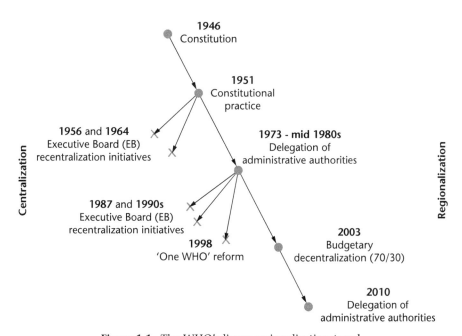

Figure 1.1. The WHO's linear regionalization trend.

as in the 1950s, the Executive Board has repeatedly bargained over proposals to enhance centralized control over the regional offices. Yet none of these initiatives, even those submitted by powerful members such as the United States (US), ever succeeded (see Chapters 3 and 4). Likewise, the "One WHO" reform launched by DG Gro Harlem Brundtland in 1998 failed in its attempt to increase centralized authority over regional programming and budgeting (see Chapter 5).

One may suggest that this unique—and robust—regionalization trajectory is the reflection of uniquely federal tasks that the WHO has to fulfill. Indeed, few would question that the WHO must entertain some field presence to be able to provide technical advice to health ministries and respond to regional and national diversity regarding heath systems and conditions. However, the record of external evaluations and internal self-assessments of the WHO's technical cooperation work here paints a different picture. Regionalization is, rather, referred to as one of the WHO's main structural weaknesses and an impediment to field level effectiveness (Godlee 1994a; Graham 2014; Robbins 1999). For example, the UN Joint Inspection Unit came to the conclusion that the WHO was in a state of "fragmentation verging on disintegration" that jeopardized the WHO's health development work (Daes and Daoudy 1993, p. 34). Another study of the WHO's field work commissioned by the Danish Ministry of Foreign Affairs came to similar assessments and admonished that regional politics rather than country needs determined resource allocation, and that the resources were absorbed by the regional offices instead of channeled to the country level. The report called for a "basic review and reorganization of the function and staffing of WHO's regional offices" (Danida 1991, p. iv). But also internal reports such as the evaluation of the Roll Back Malaria (RBM) partnership made regionalization responsible for RBM's failure in one of the WHO's core domains of work, the development of global policy standards (Roll Back Malaria and World Health Organization 2002, p. 59).

Given the record of centralization attempts and the longstanding criticism of regionalization in the WHO, a purely functional explanation of this federal design seems inadequate. From a "rational design" point of view, the WHO's regionalization should reflect the member states' joint goals, and its adaptation over time should correct for perceived dysfunctions and pathologies rather than exacerbate them (Koremenos et al. 2001a). Likewise, the WHO's second dimension of fragmentation, the rise of special programs, defies simple functional explanations.

The Budgetary Shift and the Rise of Special Programs

The second fragmenting trend in the WHO is the organization's increasing reliance on voluntary, so-called "extra-budgetary" donations. These

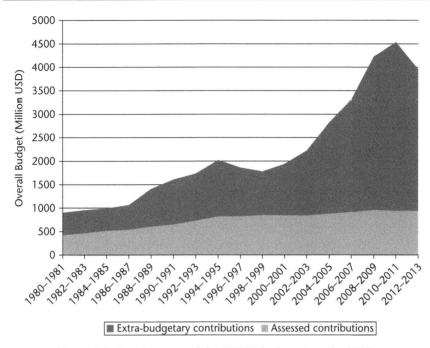

Figure 1.2. Development of the WHO's budget since the 1980s.

contributions supplement the declining share of the member states' regular assessed contributions to the WHO budget, which have not been raised since the 1980s. Since the early 1990s, assessed contributions have not even been adapted to inflation, which means that they are factually shrinking (Lee 2009, p. 39). By contrast, the share of extra-budgetary funds has grown almost linearly, from 25 percent in 1971 (Walt 1993) to 80 percent in 2010 (WHO 2010, p. 2). These funds are provided by member states, other UN organizations, companies, and foundations, with member states paying the largest part.[12]

The surge in voluntary contributions since the 1980s is summarized in Figure 1.2. This trend is, on the one hand, a sign of continued support for the WHO, whose total program budget has grown considerably since the 1980s. On the other hand, the shift to extra-budgetary funding impairs the coherence and impact of the WHO's work. Voluntary donations are granted for short-term periods of usually one to two years and paid much more erratically than assessed contributions. This makes them an uncertain basis

---

[12] In the 2012–13 budgetary biennium, member states contributed 53 percent of the WHO's extra-budgetary income, followed by the UN and other international organizations (22 percent), foundations (19 percent), non-governmental and other institutions (5 percent), and finally the private sector (1 percent), see WHO (2014b, p. 6).

for budgeting and also for staffing, with employees increasingly sitting on short-term contracts (Lee 2009, p. 106).[13] But most importantly, extra-budgetary contributions are mostly conditional, i.e. "earmarked" for specific projects and usages.[14] Donors decide which policy or program to support with their contribution, and often also specify the specific component of a program they are willing to pay for, such as vaccines for particular parts of the population in specified areas, bed nets to protect against malaria mosquitoes, or specific research endeavors. These conditions are laid down in specific donor agreements that determine the targets of individual programs that are subject to distinct, often public-private, governance schemes.

Hence, behind the trend toward voluntary financing stands the rise of "special programs" in the WHO: departments and projects that are set up for specific and circumscribed goals and partially exempted from the WHO's administrative rules due to their separate governance structures and reporting lines.[15] While from one perspective these special terms increase the programs' dependence on external donors, from the other they make them less dependent on the WHO directorate and allow successful fundraisers to rebut attempts at centralized steering (see Chapter 5).

This gradual autonomization of thematic subunits in the WHO again defies simple functional explanations. Certainly, the internal competition that voluntary funding has brought to the organization could be viewed as an efficient design that cuts waste and selects for the best programs (see Frey 2008; Hawkins et al. 2006b, p. 30). The competition for donor funds—both within the WHO but also between the WHO and other international health agencies—could therefore bear the advantage of allocating notoriously scarce resources to where they are best used (see also Koremenos et al. 2001b, p. 1077). However, there exists neither a shared benchmark for the value of WHO projects nor a market mechanism that would select for the "best activities." Instead, two recurrent criticisms of the turn to special programs question the functionality of this fragmented design. First, despite all pledges to the contrary, the competition for donor money has not led the WHO to focus on its "comparative advantage" (Lerer and Matzopoulos 2001, p. 415)—that is, normative and emergency response functions rather than technical cooperation activities that are also performed by more operational IOs such as UNICEF (Lee 2009,

---

[13] On recent steps toward making the payment of voluntary contributions more predictable via an institutionalized WHO Financing Dialogue, see PricewaterhouseCoopers SA (2014).

[14] The WHO estimated in 2009 that less than 10 percent of its extra-budgetary funds were fully (1 percent) or highly (5–6 percent) "flexible," that is, not earmarked for specific topics, programs or even concrete activities (WHO 2009, p. 14).

[15] The terminology of WHO "special programs" is historically tied to a range of programs financed by voluntary donations that the organization began to set up during the 1980s and 1990s (Godlee 1995c). I use the term in a more generic sense, referring to all WHO programs and partnerships that are based on separate governance schemes.

pp. 18–21; WHO 2010, pp. 1–2). Yet, pleas to concentrate the WHO's resources have not been consequential, and the IO remains stuck in its situation of "underfunded 'mission creep'" (Levine 2006, p. 1015; see Gopakumar and Wanis 2011; WHO 2011f). Second, the effectiveness of special programs is contested. Extra-budgetary funds are not only unsustainable for the WHO that cannot cover core running costs due to the insufficient overhead charge of about 13 percent.[16] Special programs are also criticized because they follow short-term donor preferences and bias resources toward popular and visible topics. Long-term strategies for the strengthening of health systems and disease prevention are therefore neglected (Bull and McNeill 2007, pp. 65–92; Godlee 1995c; Levine 2006, p. 1015; Vaughan et al. 1996; Walt 1993), and agreed-upon priorities of the WHO often cannot be implemented due to a lack of funds (WHO 2009, pp. 11–15). Yet, although even donors point to the problems raised by the WHO's "fragmented funding" (HM Government 2009, p. 6), a pooling of budgetary authority remains out of sight.

As the subsequent chapters will show in more detail, the dysfunctional implications of the WHO's dual fragmentation have been targeted in many reforms. The futility of these efforts suggests that there are deeper reform obstacles that obviate deliberate change in the WHO. This is not to deny that it is intentional actors—donor and recipient states, private donors, DGs, and subunit directors—which are responsible for the WHO's development. Yet the aggregate outcome of their efforts is path dependent rather than anybody's choice.

1.2 The Argument: Path Dependent IO Fragmentation

This book analyzes how historical constraints and local strategies interact in producing IO fragmentation. I reconstruct the ongoing empowerment of the WHO's regional and thematic subunits as a path dependent fragmentation process. The WHO's development is path dependent because it locks in and reinforces a historical design that was institutionalized during the organization's founding moment between 1946 and 1951. This initial design, in turn, was contingent on a historical constellation where a preexisting Pan American Sanitary Bureau was protected by a coalition of Latin American states that forced an unexpectedly regionalized structure on the WHO. The winners of this initial outcome, mostly coalitions between developing states and regional offices, henceforth defeated all recentralization attempts. Reform coalitions,

---

[16] For example in 2006, the imbalance between project money and administrative resources led donors to exceptionally allow the WHO to reallocate donations to core running costs. This remained, however, a one-time ad hoc measure (Lee 2009, p. 106).

therefore, had to work with or around the regional offices—meaning that they either granted further authority to the regions (and thereby deepened the WHO's fragmentation), or created new centers of authority such as the semi-autonomous special programs (and thereby widened the WHO's fragmentation). Hence, WHO reform takes place in the shadow of a longstanding fragmentation trap that reformers must take into account when seeking to enact policy or polity changes, and that they are induced to reinforce in their attempt to mobilize for WHO reform.

This argument combines a bureaucratic politics view of international organizations with a historical institutionalist (HI) view of institutional change. First, the *bureaucratic politics* approach emphasizes internal conflicts as determinants of IO change. I here borrow insights from resource dependence theory and its coalitional view of organizations (Pfeffer and Salancik 2003) and from sociological organization theories that focus on the strategic and distributional dynamics inherent in organizational change (Friedberg 1997; see also Michels 1989; Selznick 1966). The bureaucratic politics perspective highlights that IO change is a conflictual process in which the different coalitions draw on their local organizational resources to influence reform outcomes at two levels: the level of policy and the level of polity outcomes. As deals about policy change are deeply intertwined with the renegotiation of organizational structures and therefore power, IO reform is inherently transformative. Second, the notion of *path dependent* IO change borrows from historical institutionalism, which is an established research tradition in domestic and comparative politics,[17] but also attracts increasing attention from students of international institutions (Chwieroth 2014; Dannreuther 2011; Farrell and Newman 2010; Fioretos 2011; Hanrieder 2014a). Drawing in particular on the works of Paul Pierson (2004) and Kathleen Thelen and colleagues (Mahoney and Thelen 2010b; Streeck and Thelen 2005b), I reconstruct how actors draw on their prior institutional position in the process of reform. This reconstruction emphasizes the sequential dynamics and endogenous mechanisms that govern change in international organizations. The PDPD approach thus accounts for the endogenous dynamics which induce IO reformers to reinforce fragmentation over time.

The Fragmentation Trap

I argue in this book that fragmentation is an "absorbing state" in international organizations (see Pierson 2004, pp. 92–5), because the authorities granted to IO subunits are easier to reinforce than to reverse. This argument is based on

---

[17] For reviews of the historical institutionalist research tradition see Pierson and Skocpol (2002) and Thelen (1999).

three main propositions. First, fragmentation is *locked-in* as soon as it generates vested interests by member states that can reap local gains from coalitions with these units. States will therefore protect their favorite units and block centralizing moves undertaken by reform coalitions. Fragmentation, thus, entails a proliferation of veto positions and the concomitant joint action hurdles with regard to centralizing reforms. In the WHO case, it was mostly developing states that benefited from the regional offices' lobbying for more development assistance, and therefore strengthened the regions at the expense of the WHO headquarters (see Chapter 3). In other organizations such as UNESCO, individual states ally with those *IO sectors* that represent and protect their national policy preferences, and strengthen them through continued engagement (see Chapter 6).

Second, however, fragmentation, like any organizational outcome, is not static. Organizations constantly change as they are reproduced in the face of changing circumstances. To demonstrate their agency and legitimize their continued existence, IOs recurrently undertake *reforms,* that is, attempts at deliberate change to reflect new demands and the changing interests of their member states. Reforms are usually initiated by (incoming) DGs who, supported by a reform coalition of like-minded states, seek to enact new policies and organizational designs to demonstrate their IO's continued relevance. Along this reform trajectory, further fragmenting moves are likely to take place. The reformers of fragmented IOs need to mobilize those subunits on whose collaboration and implementation the reform hinges. To win subunit support, reformers can opt for delegating further authorities to them in exchange for policy support, and thereby *deepen* fragmentation. This internal deal of "buying" subunit support for reform has been observed for federal systems such as the Federal Republic of Germany (Scharpf 1988). In the WHO, a similar deal accompanied its first major reform that was launched in the 1970s to bring "Primary Health Care" (PHC) to the WHO and its member states, in particular developing countries. To mobilize the regional directors whose support was critical for enacting the reform at the country level, DG Halfdan Mahler endowed them with additional managerial authorities and thus deepened the WHO's regionalization. Even as the reform was not implemented and turned out to be a failure, the new authorities would remain with the regional offices and resist all subsequent recentralization attempts (see Chapter 4). A comparable dynamic of deepening fragmentation reinforced the UNESCO's thematic sectors, which were strengthened in the process of territorial decentralization, extending their power to sector-specific field offices (see Chapter 6).

Third, reformers can also seek to avoid this internal deal and still enact change in the IO, by circumventing internal blockades. In situations of internal deadlock and due to recalcitrant subunits, the "layering" of new subunits on the IO is a viable reform strategy. It allows reformers to bypass established subunits, but at the price of delegating power to additional organizational layers which make the IO more fragmented. The strategy of bypassing subunits with new layers thus amounts to *widening* fragmentation in IOs and the mounting of further obstacles to future reform. The WHO's special programs exemplify such organizational add-ons that enable policy change but undermine coherence (see Chapter 5). Likewise, UNESCO's attempts to overcome internal blockades with the help of additional "inter-sectoral" programs has added to, rather than diminished, its fragmentation along thematic sectors (see Chapter 6).

The lock-in and reinforcement mechanisms of the fragmentation trap will thus be illustrated in depth for the WHO case, and its wider validity is buttressed by the ensuing comparison between the International Labour Organization (ILO) and UNESCO. These cases buttress the claim that the fragmentation trap can be triggered via different IO units—and that it is far easier to reinforce than to escape or reverse the fragmentation pathway.

Structural Determination, not Determinism

Path dependent fragmentation is a long-term process that is marked by "structural determination" rather than one-shot causation (Pierson 2004, p. 93). The claim is that the overall tendency of fragmented IOs is to become more fragmented over time. The fragmentation trap does not plight to explain the timing and sequence of individual fragmenting moves. These single transformations hinge on a host of contextual factors such as the type of reform pressure that an IO faces and the interest and power constellations between reform and status quo coalitions. Depending on this constellation, reforms can be more or less fragmenting, and whether they involve the deepening or widening dynamic is not pre-determined (cf. Chapter 2). Yet once a move toward further fragmentation is made, it is likely to stick.

This is not to say that fragmentation is entirely irreversible. Deterministic processes do not exist in social reality, and any seeming "end of history" is also the beginning of a new one (Fukuyama 1992). The fragmentation trap rather suggests that reversing this process is extremely costly, and that individual bureaucrats and states have multiple opportunities to come to terms with this pathway without reversing it. Certainly, dissatisfied states can always choose exit over loyalty and turn to, or create, new institutions. Yet this requires bigger investments than muddling through with local solutions in an already focal IO (see also Jupille et al. 2013). Likewise, centralization proponents can seek to forge big enough reform coalitions to reverse the fragmentation pathway, relying on credible threats of exit and/or considerable side payments to status quo actors. For example, in the WHO case the biggest donor state, the US, has openly attempted to strengthen the DG vis-à-vis the regional directors, but it gave up rather quickly in the face of resistance at the Executive Board (see Chapter 4). A more determined and concerted centralization effort might well have exposed that the WHO's fragmentation pathway is not an iron law (see Chapter 4). The concluding chapter reconsiders the question of how robust the fragmentation trap is in the IO world and discusses the complex developments that can arise from this seemingly linear trajectory (see Chapter 7).

1.3 Conflict and Change in International Organizations

The argument of path dependent fragmentation contributes to two ongoing debates about institutional change: The "rationalist-constructivist" debate on IO inertia in International Relations (IR), and the "punctuated versus gradual change" debate in the HI literature.

Socialization and Choice in IO Theory

IR theorizing on IO inertia and change is commonly framed as a debate between rational choice and sociological institutionalism (see Fioretos 2011; see also Nielson et al. 2006). In this debate, IO inertia has mostly been discussed as a rationality problem. Constructivist IO theorists here argue that the persistence of IOs is a result of the socializing force of organizational cultures. In this vein, Michael Barnett and Martha Finnemore contend that IOs perpetuate themselves because bureaucrats are "disposed" to engage in rule-driven behavior, which makes them only partially responsive to demands for change. Therefore, the most significant change dynamic in IOs is their tendency to expand and to do more of the same, in that they perceive and shape the world so as to make it amenable to bureaucratic intervention (Barnett and Finnemore 2004). As a result, attempts by member states to engineer change in IOs are regularly frustrated by recalcitrant organizational cultures and scripts (see Momani 2005; Nielson et al. 2006).

IO inertia here is based on the logic of appropriateness as the dominant paradigm of action, and thus the idea that organizational actors are deeply socialized into prevailing habits and dominant scripts (but see Weaver 2008). Against this backdrop, constructivist critics of this rather static view of IOs have in particular challenged the "oversocialized" view of IO staff as forestalling the possibility of intended change. Constructivist approaches to policy change in IOs, therefore, stress that norm entrepreneurs can change IO cultures by means of argumentative action and persuasion (Chwieroth 2008; Leiteritz 2005; Park 2005).

Notably, the rationalist debate has also shifted the problem of IO inertia to the terrain of rationality assumptions. For rational choice institutionalists in particular, the persistence of international institutions is a peculiar theoretical challenge and has even been named a "paradox" (Koremenos et al. 2001b, p. 1076). In the tradition of functional cooperation theory, "rational design" scholars stress that international institutions are built to be stable because their value consists in reducing transaction costs for interstate cooperation. Their persistence then is a deliberate choice by cost-sensitive actors rather than an outcome of their socializing force (Koremenos et al. 2001a, pp. 766–7). At the same time, when institutions are too sticky to be adapted to changing demands, it becomes more and more questionable whether their persistence is still justified on the grounds of their *relative efficiency*—which is measured, for example, against sunk costs and available alternative options (cf. Koremenos et al. 2001b, p. 1076; Wallander 2000).[18] To account for patterns of institutional persistence in the face of changing cooperation problems, Joseph Jupille and colleagues have recently amended the rational choice view on IO inertia. The authors argue that institutional change may in fact be less efficient than rational design theory suggests—because their designers are not fully "rational." Where decision makers fail to anticipate the future gains to be reaped from present investments in institutional change, they may in fact stick with a second-best status quo (Jupille et al. 2013). Institutional stickiness, then, is a problem of "bounded rationality" (Jupille et al. 2013, p. 5). Similar to the constructivist account of IO inertia as based on rule-bound behavior, this explanation again refers organizational inertia to the limited strategic capabilities of actors.

The theoretical middle ground between institution-driven stasis and choice-driven change has thus been based on an agency theoretical grounding in "bounded rationality," here understood as the assumption that actors are broadly goal-oriented but not omniscient. Due to this agency theoretical focus however, an important determinant of *organizational* change has received less attention: the fact that IO change is a multi-actor and contested process, where different goals and strategies are aggregated in bringing about IO change (cf. Mayntz 2004; see Kahler 1998).[19] The *conflictual* nature of IO change is reflected most explicitly in the principal-agent (PA) literature on dynamics of delegation and control in IOs (cf. Hawkins et al. 2006a). PA theories assume that IOs are recalcitrant bureaucracies ("agents") that must be closely controlled in order to follow the orders of their member states

---

[18] Hence, rational design theory does not suggest that international institutions are *optimal*, only that they serve member state interests better than other possible solutions.
[19] On the ambiguous implications of "bounded rationality" for the salience of distributional bargaining see the discussion in Jupille et al. (2013, p. 8).

("principals"). Yet, in order to deploy mechanisms of control, states must overcome "common agency" problems among themselves (Nielson and Tierney 2003, p. 247). As long as they do not agree on how to control or change an IO, states may allow the bureaucrats to engage in mission creep and thus amplify or even transgress their mandate. PA theories thus emphasize that conflicts between principals hinder deliberate change in IOs.

Given its overriding interest in the emergence and control of agent autonomy, the PA literature does not spell out the full implications of principal conflicts for IO change, however. PA scholars stress conflict between principals as a reform break, yet the conclusion that they draw from this insight again comes back to the distinction between "the" principal and "the" agent. Periods of interstate blockades are viewed as periods of agency slack, where bureaucrats pursue their selfish agendas and member states are practically inactive (Copelovitch 2010). This perspective neglects that even where there is no principal agreement, decentralized and informal change initiatives abound and the locus of change shifts to partial alliances between some principals and some IO units (see Kleine 2013; Stone 2011; Urpelainen 2012).

The patterns of change that emerge from such local strategies within IO contexts are at the focus of this book. Hence, the underlying distinction here is not a formal distinction between principals and agents, but a temporal distinction between reform coalitions and status quo coalitions, which comprise member states and IO bureaucrats alike (see Hanrieder 2014a). In investigating how these conflicts are shaped by the outcomes of prior bargains and thus of institutional opportunities and constraints, PDPD brings in core insights of the historical institutionalist literature and its ongoing debate about the nature of institutional change.

Punctuated versus Gradual Change in HI

The HI debate on institutional change evolves around the question of whether "change" is a radical or a gradual process in political institutions. One prominent party to this debate is the "punctuated equilibrium" view of institutional development. According to this view, formal institutions stay the same as long as their development is not "punctuated" by exogenous shocks such as major wars, economic crises, or natural disasters (cf. Krasner 1984). "Path dependence" here takes on a deterministic and practically static meaning, where institutions can only be changed through exogenous shocks, which provoke "critical junctures" for the institution. Critical junctures are historical moments where institutional constraints are relaxed and there is ample space for radical changes to occur (see Capoccia and Kelemen 2007; Mahoney 2000; Soifer 2012). In between critical junctures, however, pathways are stabilized through endogenous institutional dynamics (see Rixen and Viola 2014).

Yet over the last decade, the dichotomy between extended periods of path dependent stasis and episodes of radical change has been challenged by a body of HI theorizing that stresses the endogenous dynamism of political institutions (Streeck and Thelen 2005a). Recent conceptualizations of *gradual* institutional change rather emphasize that the reproduction of institutions is itself transformative (Thelen 2004; see also Greif and Laitin 2004). For example, the actors reproducing an institution may slowly add new elements ("layering"); a changing environment may alter the impact of an institution ("drift"); or new elements may slowly overtake established ones ("replacement," cf. Streeck and Thelen 2005b). These accounts thus stress the *endogenous* dynamism of institutions rather than the impact of exogenous factors on institutional change.

Taking a nuanced view on stability *and* change in institutions, this book builds on both accounts of institutional change. On the one hand, it starts from the insight of "gradual change theorists" that IO persistence is based on ongoing adaptation efforts and thus inherently dynamic. However, the PDPD account of IO design and reform also differs from the "internalist" view of institutional change adopted in this body of literature, that is, a view where dynamism arises from the institution's endogenous processes alone. Given that IOs are not closed systems, their reproduction is never purely endogenous but shaped by external triggers as well. The IO fragmentation trap, thus, is triggered by design and reform attempts that do take up "external" demands for IO change. These demands result from a discrepancy between the institutional status quo and evolving expectations in the IO's environment and thus have an external origin. On the other hand, however, this does not amount to a punctuated equilibrium account of IO change either. Rather, instances of institutional change—and even of institutional creation (see Chapter 3)—need not be radical departures from institutional pathways but are often institutionally mediated responses to exogenous demands. Processes of IO design and reform are not radical and "contingent" critical junctures in the sense of being unpredictable (on historical contingency see Section 2.1). Rather, preexisting institutional conditions such as the positioning of reform and status quo-oriented actors shape how IOs absorb external stimuli and thus the direction of institutional change. In this nuanced account of IO design and reform, thus, change and continuity are not opposed but closely intertwined. The case design and structure of the book reflects this emphasis on path dependent reform outcomes.

1.4 Case Selection, Data, and Chapter Outline

As most works standing in the HI tradition, the present book is the result of a problem-driven research strategy (Pierson and Skocpol 2002, p. 696). It starts from the WHO's extreme fragmentation trajectory, and the puzzling observation that attempts to reverse this pathway have further reinforced rather than reduced it. This history of reform failure in one of the largest specialized agencies of the UN, whose performance affects the health of billions of people, is relevant in itself. Furthermore, given its long record of futile recentralization attempts, the WHO case provides an empirically rich source for theorizing path dependent constraints on IO design.

Thus, following the introduction of the WHO puzzle in this introductory chapter, the theoretical logic of the fragmentation trap is outlined in Chapter 2. The chapter first introduces the PDPD approach to IO design. I explicate that time is fateful in institutions, because they perpetuate the outcomes of historical struggles through formal rules and by generating vested interests. In this connection, I discuss the meaning of historical "contingency" in path dependent explanations and claim that even during founding moments, IO design is not random but shaped by prior conditions. It is fateful nevertheless because of the lock-in and reinforcement mechanisms that stabilize institutions. Given that path dependence explanations tend to focus on the development of regulatory institutions, the chapter goes on to discuss the specific reproduction requirement of formal *organizations*. Organizations persist by mobilizing collective agency, a process which I conceptualize as an "economic-political game" where policy and polity outcomes are negotiated in parallel. The chapter then focuses on the reform game that drives the reproduction of IOs with strong subunits: the fragmentation trap. I explicate its lock-in and the mechanisms of deepening and widening fragmentation and discuss possible exits from the fragmentation pathway. The chapter concludes with a methodological discussion of institutional causation and its empirical analysis with the help of process tracing and counterfactual reasoning. It thereby justifies the research design for the WHO case study and its focus on explicit design and reform attempts and shortly previews the main elements of this analysis (see Figure 2.2).

The following three chapters contain the empirical core of the book, the extended WHO case study. This historical narrative of the WHO's founding moment and its two major reforms covers the period from 1946 to 2014. It is the outcome of a "retroductive" research process going back and forth between theoretical expectations, empirical irritations, and further data collection. The analysis is informed by a variety of empirical sources including organizational documents, observational and interview data.

The primary evidence for the WHO case study consists of official WHO documents such as internal organizational studies and reports, minutes and summary records from the WHO's governing bodies and committees, resolutions and decisions, and speeches and reports by the DGs. For the period of the WHO's founding moment between 1946 and 1951, these public documents are complemented with sources from the WHO archives that provide further detail on the establishment of WHO's regional offices. Official IO documents are binding records of internally negotiated decisions (Neumann 2007). They constitute critical evidence for IO histories but must be interpreted in context, which requires the researcher's immersion into the organization's language and practices. This demands acquaintance with disciplinary (public health) and bureaucratic (UN) jargon, but also an understanding of what organizational documents "do," that is, how they are generated, negotiated, and drawn on in the IO. Several research stays at the WHO headquarters of altogether three months—the first in February 2009, the last in December 2014—have allowed me to engage in such immersion. As a visiting "historical researcher," I was generously provided with office space in the WHO Records and Archives unit, and could freely move around in the headquarters, talk to staff and attend brownbag seminars to get acquainted with the organization's daily life; and observe how WHO documents are bargained over at the World Health Assembly. This non-participant observation has served as a crucial background for making sense of the documentary evidence.

Furthermore, elite interviews have served as background information on the WHO's organizational practice. A few official oral histories with former staff members are kept at the WHO archives (e.g. Dorolle 1976; Siegel 1982). In addition, I have talked to more than 50 experts, meaning mostly active and former WHO staff. As it is typical for elite interviews, the selection of the interviewees was mainly based on snowball sampling, where initial contacts provided further recommendations regarding who is experienced and willing to discuss organizational issues with outside researchers (Littig 2009, p. 101). As the WHO became more transparent to me over time, I targeted further interviewees to cover missing departments and get a more comprehensive picture. Although all interviews were conducted at the headquarters, many interviewees had previously worked in WHO field offices outside Geneva, thus bringing in the regional and country perspective on intra-organizational struggles. The interviews were led as "problem-centered" conversations which combine factual questions with in-depth discussions of organizational problems (Witzel and Reiter 2012). They lasted between ten minutes and two hours, and sometimes were continued over several rounds. Most of them took place in the interviewees' offices, others more informally during lunch or coffee breaks. Respondents have generally been open to reflecting upon their workplace with an outsider on a confidential basis. Given their informal nature, these interviews only provide some complementary observations and are referred to as such, while the primary evidence consists of publicly available documents.[20]

---

[20] A further potential bias may be that it is in particular dissatisfied and highly critical staff members who are willing to talk to outside researchers. I was often approached by (and referred to)

Nevertheless, and like all historical narratives, the account offered in Chapters 3–5 is an interpretation that is inevitably selective (cf. Carr 1990). My main interest is in the fate of deliberate design and reform in international organizations, and therefore in the ways in which institutional conditions remove certain options or constrain designers and reformers over time. The narrative therefore sets in with the long founding moment of the WHO that lasted from 1946 until 1951. Chapter 3 reconstructs this founding moment and shows that it resulted in an extent of regionalization that was not foreseen in the WHO's constitutional design. This was due to the "Pan American headstart," the successful Latin American mobilization for the Pan American Sanitary Bureau which was in existence since 1902. I retrace the piecemeal bargaining process that cemented the Bureau's continued autonomy within the WHO, which was aided by the unforeseen delay in WHO ratifications and thus the belated institution-building in Geneva. As the Bureau's practice of regional elections for the post of the regional director was emulated in all new WHO regions, the result was a system of regional self-governance that violated constitutional provisions. The historical record also shows that this outcome was not an instance of hegemonic design, given that the US had pleaded to closely integrate the new regions into the WHO. The chapter concludes with a discussion of the early lock-in of regionalization in the WHO, which was based on the formation of regional coalitions that used the regional offices as venues for budgetary struggles, and that was testified by a series of futile recentralization attempts in the 1950s and 1960s.

Chapter 4 analyzes how this initial regionalization was reinforced through the WHO's first major reform, the "Health for All" reform that was launched in the 1970s. The chapter shows that this reform did not attain its policy goal of implementing the new policy paradigm of Primary Health Care, but had a lasting secondary effect in that it entailed a significant delegation of authorities to the regional offices. This reform was designed as the response to a postcolonial legitimacy crisis in the WHO, as global calls for a New International and Economic Order and the dysfunction of hospital-based health systems in the developing world created demand for new policy approaches. PHC was introduced as an egalitarian and bottom-up policy approach the implementation of which crucially relied on national ownership. Yet, as the regional offices had become organizational filters in the WHO's field work, DG Halfdan Mahler sought to implement the new paradigm by making the regional offices the main agents of change. This initiative was not successful

WHO officers who were keen to expose what they deemed scandalous developments in the organization. Similar to what Catherine Weaver reports from her research experience inside the World Bank, I was "leaked" documents through highly secretive channels, and found out only later that these documents were publicly available (see the discussion in Weaver 2008, pp. 14–16).

in that the regional offices failed to implement PHC. In the aftermath of the reform, the DG openly criticized and regretted his regionalization, and thereby provoked a wave of critical evaluations and recentralization attempts, also by the US. These attempts were again defeated so that the WHO's regional fragmentation was effectively *deepened* through the PHC reform.

Chapter 5 investigates the second major reform of the WHO, the One WHO reform that was started in 1998 by DG Gro Harlem Brundtland. One WHO explicitly sought to reverse the WHO's fragmentation process, but de facto *widened* it through the creation and empowerment of a multitude of global health partnerships. The chapter reconstructs Brundtland's reform ambitions and the economic policy paradigm that informed her approach to global health and to corporate governance in the WHO. This paradigm proposed to instill agency and coherence in the WHO through a massive rotation of staff, a unified program budget and the mobilization of high-level political support for WHO projects. However, Brundtland failed in her attempt to integrate the regional offices into the corporate budgeting and programming process, and her bid for more discretionary funds was rejected by the organization's main donors. The reform therefore relied on layering as the main technique of implementing change in the WHO, that is, the creation and empowerment of semi-autonomous thematic units ("special programs"). This turn to special programs accelerated and exacerbated a dynamic that had slowly started in the aftermath of the PHC reform, and effectively undermined the One WHO ambition. It thereby reinforced the WHO's dual fragmentation pathway along regional as well as thematic lines.

Chapter 6 explores the external validity of the fragmentation trap beyond the case of regionalization in the WHO. It starts from the observation of a broader trend toward territorial decentralization in the UN system and asks in how far different federalisms in the UN replicate the logic of path dependent fragmentation. The chapter compares the ILO that embarked on decentralization from a hierarchical structure, with UNESCO that was from the outset fragmented into thematic sectors. It argues that the ILO's turn to field-level capacity-building through programs such as the International Programme on the Elimination of Child Labour was implemented in a hierarchical manner and did not entail a major subunit empowerment. By contrast, in UNESCO the creation of field offices deepened a sector-driven fragmentation process. Its thematic sectors that have marked the organization since its creation have "parented" their own, issue-specific field offices. UNESCO's fragmentation has also been widened through the establishment of inter-sectoral programs, which became additional layers but did not surmount inter-sectoral rivalries. UNESCO's complexity and fragmentation have become the objects of ongoing reform efforts. The comparison of these trajectories lends further plausibility to the claim of path dependent fragmentation, and it shows how the mechanisms of the fragmentation trap operate in different organizational contexts such as the sectoral system of UNESCO. The chapter is based on a survey of IO documents and secondary literature, and does not engage in an in-depth reconstruction of design or reform attempts. Hence, it is intended to serve as a starting point for further empirical studies that extend and refine the analysis of decentralization and fragmentation in international organizations.

Chapter 7 discusses the book's implications for IO reform and for IO research. I first reconsider the various technologies through which IOs construct their agency and ability to change. Reform technologies are an important but neglected aspect of bureaucratic culture in IOs, which legitimate themselves as reforming organizations despite all obstacles to organizational change. I then discuss how the fragmentation of global governance at large reinforces the fragmentation of individual IOs. The chapter thereby connects the fragmentation trap model to the literatures on trans-organizational networks, regime complexity, and institutional choice. Finally, I point out problems that reformers encounter in contemporary IOs. They are faced with the temptation of goal displacement, that is, of making reform an end in itself, and have to deal with trade-offs between IO-specific and UN-wide reform outcomes.

2

The Centrifugal Reproduction of International Organizations

In the preceding chapter, I have introduced the ongoing fragmentation of the World Health Organization (WHO) and the challenge that it poses to functional explanations of international organization (IO) design and reform. The present chapter addresses this challenge and develops an institution-driven explanation of the peculiar inertia of IO fragmentation. I argue that fragmented authority structures within IOs give rise to vested interests that entrench subunit authority, and create endogenous institutional struggles whereby fragmentation becomes difficult to reverse, but easy to reinforce in the course of reform. Reforms—deliberate efforts to change an IO that are undertaken by reform coalitions of IO leaders and their external supporters— here become triggers of further fragmentation. Where the reformers of fragmented IOs are faced with recalcitrant subunits, they can either seek to buy their support through further institutional concessions—and thereby *deepen* fragmentation by further empowering these units—or they can bypass internal blockades by creating new and partially independent subunits, which amounts to a *widening* of fragmentation to additional organizational "layers." Hence, the reproduction of fragmented IOs tends to be "centrifugal" in that it strengthens the subunits at the expense of the directorate. This fragmentation trap explains the peculiar development of the WHO (which I will show in Chapters 3–5), but is also triggered in other United Nations (UN) organizations that harbor powerful subunits, such as the United National Educational, Scientific and Cultural Organization (UNESCO, see Chapter 6).

The argument put forward in the present chapter combines historical institutionalist concepts and insights from resource dependence theory and theorizes fragmentation as a power-driven, path dependent organizational dynamic. Power-driven path dependence (PDPD) focuses on the distributional struggles—both between organizational actors and their external allies—that *lock in* fragmented IO structures, and the conflictual dynamics that *reinforce* fragmentation in the course of reform. While the endogenous fragmentation mechanisms spelled out in here are generic and can be found in different kinds of formal organizations, the chapter is tailored to the IO context. It focuses on how the agents involved in IO reform—bureaucratic units and their state and non-state allies in the organizational environment[1]—struggle over policies and institutions, and how they capitalize on their control of institutional resources that are critical for the reform effort. The more reform-critical resources IO subunits control, and the better they are protected by external allies, the easier it becomes for them to reap *increasing returns* from their power position in the process of reform.

With this theoretical account, I seek to make a threefold contribution to the scholarly debate about IO design and IO change. First, I offer a genuinely dynamic approach to IO development. Processual approaches are still rare when it comes to explaining change and even inertia in IOs.[2] To date, a wide range of causal factors such as state interests (Nielson and Tierney 2003), bureaucratic dispositions (Barnett and Finnemore 2004), external socializing agencies (Park 2005), internal norm entrepreneurs (Betts 2009b; Leiteritz 2005), or combinations thereof (Vetterlein 2007) have been advanced as conditions of change in IOs. What is largely missing from this debate, however, are theories about how IOs grow older; that is, what makes them robust over time, and how organizational structures bias the course of adaptation and reform. Drawing from historical institutionalist accounts of path dependent institutional change, PDPD serves to theorize how IOs are reproduced in time, and to specify the endogenous mechanisms shaping IO reform.

Second, by explaining the forces of IO *fragmentation*, the chapter balances the present centralization bias of the IO literature. Certainly, *inter*-institutional fragmentation in the form of "legal fragmentation" (Benvenisti and Downs 2007) and "regime complexity" (Alter and Meunier 2009) attracts growing attention by students of international institutions who seek to conceptualize the endogenous dynamics arising from a fragmented global polity (Gehring and Faude 2014; Raustiala and Victor 2004). The prevailing ontology of IOs, however, is based on the assumption of the integrated IO actor, which underlies rationalist as well as constructivist IO scholarship. Constructivists have used Weberian analogies to conceptualize IOs as centralizing bureaucracies (Barnett 2002). Rational design scholars have put forward efficiency arguments for the delegation of authorities to IOs (Abbott and Snidal 1998), equating such delegation with "centralization" (Koremenos 2008, pp. 152–3). The principal–agent

---

[1] Private actors become more important when the "layering" strategy is chosen that can bypass the formal prerogatives of member states (see Section 2.3).

[2] Exceptions include Chwieroth (2014); Farrell and Newman (2010); Hanrieder (2014a), and for the population level Shanks et al. (1996). For an argument about institutional choice in context, see Jupille et al. (2013).

literature draws on this assumption and conceives of IOs as coherent and integrated "agents" (Hawkins et al. 2006a). Yet, many IO bureaucracies are far less hierarchical than the centralization-cum-agency ontology suggests, and harbor multiple and overlapping centers of authority. Fragmented IO designs defy prevailing ontologies and thereby also theories of IO agency, delegation, and control. They are prone to engage in self-defeating behavior (Hanrieder 2014b) and difficult to steer by a collective principal (Graham 2014). Organizational fragmentation thus sheds a new light on the causal dispositions of IOs, and its self-stabilization provides new insight into the "institutional choices" through which IO designs are reproduced and changed.

Third, by offering a distributional rationalist approach to path dependence, the fragmentation trap model responds to the challenge of bringing power to institutional analysis (Barnett and Duvall 2005; Gruber 2000; Stone 2009). While students of rational design foreground considerations of collective efficiency in their explanations of IO outcomes (Koremenos et al. 2001a,b), historical institutionalists stress that concerns about institutional power are critical determinants of IO design and reform (Krasner 1988; Hall and Taylor 1996).[3] I will argue, in this vein, that institutional power resources—formal decision rights as well as administrative control over budget and personnel—are constantly renegotiated as organizations are reformed, and that power-sensitive actors defend institutional structures even when this involves collective and/or individual welfare losses. In fact, it is precisely these resources that they may bring to bear on the next round of reform in order to attain their desired outcome. Hence, IO reform is an "economic-political" game, where the proponents and opponents of IO reform strive for immediate material ("economic") gains as well as long-term and structural ("political") advantages (see Section 2.2). This distributional perspective transcends the functionalist leaning of the IO design literature without rejecting rational choice altogether; for IO inertia here does not rest on deep socialization (Barnett and Finnemore 2004) or on "bounded rationality" (Jupille et al. 2013), and thus is not a metatheoretical challenge to prevailing explanations in rational institutionalism. I instead offer an institutional account of the time horizons and strategic capacities of rational actors. From the viewpoint of the economic-political game, it is long-term concerns about institutional power positions, and not the psychological inability to anticipate efficiency gains, which induce actors to protect the status quo. Likewise, reinforcing the status quo is not a matter of efficiency gains and the collective "increasing returns"

---

[3] It should be clarified that the power-centered approach constitutes one (prominent) variant of historical institutionalist reasoning, but not historical institutionalism (HI) per se. Other International Relations (IR) scholars drawing on this tradition take a more sociological and norms-centered approach to international path dependencies (Dannreuther 2011; see also Mahoney 2000).

that can be reaped from the institution, but of the "increasing returns to power" that reforms yield for well-positioned actors.

It should also be noted that my take on path dependent fragmentation bridges (or ignores) an apparent divide between "punctuated equilibrium" and "gradualist" approaches to institutional change. Punctuated equilibrium—the idea that institutions are self-stabilizing until a shock or "critical juncture" triggers change (Krasner 1984)—is often opposed to gradualist approaches that focus on the ongoing transformation of institutions in the course of their reproduction (Streeck and Thelen 2005a). The fragmentation trap model, like in fact most arguments about path dependent change, combines both perspectives: It argues that institutions respond to external stimuli, but do so in a directed way because their response is shaped by preexisting institutional conditions (see also Mahoney and Thelen 2010a). Hence, I do not make a philosophical argument about the nature of "change", but postulate empirical mechanisms that reforms tend to trigger in fragmented organizations.

The chapter proceeds in four main steps. I first discuss the temporality of institutions that is due to the fatefulness of early historical causes (see Section 2.1). Next, I turn to the mechanisms of organizational reproduction which underlie the lock-in and reinforcement of IO outcomes (see Section 2.2).[4] The third section uses these elements to theorize the lock-in and reinforcement of fragmentation in IOs (see Section 2.3). Finally, I discuss the methodology of analyzing path dependent IO change and lay out the research design for the ensuing empirical chapters (see Section 2.4).

2.1 Path Dependence: Necessity out of Contingency

In their still relevant contribution to the fiftieth anniversary volume of *International Organization*, the organization theorists James March and Johan P. Olsen discussed the difficulty that International Relations (IR) institutionalists have in accounting for "inefficient history" (March and Olsen 1998). Challenging rational choice theory's inclination to engage in post-hoc rationalizations of institutional outcomes, and the comparative statics perspective that IR usually adopts, March and Olsen emphasized the importance of endogenous institutional dynamics, also for international politics. They claimed that institutional dynamics could not be reduced to current conditions and motives, and were seldom rationally intended. With institutional inertia and lags in

---

[4] In the following, the term "institution" refers to explicit and formal institutions only, in line with historical institutionalist uses of the term (Hall and Taylor 1996, p. 941; Mahoney and Thelen 2010b, p. 7). Organizations are understood as a subset of formal institutions whose particular feature is that they persist through mobilizing collective action. Hence, I will turn to the specifics of organizational change in the sections on reproduction mechanisms (see Section 2.2 and Section 2.3).

adaptation pervading institutional change, and in the absence of a market-like mechanism selecting for well-adapted institutions, historically "inefficient" (i.e. ill-adapted) institutions could easily endure (March and Olsen 1998, pp. 954–6).

This "sociological" intervention into IR institutionalism was widely received, yet mostly due to its stress on the "logic of appropriateness" as a non-rationalist theory of agency. The logic of appropriateness was used to explain institutional inertia on the grounds that actors were impregnated by organizational cultures and bureaucratic scripts, and thus that their appropriate behavior prevented sweeping change in IOs (Barnett and Finnemore 2004; Weaver 2008; cf. critically Chwieroth 2008). Rationalists, by contrast, offered models of deliberate change and thus efficient history, mostly through the "rational design" approach. Rationally designed features of IOs here are seen to reflect the functions that organizations fulfil for realizing joint gains for member states. IO features have not only been rationally chosen in the past, but they also have been regularly updated later on, because intelligent designers are capable of adapting their creatures once these grow dated or dysfunctional. Rational design therefore determines both institutional creation and it is the "overriding mechanism" (Koremenos et al. 2001a, p. 766) in the process of institutional change.

This rationalism-constructivism divide has engendered rather static juxtapositions of constructivist and rationalist determinants of IO change (Nielson et al. 2006), which also led to attempts to bridge that divide, for example, by referring institutional inertia to the "bounded rationality" of political actors (Jupille et al. 2013). Still, the relevance of process and historical timing has not gone unnoticed. Rational choice scholars have pointed out the "'stability/ instability' paradox" (Koremenos et al. 2001b, p. 1076) that is involved in building international institutions and the challenge it poses to rational design: Institutions are designed to stabilize expectations and thus perpetuate historical choices into the present, and at the same time they shall remain flexible so that they can respond to new demands. For rational design scholars, this conundrum is about choosing the right flexibilities right at the beginning (see Thompson 2010). However, it has also been stressed that stability increases over an organization's lifetime, which points to the importance of organizational age for the propensity of IOs to change, or die. IO inertia tends to increase with age, so that early adaptation is easier than later changes (Weaver 2008, p. 37). Additionally, decreasing flexibility does not seem to be a disadvantage. On the contrary, beyond a certain age (of about fifty years), IOs are much less likely to be discarded than in the uncertain years of their adolescence.[5] Although Susan Strange's polemic that international

---

[5] Paul Ingram and Magnus Thor Torfason have confirmed the "age dependence of IGO [intergovernmental organization] failure" and come up with "an ∩-shaped failure rate, which peaks at an IGO age of twenty-five, and crosses the origin at an age of fifty. The most robust IGOs are the oldest, after an age of fifty" (Ingram and Torfason 2010, p. 23).

organizations "never die" (Strange 1998) is an exaggeration (Rittberger et al. 2012, p. 68), these observations suggest that international institutions are not only outcomes, but they also become determinants of institutional choices (see Greif and Laitin 2004).

Historical institutionalism (HI) and its concept of path dependence help to make *theoretical* sense of such observations. Path dependence means that *institutions lock in and reinforce historical outcomes through endogenous institutional mechanisms.*[6] Time here assumes a theoretical status because it is "fateful" (Sewell 2005, p. 6) for IOs, which perpetuate historical choices into the present. This fatefulness of history can be most visually grasped when looking at the fossil-like shapes of many congressional districts in the United States (US), which resemble salamanders much more than geometric units or geographical delineations.[7] These districts are the outcomes of decades of "gerrymandering"; that is, the repeated strategic reapportionment of voters to congressional districts by the incumbents: Every ten years following the decennial census, the districts are adapted to shifting population numbers. Power-holders seize this opportunity to increase their chances in future elections by creatively re-designing electoral districts. The outcomes of these reapportionments are not linear reflections of democratic principles in that they undermine the "one person, one vote" principle. Yet, neither are they linear reflections of contemporary power constellations, because redistricting can only shift the status quo within a range of legal and structural restrictions (Seabrook 2010). They represent the cumulative outcomes of hard-to-reverse, historically specific junctures of political struggles within institutional constraints, which current actors can only modify to some extent.

The status quo bias of institutions is not limited to domestic institutions. Similarly, the composition of the UN Security Council (UNSC) with its five permanent veto positions still reflects the post-World War II power constellation. Its historical design strongly circumscribes the prospects for future reform (Hosli et al. 2011). In particular the permanent veto positions are hard to overturn due to their "self-referencing" character (see Pierson 2004, p. 145): They can only be abolished with the consent of the veto powers themselves. The UNSC's decision rules thus freeze past power constellations. In other words: The Council's current shape is "contingent" on the historical causes at work during its founding moment.

---

[6] For a more generic use of "path dependence," see, e.g., Barnett and Finnemore (2004, p. 43). On the narrower conceptualization of path dependence, see Mahoney (2000); Page (2006); Rixen and Viola (2014).

[7] For a "best of" gerrymandered districts, see <http://pajamasmedia.com/zombie/2010/11/11/the-top-ten-most-gerrymandered-congressional-districts-in-the-united-states/> (accessed November 24, 2010).

The historical "contingency" of institutional pathways must not be mistaken for sheer unpredictability or random, though. In other words: International institutions are not mutations.[8] Certainly, especially during founding moments, institutional constraints are relaxed and the new design inevitably transforms preexisting pathways (see Capoccia and Kelemen 2007). Still, no IO is created on a blank slate. Even during founding moments, intentional actors draw on existing resources in their struggles over an IO's design. The remnants of previous institutions, domestic or international blueprints, and coalitions established in previous collaborative efforts are all brought to bear on an IO's founding design.[9] IO founding moments may appear more uncertain and their outcomes less predictable where multiple pathways combine in a complex way, so that the design outcome is hard to forecast from the viewpoint of the participating actors. It then appears "unintended" even though it was created by intentional and goal-oriented actors (Lindner and Rittberger 2003, p. 445).[10] This will in particular be the case where no dominant actor or coalition can impose its preferred design for the new organization. We will see in Chapter 3 that the WHO's founding moment was marked by such complexity and conflict, which allowed a Pan American pro-regional coalition to undermine the deliberate design that has been forged by the enacting coalition. However, it can also be the case that the enacting coalition is dominant enough to actually provide and enforce a "master plan." This seems to have been the case for the UNSC, whose design was prepared in advance to the 1945 San Francisco conference and imposed by the great powers, the future Permanent Five. They manipulated the negotiation procedures in such a way that the other states had to agree to this peculiar design (Luard 1982, pp. 43–4). Still, in both cases, once the IO was established, the historical outcome constrained future adaptation. The long-term organizational outcome therefore was "contingent on" the historical outcome of the founding moment. It is for this reason that temporal sequence is so crucial for IO design: Early causes are privileged over later causes, the impact of which will be smaller once an institutional pathway is enacted.

Still, to become fateful, historical outcomes must be institutionalized. Institutions do not persist by filling some empty space; they must be constantly reproduced in political practice (Thelen 1999, pp. 391–2). Formal institutions

---

[8] On such strong notions of contingency as unpredictability from initial conditions see Goldstone (1998). On the theory-laden notion of contingency in institutional explanations see Mahoney (2000).

[9] Hence, although founding moments are plausible cut-off points for historical narratives, in principle one could embark on an infinite regress of going ever deeper back in history in order to explain an IO's specific pathway (see the discussion in Büthe 2002, pp. 487–8).

[10] An instructive discussion of the renaissance origin of contingency as unintendedness or "fortuna" that marks the limits of deliberate choice or "virtù" is provided by David Wootton (2007); see also Lebow (2010, pp. 96–7).

owe their persistence to the activities of the winners of a path dependent outcome who orient their strategies and resources to the institution and generate a vested interest in preserving a chosen pathway. Their "positive feedback" to the institution hinges on the distributional benefits they reap from a given pathway. Their ability to resist challenges to the status quo is aided by the formal side of institutions such as the decision rules that govern treaty revisions. Often these rules entail demanding quorums, majorities, or the consent of veto players like in the UNSC case, rules which make it easier for blocking minorities to protect the status quo. In addition to such procedural advantages, early winners in an institution assume control of strategic resources and positions, which, in turn, helps them to reinforce their power position and further cement the status quo. Hence, even though all-out irreversibility hardly exists, ceteris paribus status quo coalitions can dramatically raise the costs of reversing a given pathway.[11]

At the same time, even conservative strategies in institutions have a dynamic component. Practices of institutional reproduction are always potentially transformative in that they alter their own institutional preconditions (Greif and Laitin 2004). They reshape incentive structures, redistribute power among participants, and realign the coalitions that sustain institutions. The inherent dynamism of institutional reproduction has been particularly stressed in recent HI works on gradual institutional change. These works mostly focus on the reproduction of regulatory institutions such as laws and formal policies, which are reproduced and reshaped through the compliance of their rule addressees (Mahoney and Thelen 2010b; Streeck and Thelen 2005b). In order to understand the dynamics of reproduction in formal *organizations*, special attention must be paid to the way in which they generate collective agency. Drawing on resource dependence theory (Pfeffer and Salancik 2003) and strategic organization theory (Friedberg 1997), in the following section I conceptualize IO reproduction as an economic-political game, the stake of which is the mobilization of common agency for organizational goals.

2.2 Reform and the Politics of Organizational Reproduction

The reproduction of formal organizations is an ongoing cooperation problem. Being instituted as instruments of collective agency, organizations need to

---

[11] Note that from the PDPD perspective, the persistence of the pathway thus does not hinge on its relative efficiency—or the "increasing returns" the institution yields from a collective point of view (Pierson 2000)—but on the ability of early winners to defeat attempts at reversing a given pathway, that is, "increasing returns to power" (Mahoney and Thelen 2010b, p. 7). For an efficiency-based explanation of institutional inertia in IR see Celeste Wallander's account of how the North Atlantic Treaty Organization (NATO) survived and was adapted after the end of the Cold War (Wallander 2000).

constantly mobilize actors and resources toward organizational goals in order to persist (Brunsson 2006, p. 2). This does not imply that organizations are themselves quasi-actors. Their reproduction is performed by coalitions that rally around and jointly realize their organizational goals in repeated rounds of organizational reproduction (Pfeffer and Salancik 2003, pp. 24–32). Therefore, even what looks like "continuity" is an ongoing collective achievement through which organizations are adapted to changing circumstances (cf. Barnes 2001, pp. 32–3). Technological or financial changes, new standards of efficiency and effectiveness, or changes in organizational membership all need to be actively incorporated in order to reproduce organizations in time and to keep stable what are regarded to be an organization's core functions. This requires continuing decision making so as to re-enact organizational rules and policies (Gehring 2009; Koch 2009), and to mobilize resources for the organization's maintenance (Pfeffer and Salancik 2003)—for inactivity would eventually result in "drift," that is, the organization's fading into irrelevance due to insufficient updating (Hacker 2004; Hanrieder 2014a).

This also applies to IOs, in that, like all organizations, IOs must mobilize resources and actors from their environment in order to survive (see also Weaver 2008). They collect membership fees and voluntary contributions, recruit staff, convene expert committees, mobilize state delegates to participate in the governing bodies' work, and enlist non-state actors who contribute their expertise and legitimacy to the IO activities. These ongoing activities ensure that an IO is adapted to the organizational "environment," that is, those actors and actions that are not participating in reproducing the IO but dispose of resources that the IO needs for its maintenance (Pfeffer and Salancik 2003, pp. 29–32).[12]

The central means of IOs to legitimate themselves vis-à-vis their supporters and thus tap critical resources is organizational reform. Reforms are joint undertakings that seek to enact a collective decision for change. Reforms demonstrate agency, enact new ideas through policy change, and re-engineer organizational structures that have grown dated or dysfunctional (Brunsson and Olsen 1993). In international organizations, reforms are usually pursued by reform coalitions that comprise IO leaders as well as like-minded states that provide ideational and material support for organizational change. They are based on new ideologies and organizational blueprints that shall demonstrate the IO's continued relevance for global cooperation, its ability to take on new problems and work with changing partners. IO reforms are explicit in that

---

[12] This implies that "states" can be both parts of the IO and of its environment: The department (e.g. environment) of the government that sends delegates to the (environmental) IO is a participant, yet the other departments and cabinet members of a government—who co-decide on the share of the budget that is allocated to the IO—are part of the IO environment from which resources must be extracted.

they are sanctioned in governing body decisions, and mainstreamed in the IO's program budget, to be implemented in the operations of the relevant subunits. Especially in times of legitimacy crisis, when an IO's policies or structures are contested and appear out of tune with surrounding developments, the IO's willingness to engage in reform is essential for ensuring the continued support of external actors.

The enactment of IO reform hinges on the resolution of collective action problems—with all the distributional concerns and power asymmetries involved in cooperation. In this process, state and IO players will bring their external and institutional resources to bear on the terms of cooperation so as to influence outcomes in their favor. The "reform designs" will thus reflect the power constellation among the participating actors who draw on their material resources, organizational decision rights, bureaucratic capacities, and ties with critical allies in order to influence reform policies in their favor. Yet importantly, this relationship between power resources and reform policies is recursive, for reform deals entail policy changes as well as structural changes in organizations. As the sociologist Erhard Friedberg has elaborated, cooperation in organizations is always about two dimensions: the "economic" question of which organizational policy is to be pursued, and the "political" negotiation and re-negotiation of underlying rules and institutional power positions (Friedberg 1997, pp. 84–7). While the economic level of organizational decisions concerns problems of substantive policy and immediate material gains, the political dimension refers to how decisions restructure the institutional conditions for future cooperation. Both dimensions are interlinked, either formally or informally. Formally, policy change often involves reorganization. This is exemplified by reforms such as the "greening" of state policies since the 1960s, which was accompanied by the establishment of environmental ministries and agencies in all Western governments (Dingwerth and Jörgens, forthcoming 2015). The interlinkage of policy and structural change can also be observed at more informal levels. For example, a political party's ecological turn after an environmental disaster is likely to empower those branches and actors within the party that possess environmentalist expertise and credibility, and are needed to reposition the party under altered circumstances.

Hence, the deals or "games" through which organizations are reproduced do not only pertain to the policy outcome of cooperation, but also to the structural consequences following from their enactment. This can also be observed in international organizations, where the negotiation of policy goals is often linked to polity innovations such as the creation of new committees, or the empowerment of units that are critical for executing a particular policy. For example, the World Bank's "greening of aid" empowered environmental specialists within the Bank, but also entailed a broader restructuring in that board members were involved much earlier in the loan approval process than they had been before the environmental shift (Nielson and Tierney 2005, p. 791).

This two-dimensionality makes organizational reproduction inherently dynamic, because organizational players, be it states or IO bureaucrats, can seek to capitalize on their power to strengthen their position for future rounds of reproduction. They can exploit their position insofar as others are dependent on them for realizing their material or policy goals, and thus may be willing to pay the price of institutional concessions. Depending on the organizational context and the goals of the reform, this game can play out differently and take on potentially endless variations. In the following, I will focus on how reform deals play out on the bureaucratic structure of internally fragmented IOs, where subunits control resources that are critical for IO reform. This constellation deserves special attention because its internal dynamics qualify the "iron law" postulated by the sociologist Robert Michels, according to which organizational change redistributes power to organizational leaders.[13] As I will discuss in the following section, power concentration can also occur at the level of subunits—and thus produce a fragmentation trap for the leaders engaging in organizational reform.

2.3 The Fragmentation Trap

Fragmentation is, on the one hand, a distinct organizational *outcome*. It is determined by the extent to which subunits—functional subunits such as the thematic sectors into which UNESCO is divided, or territorial subunits such as the regional, sub-regional and country offices entertained by many UN organizations—control their own power resources: They hold procedural rights in the decision making process, for example, when they prepare the budget or design programs in their domain. They control administrative capacities when they decide on their share of the budget or make their own staffing decisions. And subunits can control the IO's access to vital resources where they entertain separate ties with supporters in the environment, most importantly states, but also non-state supporters and funders (Hanrieder 2014b). The greater the extent of these subunit authorities, the more fragmented and the less hierarchical is an IO.[14]

---

[13] "Als Regel kann man aufstellen: Die Macht der Führer wächst im gleichen Maßstabe wie die Organisation" (Michels 1989, p. 21).

[14] This deliberately parsimonious conceptualization views fragmentation as an authority *structure* within IOs and thereby excludes other connotations of the term such as preference divergence or policy fragmentation (see Graham 2014, p. 5). Given that the causal relationship between structural fragmentation and policy fragmentation is ambiguous (Genschel 1997, see also Zürn and Faude 2013), this book only offers case-specific—not general—conclusions about the behavioral implications of IO fragmentation.

IO fragmentation is a matter of degree, and assessing its extent requires a detailed and context-sensitive examination of the resource distribution and reproduction requirements in individual organizations—or organizational complexes such as the UN. In fact, fragmentation is a longstanding feature of the UN system as a whole, which is marked by interagency competition and a duplication of authorities between the various programs, funds, and specialized agencies (Kennedy 2006; Müller 2010). But also individual UN organizations can be considerably fragmented (Graham 2014). The WHO with its strong regional offices (see Chapters 3–5), but also the UNESCO with its entrenched thematic sectors (see Chapter 6) are eminent examples of fragmented IOs. Likewise, the increasingly complex European Union (EU) with its differentiated organizational layers and semi-autonomous regulatory agencies harbors multiple centers of authority (Leuffen et al. 2013; Rittberger and Wonka 2011). Cutting bureaucratic complexity or centralizing authority in the EU is daunting due to the vested interests that states have in particular units, such as "their" commissioner in Brussels. Therefore, and although the Lisbon Treaty foresaw a reduction in size upon enlargement, upon the accession of Croatia in July 2013, the EU's member states decided to prolong the "one commissioner per country" rule until 2019.[15] This observation also indicates that fragmentation understood as a *process* tends to be easier to reinforce than to revert.

Fragmentation may often be inefficient from a collective point of view, when duplication and internal competition hinder corporate agency or reform. However, from a distributional perspective, fragmentation tends to generate many winners and receive positive feedback from those member states that reap local gains from their ties with particular subunits (see Hanrieder 2014b). States that benefit from the persistence of specific regional or functional bureaus within IOs will be unwilling to undermine these subunits, even if centralization was collectively efficient. Re-designing a fragmented IO in a way that endows the leaders with more centralized control will always go against the interests not only of these subunits, but also of those member states that have a vested interest in their persistence. Hence, given the plurality of local gains to be reaped from alliances with distinct subunits that fragmented IOs offer, it is likely that fragmentation gives rise to blocking minorities that are keen to defeat centralization attempts. Just as in the case of EU commissioners, a collective (majority or super-majority, depending on the specific requirements of the IO) decision to take away such local privileges is difficult to attain. Fragmentation is thus easy to *lock in* for blocking minorities thanks to the collective action hurdles that are faced by coalitions of centralizers. The first proposition of the fragmentation trap, therefore, reads that:

(P1)   Due to local gains that member states reap from fragmentation and the joint decision hurdles for centralizing reforms, it is unlikely that fragmentation is reversed.

This first proposition resonates with, but also differs from, the "common agency" problem discussed in principal–agent (PA) theory. The PA perspective highlights that positional differences among member states arise from exogenously given differences about IO policies (Copelovitch 2010). A path dependence approach adds to this perspective that positional differences are also endogenous to IO structures. They are shaped by the coalitions and channels of influence that member states entertain with specific units of the IO, coalitions that allow them to reap local gains independently from joint decisions by the collective principal. Thereby, endogenous institutional dynamics exacerbate common agency problems among IO member states.

Fragmentation is not a static constellation, nonetheless. It also engenders a distinct, centrifugal dynamic of IO reproduction, because the reform game in fragmented IOs is asymmetrically structured to the disadvantage of reformers; namely, IO leaders. In this game, IO leaders often are at the center of specific reform coalitions for IOs—coalitions which entail both member states and other external and internal allies. Many IO leaders take office with an explicit reform promise and an agenda for change. For example, Kofi Annan's takeover as UN Secretary-General in 1996 was accompanied by a major reorganization effort that should make the UN more efficient and coherent, and update its bureaucracy in the light of contemporary new public management standards (Annan 1998). Likewise, the Presidents of the World Bank Group have launched major policy and organizational reforms, for example Robert McNamara (1968–81), who centered the Bank's activities on fighting poverty and aiding rural development, or James D. Wolfensohn (1995–2005), whose Strategic Compact aimed at an encompassing overhaul of the Bank's working methods and business practices. This identification of IO leaders with IO reform implies that they are the first to be held accountable for delivering visible reform outcomes. Their time horizon thus tends to be fixated on immediate reform results that they can report to their reform coalition.

Where, however, reformers are confronted with recalcitrant subunits that can count on the support of a status quo coalition or a number of status quo states, they will need to make major efforts to mobilize these subunits for the reform endeavor.[16] Thus in fragmented IOs, powerful subunits are in a position to formally or informally veto policy change. Veto power can be exerted

---

[16] On the varieties of institutional dynamics which can arise from the interplay of reform and status quo coalitions, see Hanrieder (2014a).

at the level of decision-making, but also at the level of policy implementation. For example, an evaluation unit holding back a report without which a project cannot be implemented can factually veto this project. By implication, sub-unit powers can have different sources. They can rest on formal positions in the decision-making process, but also on the resources—funds, expertise, operational capacities—that a subunit commands. The less these resources are centrally controlled—for example, when an issue-specific department earns independent donations—the more easily these capacities can become sources of veto power. Special ties with actors in the organizational environ-ment can also endow subunits with veto opportunities. These ties need not rest on monetary donations. Where the success of an organizational policy critically depends on external collaborators, those organizational units having access to supporters in the environment can threaten to block or significantly delay the collective policy. Assuming that the subunits care about this critical position, they will seek to maintain it, and possibly even be able to capitalize on it over repeated rounds of reproduction. This is what makes fragmentation in IOs a structural trap. It is not only a difficult-to-reverse *outcome*, due to the structural asymmetry in favor of the subunits, but it can also become a self-reinforcing centrifugal *process*. Whereas fragmentation-the-outcome is the opposite concept to organizational hierarchy, fragmentation-the-process is opposed to the process of centralization, i.e. the accumulation of control in the directorate of an IO.

There are two *organizational mechanisms* through which fragmentation is reinforced over rounds of reproduction: First, fragmentation is *deepened* when subunits reap increasing returns from their power positions, that is, when reformers have to buy subunit support for their reform projects. Second, fragmentation is *widened* when reformers seek to circumvent internal veto players by creating new organizational subunits that are vested with inde-pendent powers—a mode of change that has been labeled "layering" in recent historical institutionalist contributions (Streeck and Thelen 2005b, pp. 23–4). Whether and when these mechanisms of centrifugal reproduction will be triggered in IOs depends on contextual factors—just like the physical concept of "centrifugal force" refers to a power that is inherently relational and only exists within a given rotation system.[17] Generally speaking, the activation of the fragmentation trap depends on a constellation where the organization's leadership has to overcome subunit vetoes in order to enact policy or structural reforms. As long as they work within organizational constraints—that is, strat-egies that do not seek to abolish the vetoes but work with them—reformers are

---

[17] Contrary to centripetal force, according to Newton's laws centrifugal force is not a "real," but a "fictitious" or "inertial" force, i.e. it is endogenous to a *moving* system. I thank Duncan Snidal for bringing to my attention the contested ontological status of centrifugal force.

induced to deepen or widen fragmentation as they mobilize IO offices to participate in a reform.

The first mechanism, *deepening* fragmentation, shapes organizational change in constellations where reformers can and do trade organizational power for policy support. Where powerful subunits need to be mobilized for collective policies or reforms that they have no immediate interest in, they will need special incentives. Also, the package deal that leaders can most easily offer is the delegation of authority to decentralized units (the "political" deal) in exchange for their policy support (the "economic" deal). This deal generates increasing returns to subunit power. The fact that power tends to be redistributed centrifugally where federal units are strong has also been observed for feudal systems such as the German Empire (Spruyt 1994, pp. 109–29) and for contemporary German federalism, which is the prototype of Fritz Scharpf's joint-decision trap:

> And if the [German] federal government insisted upon its objectives, it often had to buy support for national policies at the expense of permanent improvements of the institutional and financial position of the *Länder*. Thus, just as the emperors of the Holy Roman Empire were forced to expend their dynastic possessions and, finally, the imperial prerogatives, in order to maintain the loyalty of their vassal princes, so the German federal government has seen its share of total revenue reduced from 53 per cent in 1970 to 48 per cent in 1983.
>
> Scharpf 1988, p. 255.

For Scharpf, this joint-decision trap is first and foremost a cause of policy inefficiency (Falkner 2011; Scharpf 1988). Yet, from an institutional perspective, it is also an endogenous determinant of organizational change. Centrifugal reform deals fuel the accumulation of subunit power and thereby leave the subunits even better positioned for the next round of reform, for example, when they extend their budgetary control, assume more discretion with regard to policy formulation, face less reporting duties vis-à-vis the directorate, or enjoy more discretion in the selection and appointment of staff. This fragmenting dynamic thus makes organizations even less capable of corporate agency in the next round of reform. The mechanism of deepening fragmentation can be summarized in the second proposition of the fragmentation trap:

(P2)   Fragmentation is deepened when IO subunits are in a position to make their cooperation with the reformers conditional on structural concessions.

This fragmentation pathway is depicted through the left loop in Figure 2.1 below, which specifies how the reform strategy of buying subunit support leads to the devolution of powers to existing subunits, thus deepening fragmentation by generating better veto opportunities for the subunits. The

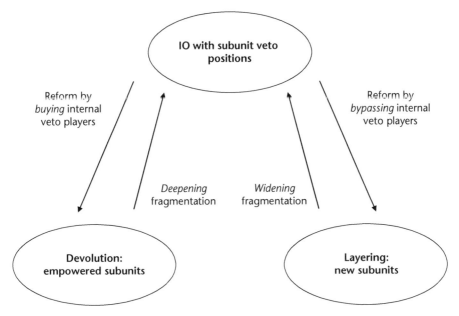

Figure 2.1. The fragmentation trap.

model further specifies the second fragmenting pathway, the layering of new power centers upon existing structures.

As long as internal reform deals can be struck within a fragmented IO, subunits can maintain and strengthen their position. This game reaches its limits, however, when the reformers and the subunits cannot agree on such a deal—either because reformers eschew the concessions they would have to make, or because the subunits prefer to block reform projects. When exactly such deadlock is reached is difficult to predict ex ante. In principle, it can occur at different "levels" of fragmentation as long as conflicts over IO reform are too entrenched to be accommodated by specific deals between reform proponents and opponents in the IO. Deadlock becomes more likely, though, the more authority is delegated to the subunits. For ceteris paribus, more autonomous subunits are more costly to mobilize than dependent subunits. As a reaction to such obstacles, leaders can seek to escape internal blockades by creating new organizational units that are "layered" upon established structures, and thereby *widen* organizational fragmentation. The timing of such moves will depend on blockades over concrete reform goals that provoke this mode of "internal exit," yet the structural preconditions are set by the fragmentation trap.

Creating add-on organizational elements allows IOs to change where all-out transformation or concerted reform cannot be achieved (see Shanks et al. 1996, p. 621). Layering is an important reform strategy in many IOs, in particular in the EU with its many adjunct agencies (Kelemen and Tarrant 2011; McNamara and Newman 2009). It can also be found in global IOs such as the World Bank, which is increasingly using Trust Funds that are only accountable to a subset of the Bank's membership (Distler 2012), or in the WHO with its manifold special programs and public-private partnerships for health (see Chapter 5). Layering is a means to accommodate new goals or demands through additional structures, and even new players who are not well-positioned in the IO's established structures. For example, non-state donors or other IOs that cannot have a seat at the governing bodies of an IO can become participants in newly designed add-ons to the organization. Through special agreements for specific projects or partnerships that are more or less closely integrated with the IO, but autonomous enough not to work through established internal structures, new layers allow reformers to ensure the continued influx of resources into fragmented IOs.

Thus, from a corporate perspective, layering ensures that organizations with internal reform blockades do not "drift" into irrelevance and remain able to secure support from their environment. Obviously, this mode of organizational change entails the risk of exacerbating institutional incongruence and thus policy fragmentation (Fioretos 2011, pp. 389–90; Streeck and Thelen 2005b, p. 24). In institutional terms, it is a pathway to further fragmentation. To effectively circumvent the blockades by established vetoers, new organizational units must be entrusted with independent powers. Layering may thus be a rational avenue for organizational reformers, but only against the backdrop of locked-in historical constraints that raise the organizational costs of concerted reform: In fact, the structural by-product of this reproduction technique is further fragmentation—in this case, a "horizontal" power transfer to additional subunits rather than a "vertical" transfer to existing subunits (as in the case of widening). The third proposition of the fragmentation trap therefore reads:

(P3)   Fragmentation is widened to new organizational power centers when the mobilization of internal veto players becomes prohibitively costly for organizational leaders.

The two mechanisms taken together make fragmentation a self-perpetuating institutional design or, to use Paul Pierson's expression, a "deep equilibrium" (Pierson 2004, p. 157). Fragmentation is a design that is difficult to escape from, but is easily reinforced over rounds of reproduction. This is not to say that each and every reform in fragmented IOs will also lead to further fragmentation. The fragmenting dynamic can always be halted or slowed down, and the timing of further fragmenting moves depend on myriad contextual factors that pitch reform and status quo coalitions against each other in IOs.

Long periods during which fragmentation comes to a halt may be followed by major widening or deepening episodes. In total, however, fragmenting moves are likely to be more sustainable than centralizing ones. Due to the local gains that can be reaped by defenders of fragmentation (Proposition 1), the need to win subunits for reform (Proposition 2), or to bypass them if their support is too costly (Proposition 3), fragmentation becomes for IO reformers what superglue is for the frog in Charles Cameron's metaphor: In the metaphor, a frog hopping from lily pad to lily pad will ultimately stick to the one lily pad that is coated with superglue. The timing of this landing may vary, but the probability of the eventual outcome is very high (quoted in Pierson 2004, p. 94). For IO reformers, this means that, of myriad reform attempts with and without fragmenting implications, those that transfer authorities to IO sub-units tend to be particularly sticky—costly to reverse. Evidently, even then centralization does not become all-out impossible, because no pathway is ever fully irreversible. Yet the costs of reversing fragmentation rise as it widens and deepens over time. Only where centralizers are committed to bearing these costs—which means, in particular, that they offer substantial side payments to the opponents of centralization—can fragmentation be reversed. The easier and less costly option is, however, to strive for local gains and muddle through, for example, by compromising with established structures or working through new organizational layers.

The two centrifugal loops that reproduce fragmented organizational structures can occur sequentially, but also in parallel. Likewise, the timing and sequence of the two mechanisms can vary. As outlined above, which mechanism is triggered at what point in an organization's history depends on whether in specific constellations the reform game can better be resolved internally (deepening fragmentation) or externally (widening fragmentation). Still, as the institutional choice literature also confirms, the participants to an institution will ceteris paribus prefer to use existing institutions before they opt for changing or even abandoning it (Jupille et al. 2013). We may thus expect that deepening fragmentation is the dominant fragmentation logic in earlier phases of an organization's history, while layering becomes more important as the organization ages (see also Mintzberg 1984).

At the same time, both mechanisms can also occur simultaneously and interact in nonlinear ways, depending on which subunits are reinforced through IO reform. The institutional dynamics unclenched by the fragmentation trap are thus manifold and may also lead to nonlinear developments that subvert one or the other fragmentation trajectory (see Chapter 7). For unless an IO is formally abandoned, organizational reproduction never reaches an endpoint (or the final lily pad), and even in the absence of exogenous shocks, the mechanisms that sustain a configuration can, at some point, also lead to a switch in pathways—by provoking adverse reactions

(Mahoney 2000; Zürn 2015) or empowering players who are interested in more far reaching reform (see Mahoney and Thelen 2010b). Still, the staying power of fragmentation should make it a difficult to overturn organizational outcome and process.

One further limitation of the fragmentation trap model should be noted in here, namely its focus on single IOs that leaves out relationships with external competitors. Hence, the ultimate option—that is, exit—is not captured by the fragmentation trap. Discontent states can, after all, withdraw from an IO and its reform coalition if they deem the costs of reform to be too high. They may thus choose exit over layering, which, in this sense, is a form of loyalty or voice (Hirschman 1970) that keeps reproducing the IO, albeit in a conflictual manner. The option that states shift resources to bilateral channels, turn to other IOs, or play different IOs against each other, is not grasped by the fragmentation trap model. It does not specify how inter-organizational competition may feed back into the reproduction process, but focuses on individual organizations and on how layering helps them to avoid exit and thereby drift. A priori, the effect of exit options seems to be ambiguous: They may strengthen the bargaining position of reformers inside the IO, because they can credibly threaten to entirely work around the IO. In that scenario, outside options would indeed weaken the strength of the fragmentation trap. However, exit options also serve to divert reform pressure from IOs, because dissatisfied states can more easily accept an organizational set-up as long as they can also opt out and pursue their aims outside the IO (see Chapter 7). They may thus sustain a fragmented IO and use it in a more erratic manner rather than putting all their efforts into reforming it, potentially even through expensive package deals with strong status quo oriented states. As long as such an effort is not made, its centrifugal forces make IO fragmentation a paradoxically stable organizational trajectory that is hardly reverted, but often reinforced through attempts at organizational reform.

2.4 Conclusion: The Methodology of Studying Path Dependent Fragmentation

Based on a historical institutionalist approach to IO design, this chapter has theorized the dynamic of organizational fragmentation. I have emphasized the importance of power driven path dependence (PDPD), and thus of distributional conflict within organizations, and specified the reform strategies through which IO fragmentation is locked in and reinforced over rounds of organizational reform: The strategy of buying subunit support leads to deeper fragmentation because it further empowers existing subunits, and the strategy of bypassing subunit blockades leads to wider fragmentation because it empowers additional subunits that are layered on the IO.

The ambition of this PDPD account of fragmentation is to lay bare institutionally determined patterns of IO change. It shall grasp how IO design and reform attempts are affected by institutional preconditions, and hence the importance of "structural determination" (Pierson 2004, pp. 92–5) for IO development. Therefore, the fragmentation trap seeks to theorize the direction of institutional change, but not the timing of individual transformations. It is about how fragmentation constrains the choices of actors, removes certain options while offering others, and thus directs their efforts toward institutional outcomes (Bachrach and Baratz 1962). This ambition requires research designs that can capture subtle and long-term institutional effects on IO reform rather than the effects of single conditions or events—and hence a combination of *overtime analysis* grasping the direction of change in IOs and *counterfactual probes* of path dependent effects on IO development.

First, a macro historical and longitudinal perspective on IO change is required to assess the overall direction of change in an organization. From a macro perspective, coherent processes of IO change become visible that escape the condition-centric approach of comparative statics designs. An overtime analysis assesses which transformations stick with an organization in the long run, and thereby captures long-term design and reform outcomes in an organization. This processual approach is not to be mistaken for what is usually referred to as process tracing in the case study literature, however. "Process tracing" describes a method that seeks to reconstruct uninterrupted causal chains, and often it implies the search for micro foundations, that is, individual-level motivational accounts (Checkel 2005; George and Bennett 2005, pp. 205–32). An analysis of macro processes (and outcomes) is different from process tracing in two respects: It focuses on aggregate trends rather than complete and linear causal chains;[18] and it seeks to explain "macro phenomena" (Mayntz 2004) such as IO outcomes through institutional dynamics rather than individual decisions. Such an explanation does not primarily hinge on unveiling the players' true motives. Assuming that actions are broadly goal-oriented, an explanation of institutional outcomes needs to be based on genuinely institutional mechanisms which organize the actions, and thus uncover the mediating role of institutional constraints (Mayntz 2004, p. 252). This overtime analysis will be performed for all three IOs investigated in this book, which retraces the histories of the WHO (Chapters 3–5) and of the

---

[18] The assumption that variables enter the historical stage in a neat sequence that only must be observed by the researcher is in any case an idealization that is hardly matched by the practice of historical research. Chains of causation usually overlap and interact with—rather than succeed—each other, so that their impact cannot be but estimated via counterfactual inference (Lebow 2010).

International Labour Organization (ILO) and UNESCO (Chapter 6). These organizations' different trajectories that started from, and reinforced, their initial designs will lend plausibility to the claim of path dependent fragmentation.

Second, and moving beyond correlations, the causal impact of endogenous institutional constraints must be investigated. This is the central task of the extended WHO case study presented in the following three chapters. However, path dependent determinants of institutional change often elude scholarly attention because they transcend the level of manifest choices. To assess endogenous institutional effects, we must rely on a *counterfactual* analysis of potential alternative choices. "Factually," in each and any instance of organizational transformation one may identify actors that attain their goals within the given contextual constraints. Most of the time, actors already anticipate institutional obstacles and take them into account in the very formulation of their goals (Fearon 1998). Therefore, it is often difficult to pin down path dependent constraints empirically. In how far did the institutional context preclude some options that the actors would have chosen otherwise? Manifestly, we are most likely to observe a series of voluntary choices, and no overt coercion, even if the actors may have preferred a world without the given institutional constraints (Gruber 2000). From that perspective, each institutional outcome could be interpreted as rationally chosen (Wendt 2001). One option to meet this challenge would be to rely on theoretically deduced counterfactuals. Thus, the analyst may determine which institutional outcomes would have been more optimal, or how far certain outcomes violate the interests of the participating actors (see Gruber 2000). However, to be able to make such an inference scholars need to externally impute which institutional reality the actors would have preferred, either collectively or individually. Given the complexity and trade-offs involved in concrete IO designs, such an approach risks not doing justice to the cases at hand.

To avoid this problem, the WHO case study pursues an alternative strategy. It investigates three *real-world attempts at organizational design and structural reform* in the WHO: Its founding moment in the 1940s and early 1950s (Chapter 3), the "Health for All" reform of the 1970s and 1980s (Chapter 4), and the "One WHO" reform undertaken at the turn of the millennium (Chapter 5). Deliberate designs, for example in constitutions or through member state resolutions, and formally agreed organizational reforms differ from everyday adaptation in that they seek to deliberately shape organizational structures. They are not the outcome of decentralized choices, but of collective and official decisions, which are usually driven by broader reform coalitions that channel new stimuli into organizations (see Section 2.3). Since such attempts are only sometimes successful, and often produce their effect only in interaction with preexisting organizational constraints, they provide good entry points for uncovering path dependent dynamics in IOs. Strong evidence for path dependent design and reform is provided where the outcome deviates from declared design and reform goals, in particular if these goals were pursued by a coalition of powerful states and/or bureaucrats.[19]

In addition to measuring reform outcomes against initial designs, each within-case study will investigate later attempts at reversing the outcome to prove its lock-in. Again, the lock-in or organizational "robustness" of path dependent outcomes will be strongest where it resists major "shocks" (Hasenclever et al. 2004). Hence, cases where strong states or bureaucrats sought to reverse fragmenting outcomes, and failed in their attempts to do so, will be strong evidence for PDPD.

This analytical focus on explicit design and reform uses a demanding benchmark for path dependence. It only examines instances where path dependence is explicitly challenged by intentional designers, while, in reality, path dependence should also be at play in myriad non-events that are left out by this design. IO designers and reformers are usually aware of, and anticipate, institutional constraints and may, therefore, refrain from certain options from the outset. An analysis centered on explicit struggles omits such anticipation effects that could further strengthen the claim of path dependent change in the WHO.

Figure 2.2 summarizes the main elements of the WHO analysis presented in Chapters 3–5, with each column symbolizing the narrative of one chapter (and the arrow on the right signifying the open horizon of the WHO's future

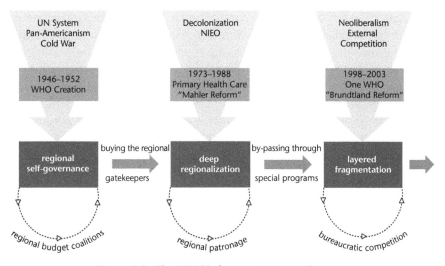

Figure 2.2. The WHO's fragmentation pathway.

<hr />

[19] Certainly, no organizational agenda will ever be fully realized, and some noise and dysfunction are always to be expected. This approach is based on a basic rationality expectation, and requires assessments of the design and reform circumstances in specific organizational settings.

pathway). The historical macro conditions and exogenous triggers for design or reform initiatives are depicted at the top of the three vertical arrows. Their organizational outcomes—regional self-governance in the 1950s, deep regionalization in the 1950s, and layered fragmentation in the 2000s—are depicted in the three central boxes. The feedback loops at the bottom signify major mechanisms of reinforcement that stabilize these outcomes, and the horizontal arrows signify the endogenous dynamics by which institutional outcomes have co-determined subsequent organizational development. This is, evidently, a stylized and simplified picture, which only grasps main aspects of the narratives presented in the following chapters. What it illustrates, though, is that this historical analysis of path dependent development is based on a combination of external and internal conditions of change. It is not an entirely internalist account where all changes are generated by the institution itself. Rather, exogenous stimuli create incentives for institutional change, which the institution receives in a path dependent way.[20]

It goes without saying that the WHO case study does not provide a strict test of the fragmentation trap in the positivist sense, given that the model was developed against the backdrop of this case. The WHO, rather, serves as an extreme case study where fragmentation can be observed to a large extent, and which therefore provides rich empirical material for exploring the underlying dynamics. Additionally, and as outlined in Chapter 1, the WHO is a hard case for fragmentation from the viewpoint of functionalist IO design theory. Its regionalization not only violates constitutional provisions, but its fragmented structure is also deemed to be dysfunctional rather than rationally designed. That the organization moves on along the fragmentation pathway despite repeated centralization attempts thus provides strong evidence for a PDPD explanation. Chapter 6 will then extend the analysis to two other UN specialized agencies, the ILO and UNESCO, to assess the external plausibility of path dependent fragmentation. This chapter compares "varieties of decentralization" in these IOs and thereby gauges how IOs institutionalize field services depending on their previous level of fragmentation. The contrasting decentralization pathways of both IOs—top-down "decentralization" in the ILO, but widening and deepening fragmentation into thematic sectors in UNESCO— suggest that path dependent fragmentation is relevant beyond the WHO case.

---

[20] Certainly, this external-internal distinction is never clear cut in reality. IOs also shape their environment and thus the "external" conditions for their reproduction (Greif and Laitin 2004), and IO reformers are to some extent always by-producing the legitimacy crisis to which they "respond" (see Section 2.2). Thus, what becomes an external trigger for change also depends on how IOs "read" their environments (Broome and Seabrooke 2012). In the case studies that follow, these causal interplays between external and internal determinants will only be studied as the background conditions that inform a specific design and reform effort. The analytical focus, however, will be on how design and reform agendas, once formulated, are absorbed by and transform the institutional trajectory of an IO.

3

Locking in a Pan American Headstart

The Long Founding Moment of the
World Health Organization

"Medicine is one of the pillars of peace." With this quote from Archbishop Spellman, the Brazilian delegation to the United Nations Conference on International Organization, held in San Francisco in the spring of 1945, was the first to raise the subject of health in postwar international politics. The initiative was well received. Although health had initially not been on the agenda, the San Francisco delegates unanimously approved the Brazilian and Chinese call to quickly establish an international health organization (WHO 1958c, p. 38). The constitution of the World Health Organization (WHO) was signed and sealed in July 1946 and entrusted the new agency to work towards "the attainment by all peoples of the highest possible level of health" (Art. 1). The WHO's mandate and functions express the joint ideals of internationally minded public health officials and their firm belief in medical and social progress.[1] At the same time, the history of the WHO's creation is a prime example of the conflict and uncertainty involved in building international organizations (IOs)—and the role that path dependence and institutional precedent play even during an IO's founding moment.

The present chapter investigates the WHO's founding period in order to retrace the historical origins and rapid lock-in of its regionalized design. From an institutional design perspective, founding moments are historical windows that offer ideal opportunities for deliberate institution-building: With institutional constraints severed, rational designers have the chance to break with the past and establish IOs that are based on contemporary preferences and ambitions. Yet as the WHO example demonstrates, distributional conflict and

---

[1] Staples (2006) gives a comprehensive account of the WHO's foundational ideals (pp. 132–60).

path dependent constraints also play out on the original design of IOs. During the WHO's creation, the deadlock between adherents of a more centralized and a more regionalized design produced a constitutional compromise that was in fact ambiguous enough to let subsequent events decide on the actual institutionalization of regionalization—events that were marked by the onset of the Cold War and a massive mobilization for the preexisting Pan American Sanitary Bureau (PASB) and thus against its integration into a hierarchical international health agency. These developments tipped the balance in favor of the regions to an extent not anticipated by the founders of the WHO. Thus, the WHO's founding moment did not end, rather it started in 1946, and lasted until 1951—the year its regional organizations became operative and developed a practice of regional self-governance. The result was an unexpectedly regionalized system that exceeded the constitutional design in that it instituted the regional directors as factual veto players vis-à-vis the director-general (DG). Nevertheless, this fragmented "design" was immediately reinforced by the winners of regionalization, especially recipient states which successfully used their regional offices as distributive vehicles in the WHO budgeting process. Regionalization was thus promptly reproduced through member state practice and locked in deeply enough to withstand several early attempts at reversal.

The WHO's founding moment is thus, both the starting point of path dependent fragmentation, and itself an illustration of power-driven path dependence (PDPD). For one, already the vague constitutional compromise that postponed the PASB's integration and only demanded that all other regional offices be firmly integrated with the WHO, reflected powers vested in existing regional arrangements, first and foremost the PASB. But also when measured against the stricter benchmark for rational design, the constitutional compromise, the actual outcome of the institution building process deviated from the negotiated design (see Section 2.4). This regionalized outcome was both shaped by the PASB's mobilizing power and aided by unforeseen developments, and in that sense bore signs of strong historical contingency as well (see Section 2.2). In particular, the unexpectedly protracted ratification process of the WHO constitution delayed institution building in Geneva, and thereby opened a historical window for the PASB to preempt its integration with the new agency. The Latin American countermobilization cemented an exceptional status for the PASB that would be emulated in all new WHO regions. Subsequently, developing states swiftly aligned themselves around their regional bureaus and thus created vested interests in maintaining regionalization. The winners of regionalization thus managed to perpetuate the pro-regional exception, which greatly affected the prospects for later reform attempts, as we will see below in Chapters 4 and 5.

The chapter covers the WHO's founding years and the early lock-in of its regionalization until the 1960s. It is based on primary documents, WHO oral history material, and secondary sources, which unveil the uncertainties, conflicts, and sequential dynamics involved in the institution building process. After giving a brief outline of the WHO's basic mission and structure in Section 3.1, I analyze the regionalization dispute in four main steps. Section 3.2 expounds the initial deadlock between regionalizers and centralizers and the constitutional compromise that it gave rise to. Section 3.3 retraces what I call the "Pan American headstart": The massive Latin American mobilization for their Bureau between 1946 and 1948, while the WHO was still on stand-by and had to accept the PASB's special status. The subsequent emulation of the Pan American "exception" in all other regional organizations will be reconstructed in Section 3.4. Finally, Section 3.5 documents the early reproduction and lock-in of the regionalization pathway in the 1950s and 1960s.

3.1 The First Universal Health Organization: Mandate and Basic Structure

The WHO's constitution was designed in two steps. A so-called Technical Preparatory Committee (TPC)[2] met in Paris from March 18 to April 5, 1946, to prepare the International Health Conference (IHC), the inter-governmental constitutional assembly that would meet in New York from June 19 to July 22 of the same year. The Committee actually prepared a draft constitution that expressed the overall consensus on the WHO's mandate and structure and that would not be radically revised in New York. The founders of the WHO agreed rather quickly on the ambitious mandate of the new international health organization as well as its goal of universal membership. The WHO should incorporate and exceed the functions of preexisting international health organizations, and thereby also overcome the fragmented institutional landscape of the interwar period.

This immediate pre-WHO period had been marked by the uneasy coexistence of two international health organizations in Europe: The Paris-based Office International d'Hygiène Publique (OIHP, 1907–46) and the Geneva-based League of Nations Health Organization (LNHO, 1921–46).[3] The first of

---

[2] The Committee was composed of sixteen individuals, mostly chiefs of their national health services. Formally, they acted in their capacity as experts in international health, although de facto they represented government positions (Goodman 1971, p. 152). The experts were natives of Belgium, Mexico, Canada, Argentina, Czechoslovakia, France, Egypt, Norway, England, Poland, Greece, India, the USA, Brazil, Yugoslavia, and China (WHO 1947b, p. 5).

[3] The WHO also inherited some of the functions and budget of the United Nations Relief and Rehabilitation Administration (UNRRA, active 1943–6), a temporary relief agency whose mandate had included health services to war-devastated regions in Europe (Goodman 1971, pp. 148–66).

them, the OIHP, had been established in the context of the international sanitary conferences, which were held since the 1850s and negotiated rules for the containment of several "quarantinable" diseases such as cholera and plague, the so-called International Sanitary Conventions. The Office's foundation was initiated at the eleventh sanitary conference in 1903, at a time of major breakthroughs in the study of disease transmission, which gave a boost to international cooperation in the domain of disease control. The Office was constituted by a committee of twelve member states initially, nine of which were European, and its main task was to oversee the application and development of the sanitary conventions, mostly through informational activities. The OIHP also worked on a range of other health topics such as the standardization of anti-diphtheritic serum or venereal diseases (WHO 1958c, pp. 15–29). Yet by the end of World War I, broader visions of public health were gaining ground that went beyond the focus on epidemiology and the control of contagious disease. These new ambitions became part of the mission of the LNHO, which was established after the end of World War I as the League's technical body for public health. The fact that the LNHO did not build on or incorporate the OIHP was mostly due to the US, who stayed outside the League but continued to be a member of the OIHP (Howard-Jones 1978). In parts, for example with regard to epidemiological intelligence, both organizations cooperated. In other respects, they diversified, for example as the LNHO took on new topics such as housing and nutrition. Still, the coexistence of both agencies was ripe with tension, legal confusion as to the status and relationship of both bodies, and overlapping activities in the expanding field of (international) public health.[4]

The new agency should transcend this deadlock and become truly universal, regarding both its mandate and its structure. Its policy ambitions are expressed in the preamble to its constitution (WHO 2006), which stipulates an ideal of health as "a state of complete physical, mental and social well-being and not merely the absence of disease or infirmity." This vision, or utopia, expresses the aspiration of many of the WHO's founders to go beyond disease-oriented "biomedical" public health work to also address the social conditions affecting human health and well-being.[5] Accordingly, the WHO's domains of activity are defined very broadly, taking up and further developing the agendas of both its predecessor organizations. Article 2 of the WHO's

The WHO only received a share of UNRRA's funds, while the larger share was transferred to the United Nations International Children's Emergency Fund, renamed United Nations Children's Fund (UNICEF) in 1953 (Farley 2008, p. 68; cf. Soper 1977, p. 320).

[4] Detailed accounts of pre-WHO international health cooperation are provided in (Goodman 1971, pp. 23–150; Howard-Jones 1978; WHO 1958c, pp. 3–34).

[5] On the debate between biomedical and sociomedical approaches to public health see Lee (2009, pp. 5–9, 16–21).

constitution lists no less than twenty-two functions and activities for the new agency.[6] The WHO should not only combat infectious diseases through, for example, its epidemiological services, but also work on nutrition and housing, economic and working conditions, maternal and child health, mental health, and environmental health. To do so, its competencies range from informational, promotional, and educational activities to technical services at the country level. The WHO's overarching function is its normative leadership role, i.e. it shall "act as the directing and coordinating authority on international health work" (Art. 2 (a)). It provides guidance to member states and their public health authorities, but also to other health-related IOs, through technical standards, conventions, and recommendations.[7]

Universality was also a structural aspiration for the WHO, which was deliberately named "World" Health Organization, and not "International" or "United Nations" Health Organization to express its global outlook (Sharp 1947, p. 514; WHO 1958c, pp. 40–1). Special emphasis was laid on the principle of inclusive membership. The WHO is open to all states, including states that are not members of the United Nations (UN) but can be easily admitted by means of a simple majority vote (Burci and Vignes 2004, p. 21). All member states are represented in the WHO's supreme governing body, the World Health Assembly (WHA), which determines the WHO's policies, program, and budget. The Assembly designates the states entitled to send individuals to the Executive Board,[8] the organization's central executive organ. The Board prepares and enacts the Assembly's work and decisions through its reports and prepares the program of work. Its central role in the organization becomes apparent through its competence to recommend a person to the Assembly for appointment as director-general (DG)—which means that de facto this decision is made by the Board and merely endorsed by the WHA (Burci and Vignes 2004, p. 48; Lee 2009, p. 27). The DG is the technical and managerial head of the secretariat and appoints its staff. Like all international civil servants, the DG and the secretariat staff are formally independent from member state instructions.[9] Figure 3.1 depicts the relationship between the

[6] The WHO's myriad constitutional functions and activities are not easily categorized. Over time, a conventional distinction between "technical" cooperation and "normative" directing activities has become dominant (see Burci and Vignes 2004, pp. 119–20).

[7] For example, UNICEF traditionally used WHO guidelines for executing vaccination campaigns (cf. Hanrieder forthcoming 2015).

[8] Originally, Executive Board members were defined as independent experts and not as state representatives. This constitutional rule led to a situation of open hypocrisy accompanied by rather awkward diplomatic language (with formulations such as "in the country I know best . . ."). Formal rules were adapted to actual practice in 1998, when the Assembly decided that Board members should henceforth act as "government representatives" (Burci and Vignes 2004, pp. 45–6).

[9] For a detailed description of the WHO's structure and constitutional practice see Burci and Vignes (2004, pp. 35–66).

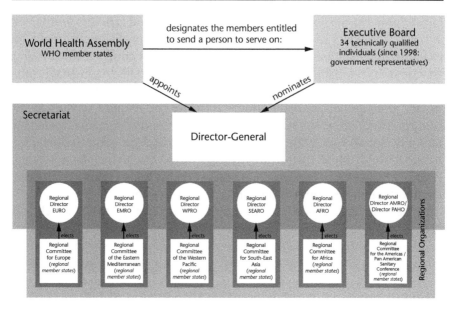

Figure 3.1. Structure of the World Health Organization.

WHO's main constitutional organs, including the special status of the regions, which was negotiated over several years.

3.2 The Foundational Deadlock: "Let Future Decide ..."

It was mainly in one respect that the WHO's future structure was contested: The negotiators could not agree on the creation and status of regional units within the WHO. That some regional layer within the organization was required was uncontroversial—and yet, positions on the extent of regional autonomies diverged too sharply to be accommodated. The major source of complexity and conflict that jeopardized the negotiations was the problem of what should become of the Pan American Sanitary Bureau (PASB).

The PASB was not the only regional organization that preceded the WHO's creation. Other regional bodies that existed at the time of the WHO's creation, such as a range of sanitary councils in colonized territories, and the regional bureaus of the OIHP and LNHO, had also been in operation for decades. Still, the question of their continued autonomy was never seriously raised (Goodman 1971, p. 318). This even held for the most important of the regional sanitary councils, the Egyptian Quarantine Board located in Alexandria. This body had administered the sanitary regime of the Suez Canal, monitored the Mecca pilgrimage, and entertained quarantine stations and their laboratories; and it is moreover considered the oldest international health organization (Goodman 1971, pp. 319–20). After World War II Egypt re-established the Board as the "Pan Arab Regional Health Bureau." Nevertheless, its maintenance as a separate entity was not seriously considered while the WHO was being established (Howard-Jones 1981, p. 17).

The PASB, by contrast, was protected by a determined coalition of Latin American states that grew stronger the longer the WHO's institution-building process lasted. This development would result in a federal bargain which left all WHO regions in a stronger position than the founders had anticipated and determined in the constitution. This section reconstructs the first stage of this historical bargain, the genesis of the constitutional compromise between regionalizers and centralizers. While at the outset, the postwar status of the PASB was precarious, this uncertainty was provisionally resolved through a constitutional compromise, which postponed the PASB's integration with the WHO. In this compromise, the status of full integration into the organization was reserved for the additional regional offices, to be created in the other five WHO regions.

Squaring the Circle between Globalism and (Pan American) Regionalism

Since its creation in 1902, the PASB had acted as the health agency of all American states with the exception of Canada, Newfoundland, and the British West Indies. The Bureau administered a series of Pan American health con-ventions and delivered epidemiological, advisory, and research services in Latin America. Like the Egyptian Quarantine Board, it had additionally served as the regional epidemiological intelligence service for the OIHP since 1926 (Howard-Jones 1981, p. 13). The PASB was part of a broader Pan American system, which had its origins in the nineteenth century. Pan Americanism had become an eminent vehicle of technical assistance from the United States (US) to Latin America during World War II, and was therefore vividly defended by most Latin American states (Whitaker 1954, pp. 171–2).

The PASB as an organizational stronghold of Pan Americanism would persist even as the Pan American Union turned into the Organization of American States in 1948 (see pp. 60–1). The Bureau's evolution is summarized in the historical overview in Table 3.1. However, at the time of the WHO's creation, the PASB's independence as a continental health agency was at stake. The US was starting to withdraw from its Pan American commitments. Before World War II, Pan American cooperation had been part of US isolationism (Whitaker 1954, pp. 156–7), yet US entrance into the war already marked a priority shift from the regional to the global level. While constructing the postwar international order, the US government actually turned away from its hemispheric commitments and ceased its established practice of consultation through Pan American forums. Initial plans to prioritize regional

Table 3.1. Development of the Pan American Health Organization[a]

1902	Founded as the *International Sanitary Bureau* of the (usually quadrennial) International Sanitary Conferences of the American Republics, with headquarters in Washington D.C., and seven staff members located in five countries
1923	Renamed *Pan American Sanitary Bureau* (PASB, now serving the Pan American Sanitary Conferences), still seven members
1926	Designated regional epidemiological intelligence service of the Office International d'Hygiène Publique (OIHP)
1947	Becomes one of four organs of the newly established Pan American Sanitary Organization (PASO), the other organs being the Pan American Sanitary Conference, the Directing Council, and the Executive Committee
1949	Integrated with the WHO as American Regional Office (AMRO) while maintaining its separate identity as PASB within PASO
1958	PASO becomes *Pan American Health Organization* (PAHO)

[a] Cf. Howard-Jones 1981; Pan American Health Organization 1992.

over global institutions within the UN were quickly shelved by both Churchill and Roosevelt, who jointly pushed for the UN system as the prime arena of postwar multilateralism (Hull 1948, pp. 1640–7). This internationalism which shaped the UN security institutions, the Bretton Woods system and early specialized agencies such as the Food and Agriculture Organization (Luard 1982, pp. 37–8) was an evident threat to Pan Americanism.

US commitment was also dwindling with regard to its continental health agency—which had never been a strong organization in any case. The PASB operated on a tiny regular budget of about US\$115,000[10] (Soper 1977, p. 320) and suffered from its near total dependence on staff seconded by the US Public Health Service (Howard-Jones 1981, pp. 13–16). For all intents and purposes, the US Surgeon General served as the Bureau's director, who since 1924 was supported by one staff member, and the facilities of the Bureau consisted of one single room within the offices of the Pan American Sanitary Union.[11] From 1942 onward, however, the US government increasingly turned away from the PASB and began to work through bilateral channels instead of the Bureau. US funding for international health thus shifted to its newly created Institute of Inter-American Affairs, and preparations were made for working through the WHO once it became operative (Soper 1977, pp. 313–14). As a consequence, the PASB's financial situation became so acute that in 1947 it was on the verge of collapse (Soper 1977, p. 320).

This precarious situation seemed like a good opportunity for the new international health organization to step in and integrate the PASB. However, many Latin American states were unwilling to give up their continental health

[10] These resources combined with several US-funded special programs and fellowships, the PASB's total program budget in 1946 amounted to US\$600,000 (Soper 1977, p. 320).

[11] The early PASB archives have not been preserved and staff numbers are hardly documented. From available information one can infer that the office's resources were barely increased prior to 1947 (Howard-Jones 1981; Soper 1977).

agency—and expected a similar stance to be taken by the US government. Yet the US position in this regard was far from clear. It persistently oscillated between Pan American solidarity and a globalist plea for full integration. On the one hand, the US delegates to the International Health Conference were instructed to "assure the supremacy of [WHO] in all matters of world-wide concern" (quoted in Staples 2006, p. 135). Yet at the same time, PASB staff vigorously defended their organization vis-à-vis their government. The PASB could also rely on strong support from the US private sector. Its pharmaceutical industry pressured the US government to protect the PASB, due to asset-specific investments in the Latin American market (Farley 2008, p. 99). These various interest groups consequently challenged the government's internationalist aspirations and made the PASB's future a site of intricate contestation.

While the WHO's federal structure was negotiated, the contested fate of the PASB was closely linked to the general question of what status regional units should enjoy within the WHO. As can be seen from the minutes of the Technical Preparatory Committee (TPC), the regional question was controversially debated among the drafters of the WHO constitution. The four written proposals submitted to the TPC by the United Kingdom (UK), the US, France, and Yugoslavia participants already mirrored the irreconcilable positions. The British draft held that priority should be given to establishing a central organization, with regional offices only providing epidemiological intelligence services (WHO 1947b, pp. 42–5). This would have implied the practical termination of the PASB's mandate. Likewise, the French submission suggested that regional offices should merely provide advice to the central organization (WHO 1947b, p. 52), while the Yugoslavian proposal left the decision over the status of such offices to regional member state preferences (WHO 1947b, p. 57).

The US proposal was less straightforward. It suggested a "dual allegiance" solution with, on the one hand, regional offices subject to the authority of the central organization, and, on the other, the continued existence and cooperative "arrangements" with existing "regional organizations" (WHO 1947b, p. 48), that is, the PASB. Thus, although the US negotiators argued that further delegation to regional offices should wait until the central organization was firmly established (Siddiqi 1995, p. 64), they agreed a flexibility mechanism should be kept in place. As it was "not possible to determine precisely the nature or degree of regional health organization which may prove to be the most effective," experimentation with both "autonomous" agencies and "[d]ependent regional offices" (WHO 1947b, pp. 67–8) would be a valuable solution.

This proposal, however, according to which existing regional organizations would not be merged with but only "utilized" by the WHO, was unacceptable for the internationalists present on the Committee. In particular, the British,

Norwegian, and French participants voiced concerns that the coexistence of several autonomous organizations would spur "sectional interests" and "unfortunate competition" (WHO 1947b, p. 29), and thereby jeopardize the unity of the organization. The goal should rather be a "takeover" of preexisting regional organizations by the new organization (WHO 1947b, p. 28).

Despite intensive negotiations, disagreement over the extent of regionalization was so profound that in the end two alternative formulations were put into the constitutional draft for the IHC. The first version, submitted by the Argentinean, French, and Norwegian Committee members, suggested that existing regional agencies should be "fully utilized" by the new organization, but developed "as quickly as practicable into regional offices of the Organization, or parts of such offices" (WHO 1947b, p. 67). The second proposal, submitted by the US delegation, merely called for "special arrangements" for the "fullest possible" utilization of existing regional health agencies. The TPC put these alternatives to a vote, in which nine participants supported the first proposition and six voted for the flexible system proposed by the US (WHO 1947b, p. 32).[12] However, this vote was not taken as a decision on the matter. Instead, the result was communicated together with the draft containing both formulations to the founding conference. With the IHC only two months away (June 1946), the Committee members reported back home on the preparations made, and countries prepared their delegations for the decisive meeting in New York.

The Compromise Formula: Postponing Integration

The IHC was attended by all UN member states, including the Soviet states that had not been represented on the TPC and were very critical of an autonomous PASB inside the WHO (WHO 1947d, p. 23).[13] Hence, the TPC deadlock went into a new round at the New York conference. While most Latin American countries rallied behind the principle of "dual allegiance," many other delegations including Canada, the UK, China, India, Poland, South Africa and, especially, the Soviet states, insisted that existing regional organizations be integrated into the WHO rather expeditiously (WHO 1947d, p. 23).

---

[12] The minutes do not identify the adherents of the two propositions.

[13] Delegations to the IHC had been sent by Argentina, Australia, Belgium, Bolivia, Brazil, Canada, Chile, China, Colombia, Costa Rica, Cuba, Czechoslovakia, Denmark, Dominican Republic, Ecuador, Egypt, El Salvador, Ethiopia, France, Greece, Guatemala, Haiti, Honduras, India, Iran, Iraq, Lebanon, Liberia, Luxembourg, Mexico, the Netherlands, New Zealand, Nicaragua, Norway, Panama, Paraguay, Peru, Poland, Philippines, Saudi Arabia, Syria, Turkey, Ukrainian Soviet Republic, Union of Soviet Socialist Republics, Union of South Africa, United Kingdom (UK), USA, Uruguay, Venezuela, and Yugoslavia (WHO 1947d, pp. 7–11).

However, with twenty out of fifty-one delegations, the PASB had a very powerful lobby, which even acted as a bloc at the IHC—a degree of mobilization that was not met by any other country group (Farley 2008, pp. 23–4). During the Conference and its various side events, PASB director Hugh Cumming was constantly rallying against what he considered a doomed internationalist project, even seeing it as an instrument of communist infiltration of the Western hemisphere (Howard-Jones 1978, pp. 161–3; Staples 2006, p. 135). Most PASB member states were unwilling to give up their Bureau in favor of a new agency, the shape and program of which could only vaguely be anticipated. Due to this stalemate, the dispute was referred to a "harmonizing sub-committee" to figure out a compromise behind closed doors.[14] This sub-committee settled on the principle of "progressive and ultimate merger" (Sharp 1947, p. 517). The wording of this compromise was sufficiently vague to be acceptable to both centralizers and separationists (WHO 1947d, p. 24):

> The Pan American Sanitary Organization, represented by the Pan American Sanitary Bureau and the Pan American Sanitary Conferences and all other inter-governmental regional health organizations in existence prior to the date of signature of this Constitution, shall in due course be integrated with the Organization. This integration shall be effected as soon as practicable through common action based on mutual consent of the competent authorities expressed through the organizations concerned.

This compromise, enshrined in Article 54 of the WHO constitution, was of course in need of interpretation both with regard to the time-frame for integration ("in due course") and the precise meaning of "integration." That is why the Canadian delegate Brock Chisholm (who would later become the WHO's first DG) insisted that all delegations agree on the dictionary definition of "integration" as "making it whole" or "entirely becoming part of a single organization." This definition was, according to the minutes, "unanimously approved" (WHO 1947d, p. 60). The question of timing however, that is, of what "in due course" should mean, was not further specified.

The timing for establishing the WHO's other regional organizations was equally left to future decisions. The World Health Assembly should delineate regional boundaries, and regional member states were then to decide upon the creation of a regional organization in their respective area (Art. 44). What the constitution did determine, though, was that any future regional organization should be an "integral part" of the organization and subject to the "authority of the Director-General and the Organization" (Arts. 45–51). Yet, as the

---

[14] The sub-committee was composed of delegations from Brazil, China, the Dominican Republic, El Salvador, France, India, Lebanon, Mexico, the Netherlands, Norway, Peru, the Union of Soviet Socialist Republics, UK, USA, Venezuela, and Yugoslavia (WHO 1947d, pp. 23–4).

57

US delegate Thomas Parran wisely predicted, only future "goodwill and cooperation of Governments" could determine the "result" of this rough regionalization roadmap (WHO 1947d, p. 60). Indeed, the sequence of events that unfolded after the 1946 compromise would prove him right: As the onset of the Cold War enabled the PASB to preempt its integration into the WHO (Section 3.3), region-building beyond the Americas followed the example set by it and thereby diverged significantly from the WHO's founding document (Section 3.4).

3.3 The Pan American Headstart

Future developments benefited the PASB, as we will see in this section. As the Cold War put an end to the postwar internationalist moment, the balance tipped in favor of the Bureau. While the WHO was forced into an interim period of nearly two years, the PASB was significantly strengthened following a change in leadership in January 1947. Faced with a reinforced pro-PASB coalition, the interim WHO had to accept an agreement that cemented the PASB's special status as a separate organization, in spite of the constitutional integration clause.

The PASB's Headstart into the Cold War

Until the WHO constitution would enter into force, a WHO Interim Commission (WHOIC) was charged with preparing for the first WHA, which should decide on the WHO's program, resources, and the details regarding its organs. What the WHO's founders had not anticipated, though, was the long delay until the WHO became operational. The general expectation had been that "the Interim Commission would come to an end in a matter of months" (Goodman 1971, p. 167). Yet, the requirement of twenty-six UN member state ratifications turned out to be a daunting threshold at a time when Cold War tensions were rising and UN euphoria was waning, even among the originators of the UN system. In the US, anticommunism was on the rise after a group of right-wing Republicans took over Congress in the November 1946 midterm elections (Farley 2008, pp. 48–9). Their suspicion of the WHO's involvement in health insurance matters—representing the threat of "socialized medicine"—led the US to postpone their ratification until July 1948 (Siddiqi 1995, p. 102).[15] Likewise, the Soviet states only ratified in March

---

[15] The US reserved the right to withdraw from the WHO at one year's notice—an exception that was grudgingly accepted at the World Health Assembly (Allen 1950, p. 38).

and April 1948, thereby agreeing to set up an organization that they would later even quit temporarily due to mounting Cold War tensions.[16]

It took until April 7, 1948 for the necessary ratifications to be collected (see Appendix 1); the importance of this date can be read from the fact that the seventh of April has been declared World Health Day that the WHO celebrates each year. The minutes of the Interim Commission's sessions are replete with announcements of the latest ratification news (e.g. WHO 1947a, p. 9, 1947c, p. 10) during this unforeseen "long wait" (Farley 2008, p. 48). During its gestation period, the Interim Commission had to witness how other international institutions such as the United Nations International Children's Emergency Fund (UNICEF, renamed United Nations Children's Fund in 1953) took on health activities of their own (Farley 2008, p. 50). And in its function as the "acting WHO," it had to conduct negotiations with an increasingly confident PASB.

While the WHO was still operating on stand-by mode, the PASB was taking steps to preempt an integration agreement that would sacrifice its autonomy to the new health agency. Already in October 1946, the PASB's directing council convened in Havana and advised member states to protect the Bureau's identity and independence, and thus to sign the WHO constitution only with reservations (WHO 1947a, p. 103). This recommendation upset the US who had not participated in the Havana meeting, and the US delegate to the Interim Commission warned that the US government would press the American states into signing the WHO constitution without any reservations (WHO 1947a, p. 17). And indeed, the subsequent Pan American Sanitary Conference, held in Caracas in January 1947, confirmed the principle of integration. At the same time, however, it was agreed that any formal agreement with the WHO should be postponed until fourteen PASB member states had signed the WHO Constitution (Berkov 1957, p. 60). The Caracas conference did see the appointment of a new director for the Bureau, Fred Soper, who would use this time lag to considerably build up the PASB's status and resources.

Soper, who had been unanimously elected in Caracas, brought to the Bureau an enormous reputation as a pioneer in the combat of yellow fever and international health work in general. His work with the Rockefeller Foundation, at the time a major provider of international health interventions, had won him high esteem in Latin America—and good connections to many American health ministries. This standing helped Soper to overcome the

---

[16] In 1949, the Soviet Union, the Ukraine, and Byelorussia withdrew from the WHO, claiming their dissatisfaction with the organization's work. By August 1950, Albania, Bulgaria, Czechoslovakia, Hungary, Poland, and Romania also withdrew, stating that the WHO had come under American domination. These states only rejoined the WHO after Stalin's death, between 1955 (Soviet Union) and 1963 (Hungary). Formally, they returned from inactive to active membership, given that the WHO constitution does not provide for withdrawals from membership (Siddiqi 1995, pp. 104–9).

Bureau's budgetary crisis through an aggressive fundraising campaign across the continent. He managed to win extra-budgetary contributions of nearly US$1.0 million for the Bureau's 1948 budget from eight Latin American states,[17] a sum that amounted to one-fifth of what was the WHO's total budget for 1949 (WHO 1958c, p. 74). In addition, the new leadership did not only strive to materially strengthen the Bureau, but also overhauled its treaty base. By September 1947, the new constitution of the Pan American Sanitary Organization (PASO) was agreed. Thereby, the PASB's status was transformed from a mere "executive board" of the Pan American Sanitary Conferences into a full-fledged IO secretariat (Howard-Jones 1981, p. 17). The PASB, or PASO, thus did everything possible to make itself too big to be absorbed.

The WHO-PASO Agreement: Pre-empting Integration

The WHO's Interim Commission, still lacking the capacities to integrate such a sizeable budget (Soper 1977, p. 322), was thus confronted with a reinforced Bureau that had positioned itself as the main distributional instrument for Latin American states. In the negotiations between the two agencies, Soper warned the commissioners quite bluntly that the ongoing expansion of the Bureau increasingly reduced the need for American states to integrate at all with the WHO (WHO 1947c, pp. 25–7, 1948a, pp. 68–70). In this unequal state of affairs, the WHO's negotiators grudgingly accepted an agreement that cemented the continued independence of its Pan American counterpart. The agreement specifies that PASO's organs should serve as the WHO's regional committee and regional office for the Americas, but at the same time keep its independence. PASO henceforth wore two different hats, as "in deference to tradition, both organizations shall retain their respective names" (WHO 1949c, p. 382): American Regional Office (AMRO) inside the WHO and PASO in the Americas (see Figure 3.1).

Indeed, it was not until these negotiations were concluded that PASO's directing council at its October 1948 meeting recommended to American member states "the desirability of ratifying the Constitution of the World Health Organization" (WHO 1948b, pp. 57–8). After Uruguay had ratified the constitution on April 22, 1949, PASO's quorum of fourteen American WHO members was reached and Chisholm and Soper signed the agreement for their respective organizations (WHO 1949a, p. 131).

Initially, the WHO directorate and the Executive Board insisted that the agreement did not yet constitute "integration" in the sense of the Constitution (WHO 1948b, p. 27, 1949c, p. 383). Upon its signature, legal opinions

---

[17] In his memoirs, Soper (1977) lists the following contributors: Argentina, Brazil, Chile, Dominican Republic, El Salvador, Mexico, Uruguay, and Venezuela (p. 322).

were obtained as to how the PASB's full integration could be achieved.[18] However, after a fruitless visit of Chisholm to the White House (Farley 2008, pp. 100–1), the WHO gave up challenging this halfway integration. To the contrary, PASO's dual status was reinforced through an agreement between PASO and the Pan American Union's successor, the Organization of American States (OAS), concluded in May 1950. This agreement demanded that PASO preserve its identity and autonomy as a specialized inter-American organization. Despite being legally looser than the agreement binding PASO to the WHO (Calderwood 1963, pp. 23–4), the OAS-PASO agreement put an additional obstacle in front of formal integration (Farley 2008, p. 103).

Hence, it was a mix of path dependent constraints (or opportunities, if looked at from the Pan American side) and unforeseen developments (the ratification delay) that left PASO with a special status inside the WHO. The WHO-PASO agreement has remained in force until the present day. This inter-agency agreement has perpetuated a historical asymmetry between the PASO and the WHOIC that was due to historical precedent, and that was also reflected in the unequal standing of the organizations' leaders: While Soper was a prestigious international health practitioner with very good political connections, his counterpart Chisholm was a contested leader due to his eccentric and esoteric views on health and international politics (Farley 2008).[19] Chisholm would only remain in office until 1953, which would be just long enough to extend the PASO-WHO bargain to all newly established WHO regions. The Pan American headstart would thereby also bias the implementation of the design for the non-American regional organizations.

3.4 Region-building Beyond the Constitution

The constitutional design that had been determined for the WHO's new regional organizations (see Section 3.2) would not remain unaffected by the Pan American head start. This concerns in particular the standing of the regional directors vis-à-vis the central governing bodies and the DG. In this section I retrace how the rapid region-building process after 1948 and the endorsed practice of regional self-governance completed the WHO's founding moment and produced an unforeseen pro-regional outcome.

---

[18] See WHO archival file no. 955-1-3.
[19] I thank Bob Reinalda for reminding me of this asymmetry between the two leading figures of the PASB-WHO bargain.

Instant Region-building after 1948

As indicated above, the constitution left the actual geographical definition of regions to the Assembly, and also the very creation of regional organizations was made contingent on the consent by a majority of member states in the respective area (Art. 44). When institution-building started at the first Assembly in June 1948, disagreements emerged as to whether it was feasible and desirable to immediately establish new regional organizations. The US delegation questioned whether sufficient resources were available for instant regionalization (WHO 1948a, p. 270). An Irish delegate pointedly compared the WHO to a newborn child and insisted that "one does not expect a child to produce a family until it has reached the age of maturity" (WHO 1948a, p. 58). Similar positions were put forward by the Canadian and Chinese delegations (WHO 1948a, pp. 271–2). The skeptics were outvoted however, and the Assembly defined six geographical areas: An Eastern Mediterranean, a Western Pacific, a South-East Asia, a European, an African, and an American area—regions which followed geographic and political lines, but in many cases were not grounded in public health or epidemiological considerations (cf. Appendix 2).[20]

The necessary majority for the creation of a regional organization was not attained immediately in all areas. Australia and New Zealand hesitated to join the Western Pacific region as they saw no need for a regional organization on top of the WHO's global services (WHO 1948a, p. 270). In Europe, views regarding regionalization were initially divided,[21] and it was agreed that a temporary special office for war-devastated territories would be sufficient, given that the WHO headquarters would be located in Geneva (WHO 1948a, pp. 264–5, 269). Yet the majority rule ensured that by 1951, all WHO regions established regional offices.

So for the most part, region-building in the WHO was a bottom-up process. One remarkable exception to this pattern is the case of the African region, where region-building was full of friction. Consisting at the time almost entirely of dependent territories, the African region demonstrated the problems that colonial rule posed for a UN organization that was based on the principle of sovereign statehood. It became a particular legal challenge to define who would be entitled to act as a member state in a region that was, for the most part, governed from Europe. In 1948, only one independent

---

[20] A particularly politicized case was Israel, which had joined the WHO as early as 1948. Due to the ensuing Arab-Israeli dispute, the Eastern Mediterranean regional committee did not meet at all between 1951 and 1953, and only in separate sub-committees thereafter, until Israel joined the European region in 1985 (Siddiqi 1995, pp. 73–161). Likewise due to political conflicts, India and Pakistan joined different regions (see Appendix 2).

[21] See WHO archival file no. 1 905-3-1.

African state, namely Liberia, was a WHO and a UN member state (WHO 1948a, pp. 265–6). Although the French, Portuguese, and British delegations hastened to assure everyone that they would be happy to participate in overseas regional organizations on behalf of their colonies (WHO 1948a, p. 266), their entitlement to do so was heavily disputed at the Assembly. Ultimately, a ruling was found according to which each "administering power" would be represented in regional organizations, but with only one vote for all territories in the region (WHO 1949b, p. 213).[22]

Secondly, the decentralization of administrative tasks to the regional level was far from smooth in the African case, as can be seen from the WHO's documentation of correspondence on this matter.[23] Finding an adequate office site and personnel for the new regional organization proved difficult for both infrastructural and political reasons. The choice of Brazzaville, Congo, was justified on the grounds of its "modern facilities and lack of racial discrimination." Still, the office could hardly get up-and-running due to a dire lack of human resources; it was well-nigh impossible to find candidates with both public health training and regional experience. These "staff difficulties" provoked calls to temporarily recentralize certain functions, such as the administration of WHO fellowships. Yet the credo in headquarters was that administrative decentralization was to be implemented evenly across all regions (WHO 1951, pp. 56–7), leading Geneva to insist on completing administrative decentralization to the African region to the same extent as to other regional offices.[24]

Toward Regional Self-governance

The African example demonstrates that operative authorities were delegated symmetrically to the newly established regional offices.[25] However, as soon as regional organizations existed, an answer to a much more critical question had to be found, namely the question of who actually governed the regional offices. This concerned, in particular, the right to appoint the director and staff of the regional offices, an issue that the founding conference had only determined to some extent.

At the IHC, it had been decided that regional directors should be appointed by a global organ—the Executive Board—but "in agreement with the regional

[22] Similarly, in the case of the American region, which included the French, British, and Dutch Guianas, the three European colonial powers were entitled by the WHA to participate in the American regional committee (Siddiqi 1995, p. 71).
[23] See WHO archival file no. OD 20 AFRO.
[24] See WHO archival file no A3/110/2.
[25] An early account and evaluation of the WHO's administrative regionalization is provided in WHO (1953).

committee" (Art. 52).[26] This wording helped to forge a broad consensus and was greeted by most delegations as meeting their preferences—albeit their support had been justified on quite different grounds. Panama welcomed the principles of "coordination" and "cooperation" underlying the formula. Mexico said it reflected its country's position, the UK delegate felt that the provision satisfied the need to weld existing health organizations into a "single whole," and the delegate of the Union of Soviet Socialist Republics (USSR) was confident that the proposal would neither undermine democratic principles nor common discipline in the new agency (WHO 1947d, pp. 63–4). Accordingly, Paraguay only spoke for a minority of Latin American states that were protective of the PASB's self-governance when insisting on a purely regional appointment procedure (WHO 1947d, p. 64).

How exactly the "agreement" from the regions would be obtained in practice had not been further clarified. A proposal made at the IHC to specify that the Board should have the "last vote" in the case of conflict had gathered some support, also from the US delegation, but was ultimately dropped for the sake of compromise (WHO 1947d, pp. 64–6). A legal opinion published at the time assumed that the regional say would be used to block unwelcome candidates suggested by the Board: "Under this formula the initiative in nominating a regional director will presumably be taken by the Board, but the Regional Committee may force the Board to submit an alternative name (or names) if it objects to the original nomination" (Sharp 1947, p. 518).

Evidently, this projection had been made before the WHO-PASO agreement that cemented the PASB's independent status within the WHO. As the WHO's central organs did not dare to interfere with the historical prerogative of the Pan American Sanitary Conference to independently appoint the Bureau's director, in practice the Executive Board's role was confined to "rubber stamping" the election of the director as the WHO's regional director for the Americas (Pan American Health Organization 1992, p. 46; Siegel 1982).

Yet what the founders of the WHO had not anticipated was that this exception from the constitutional co-decision procedure would be emulated across the other regions, too. As the new regional organizations were established, they promptly appointed their regional directors at the regional level— to the "horror" (Siegel 1982, p. 20) of those who had preferred a more centralized procedure. Still, after their inaugural meetings, the regional committees merely notified the headquarters of their choice, which the Board duly confirmed. This reversed practice endowed the regional directors with an independent source of legitimacy that paralleled the DG's legitimation

---

[26] A similar compromise was found with regard to regional office staff, who by Constitution (Art. 53) shall be "appointed in a manner to be determined by agreement between the Director-General and the Regional Director."

through the WHA. They were thus not installed as regional administrators on behalf of the DG, but rather as delegates of their own regional constituencies.

By 1951, all regional offices were established and assumed their new roles in the WHO. Afterwards, this rapid regionalization was criticized by delegates and headquarters staff as having "gone too far" (Ascher 1952, p. 39). As one senior WHO officer put it in retrospect: "It was perhaps a little premature to establish the regional organizations before the WHO had time to get its central establishment working smoothly, but it certainly stimulated regional interest from the beginning, and ensured that centralization did not become too firmly established" (Goodman 1971). As it turned out, this "regional interest" would center on the regional offices and thereby consolidate the regionalization pathway, while attempts at containing regional autonomy would consistently fail (see Figure 1.1 in Chapter 1).

3.5 Lock-in of Regional Self-governance

It goes without saying that both the PASB agreement and the practice of regional self-governance were not the same as the design envisaged by the WHO's founders—including the US that had hoped to keep the PASB's status exceptional and pleaded for a much weaker regionalization beyond the American area. That the WHO's pro-regional bargain was not a passing phenomenon but indeed became an enduring institutional legacy was due to the way it was reproduced and reinforced by bureaucrats and member state representatives. Like all organizational pathways, regionalization did not persist simply because it had filled some empty political space, but because it created a group of winners: In this case, poor states in need of basic assistance. Their distributional claims were promptly channeled through the regional organizations and gave rise to new regional coalitions supportive of the status quo. Conversely, all subsequent attempts at reopening the regional issue were defeated by adherents of the status quo, which subsequently turned out to be a robust, if not irreversible, federal design.

Vesting Interest in the Regional Offices

Right upon their creation, the regional organizations were delegated administrative functions in the programming and budgeting process (WHO 1953, pp. 157–84). The regional directors were entrusted with drafting program budgets for their regions, drafts which they based on the needs of and demands from their member states (Ascher 1952, pp. 38–9). This practice not only generated instant support for the regional organizations among recipient member states, but also provoked a significant policy shift over the WHO's early years.

Initially in 1948 the first Assembly had defined six global priority areas on which the WHO should focus, which were called the "big six." These six priority domains should be malaria, tuberculosis, venereal diseases, maternal and child health, nutrition, and environmental sanitation (Berkov 1957, pp. 67–71). Yet, in the following years, many member states challenged this priority approach. Instead, they used the regionalized budgetary mechanism to ask for more basic assistance in order to fill their more urgent procurement gaps with regard to medical equipment. The close contact between regional organizations and national ministries of health ensured that demands for basic procurement soon superseded the Assembly's policy directions, so that they practically replaced the more disease-specific and "vertical" focus of the WHO's official program. This de facto policy shift was only gradually recognized by the DG and Executive Board who tried to insist on the priority approach (Berkov 1957, pp. 67–71). However, by 1954 the Board officially acknowledged that a change in emphasis had occurred "away from priorities" toward the provision of more general health services (Berkov 1957, p. 70).

This shift toward basic assistance significantly extended the WHO's program in the technical cooperation domain, and thereby provided developing states with a considerably greater extent of IO assistance than they could accede during the interwar period (Berkov 1957, p. 67). This extension required an important budgetary scale-up as well. In 1950, responding to pressure from the regional offices, regional allocations were increased by 20 percent—an increase that was entirely dedicated to meeting country demands (Ascher 1952, pp. 38–9). Hence, based on the budgetary competences conferred upon their regional directors, the new regional offices established themselves as chief distributional vehicles for countries seeking assistance from the WHO, countries whose health needs were scarcely met by the six global priorities.

Consequently, the regional organizations were also used as forums for coalition-building within the WHO. This became most evident in the emerging practice of regional bloc voting within the WHO's global organs. Seats at the Executive Board were henceforth distributed according to regional quota, and regions repeatedly engaged in distributive quarrels over their representation as a region on the Board (Siddiqi 1995, pp. 77–82). The fact that regional allegiances indeed superseded interest in the central organization became evident as attempts were made to re-install centralized control in the WHO.

Early Signs of Irreversibility

Although regionalization had many winners, it still remained contested. Externally, other UN organizations criticized the WHO's regionalization for its lack of coordination with the wider UN system (Lee 2009, p. 32). Inside the WHO, several member states attacked the practice of appointing regional directors independently in the regions, and sought to introduce procedures to ensure involvement by the WHO's global organs. However, none of these initiatives was successful.

A first such attempt was made by New Zealand in 1956, in a memorandum to the Executive Board entitled "Method of Appointing Regional Directors" (WHO 1956, p. 143). The memorandum criticized the practice of presenting only one candidate to the Board to be appointed as regional director. New Zealand proposed that a full list of candidates should be submitted to the Board, who could then make its choice upon recommendation by the DG. The regional committee would either confirm the appointment or could "make further presentation to the Board if it wished" (WHO 1956, p. 144). Declaredly, this procedure should ensure a technically-driven choice of an officer who had the confidence of the DG. The proposal was referred to the regional committees where it was received with solid skepticism. In Africa, the Americas, South-East Asia, and the Eastern Mediterranean, it was consensually held that "the present method of appointing regional directors is satisfactory and that no change is required," while in the Western Pacific and the European region no resolution was adopted (WHO 1958a, p. 23). Consequently, the Executive Board in 1958 confined itself to commend New Zealand's initiative and decided that "this important matter should be kept under study" (WHO 1958b, p. 40).

Australia followed up on this decision with a draft resolution stating that regional committees should nominate several candidates and leave the selection to the Board and DG (WHO 1959a, 1959b, pp. 322–3). This draft equally provoked deep divisions among Board members, so much so that the opponents of reform could not be appeased by the various concessions offered by the proponents of reform. Even suggestions that the Board should be informed about the list of candidates, their qualifications and the reasons for the actual choice were not acceptable across the Board. After lengthy debates, the USSR Board member "was becoming more and more convinced that existing practice should be maintained" (WHO 1959a, p. 342) and formally proposed not to make any change to the current procedure. This proposal won a majority of twelve votes to three with two abstentions (WHO 1959a, p. 343).

Nonetheless, the Board reconsidered the issue some years later, this time on a European initiative. Following a proposition from Ireland, the European regional committee planned to alter its rules of procedure so as to increase Executive Board involvement in the appointment of regional directors (WHO 1964c). Since this reform could have implications for the wider organization, it was brought to the Board's attention in 1964—where reform proponents and opponents alike exchanged arguments similar to those of a few years before. Again, nothing came of these discussions other than a recommendation to regional offices that they consider the European motion (WHO 1964a, 1964b). The resonance was again poor. Only the regional committee for the Western Pacific region temporarily changed its rules of procedure, but then swiftly returned to business as usual (WHO 1987g).

In sum, the aftermath of the WHO's founding moment demonstrates that despite the contestation of regionalization, for example by states having to work with a regional office or director they did not support (e.g. Canada in the American region, cf. Sharp 1961, pp. 56–7), regionalization also had many winners. In particular, poor states in need of basic assistance rallied around their regional directors to influence the WHO budgeting process to their favor. This positive feedback mechanism helped to consolidate the position of regional offices that were practically created from scratch, and it ensured that those recentralization attempts that were explicitly launched by dissatisfied member states were defeated. The futile centralization initiatives put to the Board highlighted that defenders of the status quo were well positioned to block efforts to circumscribe regional self-governance. The outcome of these initiatives may well have discouraged further centralization attempts (see Section 2.4). Yet a few decades later, the robustness of regionalization in the WHO would be put to renewed tests—for instance the US's recentralization initiative in the 1980s that followed the first major experience of reform failure (Chapter 4). These attempts would again fail, while moves toward further regionalization would turn out to be more successful and fuel a pathway of centrifugal reproduction.

3.6 Conclusion: The Historical Origins of the WHO's Fragmentation

The historical struggles over the PASB's integration with the WHO have produced an IO with regional autonomies that are unmatched by other organizations. The genesis of this design illustrates the conflicts and uncertainties that IO designers are confronted with during founding moments, and the role that path dependent constraints play even when new international institutions are built. In other words, the WHO's peculiar design was neither planned nor random. It was not planned because no coalition could dominate and deliberately design this institution-building process. Rather, the WHO's founding moment was marked by a protracted deadlock between regionalizers and centralizers that was only resolved through a constitutional compromise which granted the PASB a special status within the WHO. What is more, the central player in this bargaining, the US government, did not take a clear stance toward the WHO's design, and was certainly not "fiercely protective of the independent status of the Pan American Health Organization" (Lee 2009, p. 14). We have seen that US delegates were repeatedly striving to contain separationists within the PASB and to ensure the WHO's global supremacy. Likewise, the US delegation pushed for a hierarchical solution to the question of regional director appointments beyond the PASB. However, this more integrated design for the non-American regions, which was laid down in the WHO constitution, was undermined through the ensuing autonomization of the five new regional offices. The Pan American head start thus produced a consequential unintended by-product beyond the Americas.

Neither was the WHO's design an accident or mutation. Its foundational design conflicts were resolved over years of historically situated and piecemeal institutional bargaining. In this process, the supporters of the PASB drew on their early mover advantages and the allies and institutional resources available at the time, while the WHO's interim secretariat had to cope with the loss of momentum at the beginning of the Cold War. The WHO's regionalization thus is the aggregate product of actors struggling in a complex historical context, none of whom may have foreseen the eventual outcome of their endeavors. It is *contingent* on a plethora of historical determinants—without being random or miraculous.

Still, once the organization was set up by the early 1950s, state delegates and secretariat actors alike came to recognize that the founding moment had been "fateful." The initial contingency was transformed into path dependent necessity in the aftermath of the region-building period. Regional self-governance was sustained by their strategic role within the WHO's budgeting and programming process and by the regional allegiances this practice gave rise to. The regional directors' autonomy received positive feedback from the winners of this alignment, mostly recipient states who used the regional offices to reorient the WHO's policy outlook—which shifted from the global priorities approach to the filling of capacity gaps in developing countries. This alignment of interests around the newly created regional bureaus stabilized them and made them robust enough to resist later reform efforts. As the record of frustrated recentralization attempts in the 1950s and 1960s demonstrates, the status quo coalition could fend off those centralizing moves that were made, and discourage those that weren't made. This is a significant first test of the robustness of regionalization in the WHO (see Section 2.4). Harder tests would follow after the first round of major reform, when first the US (see Chapter 4) and then the reform coalition around DG Gro Harlem Brundtland (see Chapter 5) sought to curb regional powers.

The following two chapters will also show that regionalization not only became a self-enforcing, but even an "absorbing" (Pierson 2004, p. 94) state in the WHO. While recentralization consistently failed, all further regionalization steps, regardless of how they occurred, would be locked in and protected against all revisionist efforts. The WHO's pro-regional bias would also set the path for the way the organization responded to new demands and reform agendas. The first such major reform was Halfdan Mahler's "Health for All" reform, from which the regional offices would emerge strengthened, but also as the object of much blame.

4

The Secondary Effects of Primary Health Care

The 1970s were turbulent times for the World Health Organization (WHO). The wave of decolonization since the 1960s had greatly altered the international landscape, and thereby also the WHO's constituency. Between 1956 and 1967, thirty newly independent African states became members of the WHO, meaning that African states made up nearly one-third of the WHO's membership by 1970 (Jacobson 1970, p. 77). This systemic shift not only boosted Third World influence in the WHO, but it also transformed its operational landscape. As it was extending its activities to the newly independent (mainly African) states released from colonial rule (Jacobson 1970, p. 74), the WHO was confronted with the inadequacy of postcolonial health systems that were fashioned in accordance with Western, hospital-based models. And following the spectacular failure of its Malaria Eradication Programme (MEP) in 1969, the WHO was all the more keen to find responses to what became viewed as a major crisis in health development. The global economic crisis after the oil shock and the crumbling of the Bretton Woods system did not make this an easier task.

Yet nevertheless, or exactly for these reasons, the 1970s are also remembered as the WHO's "Golden Age" (People's Health Movement et al. 2005, p. 272; WHO 2011d, p. vii), as a visionary epoch where everything seemed possible (WHO 2008b, pp. 2–3). In the midst of an escalating north–south conflict and worldwide economic instability, the WHO became the site of one of the biggest reform movements in international public health. The organizational strategy of the period ambitiously read "Health for All by the Year 2000"—a campaign by which the WHO's charismatic third director-general (DG) Halfdan Mahler (1973–88) sought to transform the WHO from what he despised as a self-serving bureaucracy into the flagship of a social revolution. Health for All (HFA) was designed to reorient the WHO's activities toward serving basic health needs, mostly in developing countries. It was premised on the framework of "Primary

Health Care" (PHC), a community-centered approach to healthcare that should replace the practice of medical professionalism and top-down development still reigning in international health assistance. The goal was to create affordable and workable health systems for poor and peripheral areas, and even to transcend the health sector in order to tackle the social and political determinants of health in related policy fields such as agriculture or education.

This ambitious policy agenda was radical but not marginal. It was backed by the 1978 International Conference on Primary Health Care, which was attended by 134 states. The solemn Declaration of Alma Ata endorsed at this conference has become a milestone document that is continuously invoked in contemporary public health debates. Yet beyond such normative affirmation, the high hopes of the PHC movement were not fulfilled. Students and adherents of Primary Health Care point out that the policy was hardly put into practice in the WHO's target countries (Litsios 2002; Magnussen et al. 2004, p. 169). Neither have PHC and HFA principles ever been mainstreamed across the WHO's programming (Burci and Vignes 2004, pp. 160–4). Recent calls in the WHO for a "return" to Primary Health Care testify to the lasting appeal of this social health agenda, but also to its limited policy impact (WHO 2008a).

The different reasons for PHC's ineffectiveness have been amply discussed in the international public health literature (Cueto 2004; Italian Global Health Watch 2008; Thomas and Weber 2004; see also Section 4.5). Yet, what the focus on the limited policy impact of PHC omits is the lasting structural impact that the Mahler reform had on the WHO. This by-product of the HFA agenda and its organizational robustness are at the center of the present chapter. I will argue that the implementation of the HFA reform has *deepened* the WHO's regionalization. The WHO was mobilized for Primary Health Care in a path dependent way, because the regional offices could capitalize on their gatekeeper position with regard to country-level programming and policy implementation. The enactment of PHC therefore entailed a strengthening of the regions' administrative and policy authorities, which should enable them to enlist target countries for national PHC strategies. Thus, the lasting outcome of the reform was that the WHO's regional organizations moved from a practice of regional self-governance to factual operative autonomy. Although this devolution of authorities to the regional level did not generate the desired policy effects—as Mahler publicly complained toward the end of his incumbency—the organizational shift in the direction of regional autonomy would stick and defy all later attacks and criticism.

By investigating this structural legacy of the Mahler reform, the present chapter not only sheds light on a neglected side of the WHO's Primary Health Care story. It also makes a more general case to pay attention to the organizational by-products of reforms in international organizations (IOs), that is, their secondary effects which can alter the rules of the game for later reforms.

Reform by-products tend to be overlooked when the focus is laid on policy effectiveness and goal-attainment. Yet, as I have argued in Chapter 2, organizational change is always two-dimensional: It involves not only the *economic* dimension of the policies enacted, but also the *political* dimension of how organizational power is redistributed through collective adaptation. Analyzed through the lens of the economic-political game, the case study of the PHC reform demonstrates how the need for an IO's adaptation to its dynamic environments feeds into and reinforces organizational power dynamics. As the record of futile recentralization efforts since the 1980s underlines, these secondary effects can indeed become a more enduring legacy of IO reform than the intended policy effects.

The chapter is divided into five sections. The first section (4.1) presents the political and technical challenges that the WHO was facing in the early 1970s, as an increasingly assertive Third World and a sense of policy failure in the domain of health development produced pressure for change. Next (4.2), the policy response to these challenges, the Primary Health Care agenda, will be introduced. The third section (4.3) investigates the implementation of PHC in the WHO and demonstrates how this strategy fed into and reinforced regionalization. The fourth section (4.4) discusses outcomes of the reform, which were marginal in policy terms but locked in in structural terms, moving the WHO toward deep regionalization. The fifth and final section (4.5) recapitulates the argument and discusses the ambiguous relationship between the two reform outcomes, regionalization, and policy failure.

4.1 The Postcolonial Legitimacy Crisis

The 1970s were a period of structural conflict in the international political economy. While the US hegemon was in relative decline and the international economic order seemed precarious, an increasingly assertive Third World organized as the Group of 77 and mobilized against global capitalism. Starting with a UN General Assembly declaration in 1974, the movement for a New International Economic Order (NIEO) fundamentally questioned the liberal doctrines of market allocation and growth-based development (Krasner 1985, pp. 65–9; White 1975b). The NIEO principles had a marked impact across the UN system, where the principle of sovereign equality ensured that the growing number of developing countries translated into growing Third World influence,[1] and where the combat of underdevelopment was already ranking

---

[1] Influence was exerted both within existing UN institutions and through newly established ones such as the UN Conference on Trade and Development (UNCTAD, established 1964) and the UN Industrial Development Organization (UNIDO, established 1966) (Krasner 1985, p. 8).

high. The UN was entering its second development decade in 1971, the first having been completed in 1970 (WHO 2008b, p. 9). And the World Bank, under its new President Robert McNamara (1968–81), made the reduction of rural deprivation and absolute poverty its policy priority. In parallel, the Bank turned away from the top-down modernization approach that had informed its early development strategies. Instead of investing in large infrastructural and industry projects, the Bank focused rather on basic human needs and rural development (Krasner 1985, pp. 19–20).

Underdevelopment and essential needs became particularly topical in the health domain, given that social deprivation and the lack of basic health infrastructures undermined the effectiveness of medical services and disease-focused interventions. The essential role of health infrastructure had been clearly exposed in the WHO's flagship program of the 1950s and 1960s, namely its Malaria Eradication Programme. The MEP had been launched in 1955 to mobilize worldwide health resources for one common goal, namely the combat and eventual defeat of malaria. Backed by the Eisenhower government on behalf of the US, the program mobilized bilateral and multilateral assistance for this "vertical" and disease-specific intervention, which mainly relied on the deployment of DDT spraying teams in infected regions (Litsios 1997).[2] However, by 1969 the WHO's member states had to officially concede defeat in the quest to eradicate the disease. Many malariologists ascribed this defeat to the lack of basic health infrastructure in developing countries, and thus the inability to sustain early eradication successes in the face of recurrent outbreaks. Tellingly, malaria eradication had not even been attempted on the African continent, whose underdeveloped health systems did not allow for sustained anti-malaria interventions (Farid 1980).[3] The spectacular failure of malaria eradication exemplifies the confrontation of disease-specific interventions with the dire health conditions in decolonized countries. Thus over the 1960s, the problem of basic health services received renewed attention, and the perception gained ground that international health work was deficient in this domain (Chorev 2012, pp. 67–8; WHO 2008b, pp. 117–18).

---

[2] DDT is the abbreviation for the insecticide dichlorodiphenyltrichloroethane.

[3] On the Malaria Eradication Programme and the bureaucratic pathologies that contributed to its failure see Siddiqi (1995, pp. 123–91). The debate over the feasibility and desirability of "vertical" malaria eradication is far from settled (for an introduction see Farid 1998; Gladwell 2001). A success story supporting the "vertical" approach is the WHO's eradication of smallpox by 1979—the Soviet flagship project against the US-sponsored anti-malaria effort (Henderson 2009). That smallpox eradication was well under way was also recognized by Mahler as early as 1974, yet he took care to attribute this success to the involvement of national health services rather than international interventions in order to get the basic health service message across (Mahler 1974a, p. 208).

A range of studies published at the time argued that postcolonial health systems were overly reliant on Western and hospital-based health care, and therefore ill-suited to the needs of underdeveloped countries (Bryant 1969; Cueto 2004, p. 1864). The gap between the professionalized and expensive medical services provided by international agencies on the one side, and unmet basic health needs on the other, was scandalized by international health practitioners calling for a paradigm shift. Among the first to call for a rethinking of international health work were Christian missionaries. Already in the 1960s, an influential series of consultations and publications of church-related health work came to devastating conclusions regarding the value of the Christian medical mission. At the so-called "Tübingen I" (1964) and "Tübingen II" (1967) consultations, it was ascertained that hospital-based and curative services made up about 95 percent of Christian health work, but only reached about 20 percent of the populations in developing countries (McGilvray 1981, p. 60). Severe doubts were being raised as to whether Christian health work was actually doing any good at all, or whether it was merely functioning as an instrument of imperial exploitation (McGilvray 1981, p. 13):

> Christianity can be seen as mixed up with Western Imperialism and Medicine can be seen as a set of expensive technologies run by professionals who may be pursuing their own interests quite as much as, if not more than, promoting the health of communities and individuals within society.

Following up on this self-incrimination, the Christian Medical Commission (CMC) was established to serve as an advisory body of the World Council of Churches. It was located nearby the WHO headquarters in Geneva, which enabled an intensive exchange with like-minded WHO staff members (Cueto 2004, p. 1865).

Thus, the emerging epistemic community for a paradigm shift in international health found a charismatic and idealistic leader when in 1973 Halfdan Mahler became the new DG of the WHO. Mahler followed (and had been the internal candidate promoted by) Marcolino Gomes Candau, whose term of office from 1953 to 1973 had been marked by organizational consolidation and continuity, but also a rather biomedical focus on disease control and eradication (Chorev 2012, p. 57; Kaplan 1983). Mahler's background, by contrast, was a long and disillusioning field experience in tuberculosis work in India, which for him revealed the limitations of modern medicine, especially with regard to the health conditions in developing countries (Cueto 2004; Hanrieder 2013). Mahler emphasized at the beginning of his incumbency that the "widespread dissatisfaction with health services" marked a "major crisis" and "turning point in the life of the Organization" (Mahler 1974a, p. 209). Likewise, at several occasions he expressed support for the NIEO demands that were put forward by developing countries at the WHO's governing bodies.[4] Thus, although an internal candidate and successor at the director-general (DG) post, Mahler embodied and catalyzed revolutionary ambitions for the WHO's outlook on global health work.

The radicalism of the policy watershed announced by the new DG and his team reflected a broader crisis of modern medicine's legitimacy, as the golden era of medical discoveries was coming to an end. Not only for the Christian Medical Commission, this anti-medical stance with regard to public health had a spiritual dimension. The CMC despised hospitals as dehumanizing and dystopian "repair facilities" that were preoccupied with "localized patholo-gies," while neglecting the identity and wholeness of individuals (McGilvray 1981, pp. 19, 48). Quite similar spiritual ideas were expressed in an anti-modern bestseller of the time, Ivan Illich's *Medical Nemesis*, which forcefully blamed the "sick-making powers of diagnosis and medicine" (Illich 1995 (1976), p. 3). Illich's accusation that the "medical establishment ha[d] become a major threat to health" (Illich 1995 (1976), p. 3) was virtually reiterated in pronouncements by Mahler, who openly doubted the usefulness of his own profession (and organization) in statements like the following (Litsios 2002, p. 717):

> I think the first step is to close the medical schools for two years. Then we can discuss what the medical schools were supposed to do, because they really consti-tute the main focus of resistance to change.

Hence, all-out "change" and new concepts were urgently called for to meet an exacerbating health development crisis. The new paradigm that should guide this change would become known as Primary Health Care.

4.2 The Primary Health Care Agenda

Based on their somber assessments of Western medicine, a group of CMC members, and staff from the WHO and the United Nations Children's Fund (UNICEF) jointly elaborated an alternative policy framework that was cen-tered on community development as the basic means of improving health conditions (McGilvray 1981, p. 20). Inspiration for this community approach was found in exemplary rural health projects, the findings of which were intensely discussed in Geneva. To mark the shift from specialized, hospital-based treatment to healthy living conditions and community self-help, Pri-mary Health Care became the slogan for the new paradigm. The projects that informed the Primary Health Care concept typically went beyond medical

[4] On the way in which the WHO secretariat rearticulated the NIEO through its PHC agenda see Chorev (2012, pp. 42–85).

interventions and included basic assistance in agriculture, health education, and prevention, and the systematic involvement of auxiliary health staff and community health workers with basic medical training. National models such as the Cuban health system or the Chinese model with its iconic "barefoot doctors"—rural health workers whose practice combined Western and Traditional medicine (Lee 1997)—were publicized alongside grassroots health development projects in countries such as India, Iran, Tanzania, or Venezuela. A series of programmatic publications such as the UNICEF/WHO volume *Alternative Approaches to Meeting Basic Health Needs in Developing Countries* (Djukanovic and Mach 1975) and the WHO volume *Health by the People* (Newell 1975a) disseminated these experiences and elaborated policy proposals for international health assistance.

The PHC strategy that was distilled from these experiences built on and reiterated previous policies in the domain of health service provision (Litsios 2002). Its distinct contours can best be reconstructed in comparison with the "biomedical" blueprint for public health, that is, an individual-centered, professionalized, and disease-oriented approach, where health was understood as a technical rather than a social problem. This opposition is summarized in Table 4.1, which presents the major points of departure of the PHC framework. First and foremost, PHC focused on *communities* as the major site of health policy. PHC should be responsive to local conditions and life styles, and be provided in a participatory manner so as to mobilize community resources for health—and, as a by-product, foster social cohesion. Second, PHC was a *comprehensive* approach with regard to the relevant policy measures as well as policy fields. It should not only integrate prevention and cure, but also overcome "health isolationism" (Mahler 1974b, p. 311) via an inter-sectoral engagement in community development. This in fact implied that poverty

Table 4.1. The Primary Health Care Paradigm[a]

Primary Health Care		Bio-medicine
Community focus	• Orientation to local needs and life patterns • Community participation and education • Maximum possible reliance on community resources	Focused on individual
Comprehensiveness	• Integration of prevention, promotion and cure • Inter-sectoral action including agriculture, education, animal husbandry, food, industry & public works	Disease-oriented
De-professionalization	• Maximum possible reliance on auxiliary health staff • Primary health workers in communities	Medical professionalism
Social justice	• Prioritize those most in need • Overcome global inequality	Technical progress

[a] Cf. Newell 1975b; Litsios 1975, 2004; WHO 2008b, pp. 308–10.

reduction would in many cases be more important than health-sectoral services (Newell 1975b, pp. 161–2).[5] Third, at the level of health services a cost-effective *de-professionalization* was called for, that is the systematic involvement of "auxiliary" health personnel and Primary Health workers prior and in addition to the classic professions of doctors and nurses. And fourth, the guiding vision of *social justice* demanded that disadvantaged groups be prioritized in international and national health strategies, and hence that social equity served as the guiding principle for PHC-related action.

Over the 1970s, the ideas attached to PHC were debated and elaborated at all levels of the WHO (WHO 2008b, pp. 300–2). The concept was officially endorsed by the World Health Assembly (WHA) in 1975, which declared that there was an "urgent need for the provision of primary health care" and, following a proposal made by the Soviet Union, called for an international conference dedicated to Primary Health Care (Res. WHA 28.88 WHO 1985, p. 64). This International Conference on Primary Health Care, which would become *the* historical landmark of the PHC movement, was held in Alma Ata, Kazakhstan, in September 1978. Sponsored jointly by UNICEF and the WHO,[6] the conference was attended by 134 country delegations as well as representatives of more than sixty other inter-governmental and non-governmental organizations (WHO 2008b, p. 299). The central outcome of the conference was the solemn Declaration of Alma Ata, which reiterated the principles of PHC and the NIEO, as well as the human right to health enshrined in the WHO's Constitution (WHO 2008b, pp. 308–10).

The solidarity and international consensus expressed in Alma Ata signified, in Mahler's words, a "spiritual and intellectual awakening" (Mahler 2008, p. 748) for those who viewed PHC not only as an alternative approach to organizing health services, but as being part of a transformative political project. The ideals underpinning the PHC agenda were values such as social cohesion, participatory organization and, indeed, the healthy, non-alienated community (Newell 1975b, p. 162). These ideals could be and were connected to the ambitious WHO constitution and its encompassing definition of health, but they still differed from the WHO's founding myth that health

---

[5] This last aspect was often disputed as many preferred to consider PHC as an alternative concept for health services rather than an encompassing development strategy (WHO 2008b, pp. 302–3). Another point of contestation was whether Primary Health Care was a pure public sector undertaking or whether it also implied private services (e.g. Collins and Green 1994).

[6] UNICEF and the WHO were traditional partners in the domains of maternal and child health. In the classic division of labor, the WHO's technical guidelines, for example on children's vaccination, would be funded and implemented by UNICEF which disposed of greater operative capacities than the WHO (Hanrieder forthcoming 2015; Lee 2009, p. 19). Inter-organizational rivalry would grow over the decades as UNICEF upscaled its health activities, especially from the 1980s onward, as UNICEF's "Children's Revolution" challenged the political authority, and also policies, of the WHO (Lee 2009, pp. 67–8).

was a matter of scientific breakthroughs and medical progress.[7] For the PHC advocates at the WHO, the central challenge thus consisted of translating this revolutionary impetus into bureaucratic action. The reform strategy developed for this purpose not only encompassed new policy tools, but also a major reorganization effort to make Primary Health Care implementable. As the following section demonstrates, both dimensions were closely intertwined.

4.3 Reform Strategy: Health for All through Regionalization

Its grassroots affinities notwithstanding, the PHC agenda carried the classic attributes of organizational reform: The rhetoric of intentional change and learning at all organizational levels, the invocation of corporate agency and leadership, and the emphasis on rational and strategic planning (Brunsson and Olsen 1993; Schein 1985). Up-to-date health management techniques, in particular methods borrowed from contemporary systems analysis, should facilitate a maximally "rational" policy planning process (Litsios 2002, p. 717; WHO 1974, p. 22). This strategic rationality should not only be embodied in corporate procedures, but also be incorporated by the WHO's staff. Through retraining and strategic recruitment, a "new type of WHO staff member" (Mahler 1975b, p. 45) was to be created: Professionals capable of seeing the bigger picture, under whose "enlightened guidance" (Mahler 1976, p. 10) the right priorities would be chosen. Thereby, a greater share of interdisciplinary generalists should guarantee that overly specialized technical parochialism could be avoided and that the WHO's work would have a strategic impact on general health systems (WHO 1979c, pp. 24–5).

Likewise, the reform was accompanied by energetic managerialism. A series of initiatives sought to smooth the WHO's internal management, and numerous documents were produced stressing the need for "flexible and efficient" (Mahler 1975b, p. 45) procedures, integrated planning, and internal dialogue and coordination (e.g. WHO 1975a, p. 90, 1975b, 1978). Most emphatic in this respect was a Board-sponsored "Study of WHO's Structures in the Light of Its Functions"—an unprecedented managerial review touching on all facets of the WHO's working methods, from the periodicity of World Health Assemblies to the location of WHO headquarters (WHO

---

[7] To give an example of this creed, DG Candau's foreword to the decennial report of the WHO's work, covering the period 1958–67, opened with the following exultation: "The scientific discoveries and practical achievements of the past decade have stirred the imagination and roused our expectations for the future. They have also served to confirm that health is purchasable" (WHO 1968, p. ix).

1979b, 1979c).[8] In these assessments, the values of efficiency and coordination were constantly reiterated in an attempt to mobilize the entire organization for what became defined as the WHO's strategic policy target: Health for All by the Year 2000.

The declared goal of the WHO's HFA strategy was to enable all people to lead economically and socially productive lives by the end of the millennium, by granting them universal and equal access to the basic conditions of good health (Mahler 1977, p. 491). This target was not introduced as a utopian ideal—quite the contrary in fact. As Mahler put it in one of his speeches, the year 2000 deadline reflected the "realistic" acknowledgment that "it will take a generation for the world's population to attain an acceptable level of health evenly distributed throughout it" (Mahler 1975a, p. 457), and thus a humble aspiration. From 1977 onwards, the HFA strategy was endorsed in numerous WHA and Board resolutions and decisions calling on the WHO to comprehensively reorient the organization's activities toward HFA (WHO 1985, pp. 1–10). Health for All was declared the WHO's "overriding priority" (WHA32.30 WHO 1985, p. 2), meaning that all WHO programs were to be formulated and judged on the grounds of how they contributed to the HFA goal. The following two subsections reconstruct the reform implementation through the lens of the economic-political game (see Chapter 2): The immediate ("economic") policy goal of the reform being the implementation of PHC at the country level, while its long-term ("political") implication was a substantive empowerment of the regional offices, which were the central gatekeepers with regard to country-level policy changes.

The Benchmark: Implementing Primary Health Care at the Country Level

Health for All was not framed as a matter of big investments or technological advances, but as a problem of reorganizing the WHO's work to mobilize countries for the policy shift. Equitable access to the most vital conditions of good health could, at least according to the PHC ideology, be achieved through inexpensive, simple and effective measures (Mahler 1975b, 1977). The challenge, therefore, rather was to shift the focus of health work away from the medical establishment toward more basic and participatory services (Mahler 1981, pp. 15–17). PHC measures included improving sanitation, housing, water supply, health education, and increasing the reliance on

---

[8] The Executive Board regularly chose topics for organizational studies that were prepared by WHO staff in collaboration with the Board. For example, the study commissioned in 1971 on methods for promoting basic health services allowed the WHO secretariat to introduce the Primary Health Care approach (WHO 2008b, pp. 117–19). These Board-sponsored studies provide very informative self-observations that document bureaucratic changes and point out the problems and conflicts which dominate organizational practice.

auxiliary health personnel such as midwives, traditional healers, and basically trained Primary Health workers. The concrete policy package would depend on the health needs of the most disadvantaged and peripheral groups in individual countries (WHO 1975c).[9]

Hence, with HFA the focus of the WHO's work shifted to the mobilization of developing countries (WHO 1979c, p. 3). In return, many of the WHO's normative and research activities—such as the preparation of specialized manuals or technical guidelines—were considerably downgraded (Mahler 1976, p. 4). And yet, due in no small part to the WHO's limited operative resources, the policy tools envisaged for country-level operations were primarily consultative and aimed at national strategizing rather than development funding (Mahler 1977, p. 491). In order to generate a systemic impact on underdeveloped health systems, the technique of "country health programming" was introduced. It aimed at transferring the systems analysis approach to the steering of national health systems. Based on new computational methods and mathematical modeling, systems analysis techniques were heralded at the time as a "scientific" approach to management and policy-making, also at Mahler's WHO. In this vein, country health programming should enable health officials to set strategic health targets and define the priorities for PHC programs in their countries with the help of analytical models and quantitative methods (Mahler 1975a, p. 459, 1977, p. 496; WHO 2008b). To produce a real transformative impact on country health systems, the so-devised PHC strategies should mobilize resources in and beyond the health sector. It was hoped that a context-sensitive application of PHC insights that was guided by the WHO but operated at the country level would empower developing countries to deploy modern planning technologies for the development of health policies, policies which were ideally tailored to their specific conditions (WHO 1975c, pp. 116–17).

Accordingly, the WHO's field work should center on coordination and policy advisory functions. Technical cooperation programs were no longer to be framed as isolated projects, but should be integrated with national policies so as to mobilize national resources toward strategically defined goals. Ties should be created with health officials, other government sectors and multilateral and bilateral aid programs in order to ensure an integrated approach to health systems across the board. To mark this priority shift, the post of "WHO representative" at the country level was renamed "WHO coordinator" (WHO 2008b, pp. 50–3). Staff-wise, generalists were favored over

---

[9] The WHO's integrated approach to health development was also mirrored in attempts to stir inter-sectoral action for development across the United Nations, under the leadership of the United Nations Development Programme (UNDP). However, these efforts generated little effect due to persisting interagency conflicts (WHO 2008b, pp. 13–17, and see Chapter 6).

specialists, since policy planning and systems management required different qualifications to specific medical projects (Mahler 1974b, p. 310).

Yet, the most crucial factor for the success of Primary Health Care was that of national participation and ownership, without which the WHO could barely make a difference. And with great insistence, the secretariat pleaded that member states make use of the WHO's expertise and implement suitable PHC measures (Mahler 1977; WHO 1979a, pp. 4–5)—either in WHO-supported pilot projects, or at the level of national health policy (Litsios 2002). To attain this mission-critical country participation, much hope was put in the regional offices as the immediate addressees of the WHO's member states.

Organizational Strategy: Regional Empowerment

PHC-related services could only be provided "at the request of the national government" (WHO 1976a, p. 24). This requirement de facto implied that the success of the reform depended on mobilizing the regional offices for Primary Health Care. As I have laid out in Chapter 3, in the WHO's regionalized system developing country requests were addressed to the regional organizations and not to headquarters. Ever since their establishment, it was the regional offices that received country requests for WHO assistance and drafted budgetary proposals on behalf of their regional member states. Regional offices thereby served as the primary addressees and distributional tools in particular for those poor states that were the main targets of the PHC reform.

These strong regional allegiances were acknowledged by Mahler, who noted that "Member States are increasingly identifying themselves with their regions and this has been accompanied by an *intensification of work in the regional committees* in recent years" (WHO 1979c, p. 15, emphasis in original). Given that the regional organizations were positioned as *the* mission-critical gate keepers to make Primary Health Care a success, the DG envisaged the regions as a central locus of program development and implementation for Primary Health Care (Mahler 1975b, p. 45).[10] However, confronting regional directors who were independently elected and de facto not subordinated to him, Mahler had to rely on inducements rather than hierarchical authority to attain regional collaboration.

This implied, first, persuasive efforts to convince the regional organizations that PHC was a desirable policy goal, or, in the terminology of the economic-political game: A desirable "economic" goal (see Section 2.2). In his speeches before the regional committees, Mahler constantly preached the PHC agenda

---

[10] By contrast, voices in particular from Soviet states that called for a more centralized and headquarter-based implementation of the reform found little resonance among WHO staff and other member states (Litsios 2002, pp. 713, 716).

(e.g. Mahler 1977, 1980). He insisted that the necessary "political will" for PHC reforms had to be generated at the regional committees, which were closest to the "front line" of countries (Mahler 1977, p. 497) and thus the main source of "leadership" for the PHC reform (Mahler 1975b, p. 44). Formal and informal meetings were used to get the regional directors on board, and a new coordination tool was instituted in 1977 in order to closely engage the regional offices: The Global Programme Committee, consisting of the director-general, the deputy director-general, the regional directors, and the assistant directors-general (WHO 2008b, p. 46, 1979a).

The central inducement the DG had to offer was a "political" concession, speaking in the language of the economic-political game (see Section 2.2): He could delegate organizational authority to the regional units in return for their cooperation in the reform endeavor. Indeed, Mahler greatly empowered the regional organizations and made them the primary authorities in operating the WHO's technical cooperation activities. To build up country-level planning and management "on the spot," the regional offices as the most proximate organiza-tional unit were given the task of acquiring "day-to-day responsibility" (Mahler 1975b, p. 44) for the WHO's new goals: "Their responsibilities will have to be increased, however risky this may appear at first sight" (Mahler 1975b, p. 44). Hence, making use of his administrative authority, Mahler delegated budgetary authority "virtually entirely" (WHO 1993, p. 2) to the regional directors.

This transfer of authority engendered a considerable build-up of adminis-trative capacity at the regional level (WHO 1993, p. 2). Beforehand, the regional offices had mostly been responsible for drawing up plans and pro-posals for technical assistance projects. Yet in the 1950s and 1960s, the budget was still operated from Geneva and entitlements to spend regional funds therefore remained at the discretion of headquarters (WHO 1993, p. 2). This system of centralized control had been institutionalized and eagerly protected by Mahler's predecessor Candau, in whose eyes it "would be undesirable for WHO to become a federation of regional organizations lacking central con-trol" (WHO 1973, p. 451).[11]

Yet after the HFA reform, the regional directors could rather freely dispose of the regular budgetary funds allotted to the regions. They were also granted discretion over the allocation of WHO fellowships, and their authority over professional staff was equally enhanced in the course of the 1970s (Beigbeder 1997, p. 57). Furthermore, the regional offices were entrusted with the man-agement of the funds for technical cooperation provided by the UN

---

[11] A member of the WHO Association of Former Staff (whom I interviewed in June 2009 and May 2010) recalled that Candau, although he had suggested Mahler for the position of DG, was disappointed by his successor's decentralization policy, and later bemoaned that Mahler was destroying his legacy of twenty years of institution building.

Development Programme (UNDP), which made up 8.4 percent of the WHO's total expenditure in 1974 (WHO 1975b, p. 3, 2008b, p. 14).[12] Only the management of the WHO's remaining extra-budgetary funds, which at the time made up about 18 percent of the WHO's overall budget (WHO 1975b, p. 2), was excluded from this delegation and remained with the DG (WHO 1993, p. 2).[13]

In summary, the 1970s marked an organizational shift from regional self-governance, based on the regional appointment of regional directors, to a system where the regional directors also enjoyed near autonomy with regard to programming and budgeting. The control over field-level services was henceforth monopolized by the regional offices, and it was these technical cooperation services that were prioritized in the PHC reform, while the WHO's normative and research activities were considerably downgraded.[14] This system of "regional self-reliance" (Mahler 1975b, p. 45) in technical cooperation matters should help to develop Primary Health Care on the spot, with regional organizations serving as the "bearers of a new regional health conscience" (Mahler 1975a, p. 457). But the outcome of these measures would be a far stretch from what Mahler had promised or hoped for.

4.4 Reform Outcome: Secondary Effects Instead of Primary Health Care

When asked for his memories of the Primary Health Care and Health for All years in the WHO, a former WHO officer replied: "It never got off the ground." While throughout the 1970s, headquarters staff was busy "deciding what words to use in writing position papers" (Litsios 2002, p. 719), few tangible

---

[12] This delegation counteracted tendencies in the UNDP to centralize the management of United Nations development funds, which in Mahler's opinion would have threatened the WHO's regionalized structure (Mahler 1977, pp. 497–8).

[13] The authority to accept and administer extra-budgetary funds such as voluntary member state contributions, gifts and bequests, had initially laid with the Executive Board, but was transferred to the DG in the early 1970s (WHO 1993, p. 2).

[14] This relocation of budgetary control became particularly evident with the WHO's reaction to the international financial crisis after the crumbling of the Bretton Woods system. For the WHO, the demise of the gold-dollar standard meant a boost in headquarter expenses which were paid in Swiss francs and continued to rise after the reevaluation of the Swiss franc in 1971: While the exchange rate of the US dollar against the Swiss franc had been 4.32 in 1971, it had gone down to 2.5 by 1976 (WHO 1976a, p. 36). The WHA, pressured by the Group of 77, reacted to this trend in 1976 by demanding a reduction of those expenses not dedicated to "technical cooperation and provision of services," first and foremost by reducing administrative overhead at headquarters and in the regional offices (WHA29.48 WHO 1985, p. 12; and see WHO 1976b, pp. 310–33). These savings were mostly attained by reducing staff at headquarters (by 20 percent or 313 posts by 1981) and by relocating several global programs to a specific regional office (Mahler 1976, p. 14). The balance was promptly passed on to the regional organizations, bypassing any form of headquarter involvement in the usage of these funds (Furth 1977, pp. 352–3).

steps toward implementation were made at the regional level. Attempts at closing the implementation gap only exposed and reinforced what was increasingly considered as dysfunctional regionalization. At the same time, the new regional competencies to allocate funds, and posts, also generated new vested interests and thus positive feedback for deeper regionalization. Hence, even powerful subsequent efforts to reverse regionalization were prevented by the legal and political lock-in of regional autonomy. Thus, the outcome of the reform was a reinforced regionalization, yet hardly a policy shift toward Primary Health Care.

The Implementation Gap

In spite of all intra-organizational coordination efforts, the regional "health consciences" did not function as intended by Mahler and his team. To the great frustration of the DG, only a few countries adopted elements of the reform such as country health planning (WHO 2008b, p. 44) or other PHC-related measures (Mahler 1983b; WHO 1980, p. 6, 1984, p. xvi). In his characteristic colorful prose, Mahler (1983b, pp. 43–4) attributed this implementation gap to the "dachshund phenomenon":

> The dog being so long, its brain takes such a time to reach its tail that while its face shows one form of emotion its tail wags in contrasting fashion.

As a response, the principle of conditionality was introduced and endorsed by the Assembly in 1980, so that technical assistance should be tied to the application of PHC principles (WHA33.17 WHO 1985, pp. 48–50). Furthermore, to close the policy-practice gap, monitoring and evaluation became the central themes of the early 1980s (Mahler 1984). New managerial procedures were introduced to review and evaluate the use of WHO resources in recipient countries. Program outputs at the country level should be monitored in national accounting controls that would be operated from the regional offices (Mahler 1983a; WHO 1984, p. xx). These audits were designed to identify how regional expenditures would be decided upon and by whom, and how they would be implemented (WHO 1984, pp. xxxvii–viii). Moreover, guidelines for regional budgeting were issued by the DG's office, to make sure that technical cooperation funds were allocated in line with WHO policies (WHO 1984, p. xxxvi).

Still, these measures had little impact apart from revealing "widespread, inadequate programme management beneath the veneer of administrative and financial correctness" (WHO 1986, p. xxii). Thus, in the second half of the decade, financial irregularities and abuses of WHO resources were reported in an increasingly sharp tone. Headquarters were quite blunt in their assessment of managerial failures, which far exceeded coordination and communication problems. It was found that WHO research fellowships in developing countries were being awarded with little to no accountability mechanism and that the WHO's budget policies were hardly ever adhered to (WHO 1986, p. xxii). The regional offices were accused of allocating technical cooperation funds with no strings attached, due to the "habit of considering the tentative country planning figure as the property of the ministry of health" (WHO 1987d, p. 7).

The DG reacted to these evaluations by turning into the most radical critic of his own child, regionalization. In his introduction to the 1988–9 program budget (WHO 1986) and in a flamboyant speech that he gave to the 1987 Assembly,[15] Mahler stated that technical cooperation was not functioning in the WHO. Assuming responsibility for having regionalized authority in the WHO to the "absolute limits of the Constitution" (WHO 1987h, p. 4), he lamented the unintended outcomes of this move in rather undiplomatic words (WHO 1987h, p. 5, emphasis in original):

> What I *do* regret is that it [regionalization] may be leading WHO to consist of six separate regional organizations and one separate headquarters organization. What I *do* regret is the increasing tendency to appoint staff in countries and in regional offices in their great majority from within the region. That to my mind contradicts the very spirit of the Constitution. What I *do* regret is that decentralization, rather than being accepted by each and every Member State as delegation to them of responsibility for the work of WHO and accountability to the Organization as a whole for the use of its collective resources, rather than that it is all too often being regarded as a blank cheque for pocket money.

Thus, faced with the results of the first financial audits, Mahler no longer heralded his organization as a flagship for social revolution, but despised it as seriously broken and in need of fundamental repair. He did not tire of emphasizing that the failures in technical cooperation were not only threatening the legitimacy and existence of the WHO's regional organizations (WHO 1987h, p. 4). Rather, these dysfunctions raised the question: "Shall WHO make the year 2000?" (WHO Regional Office for the Western Pacific 1987, p. 15).

Mahler's disillusionment with regionalization would be followed by a series of external evaluations that were equally critical of the WHO's regionalized system. Most importantly, a report by the United Nations Joint Inspection Unit (JIU) maintained that countries were the losers rather than the winners of regionalization, since the regional offices absorbed the larger part of the WHO's technical cooperation funds (Daes and Daoudy 1993, p. 30). In particular, the report blamed the unchecked authority of the regional

---

[15] The speech also marked a rhetorical peak of Mahler's incumbency. Ever faithful to his leaning toward famous quotations (e.g. of Bismarck, Montesquieu, or T.S. Eliot), the Dane loaded his sermon with references to William Shakespeare's *Hamlet*.

directors, the "undue politicization" of their work due to the "political debts" they owed to their electors and the absence of structured working relationships with headquarters (Daes and Daoudy 1993, pp. 24–5). The study called for major reforms such as limiting regional committee meetings from two per year to one per year of every other year. It also demanded to authorize the DG to select and appoint the regional directors and to recentralize control over the WHO's regional staff (Daes and Daoudy 1993, pp. 26, 41).

The JIU recommendations were also backed by similar evaluations by other agencies, such as the study sponsored by the Danish Department of International Development Cooperation that called for a "basic review" of the WHO's regional offices (Danida 1991, p. iv). The study considered the organization's structure to be an obstacle to field effectiveness. Countries would benefit little from the resources that were centralized at headquarters and regional offices; in particular since regional office resources were mostly dedicated to politicking and election campaigns. The study further found that regional resource allocations to countries and programs were not determined by health priorities but by regional politics, and thus that the WHO contributed little to attaining its goal of an integrated Primary Health Care approach (Danida 1991, pp. i–iv).

Hence, in the aftermath of the "Mahler revolution," regionalization came to be characterized as one of the WHO's main structural problems that did not support, but undermined the organization's country-level performance. The regional offices were criticized for absorbing the main part of the WHO's technical cooperation funds instead of channeling it to the country level (Godlee 1994a), and thus for adding a "dysfunctional layer of bureaucracy" (Henderson 2009, p. 86) with not much value added.

Locking in Regional Autonomy

However, despite these accusations of inefficiency, the WHO's regionalized system also had many winners who were keen to protect regional autonomies. We have already seen in Chapter 3 that early on their strategic function in preparing the WHO's budget had made the regional offices the primary distributional vehicle especially for poor countries. In his HFA reform, Mahler had explicitly taken into account the regional allegiances of his underdeveloped target countries, and therefore made the regions responsible for enacting the reform. And even though this devolution of authority may not have strengthened country-level delivery but was mostly absorbed at the regional level, in the wake of the reform many country delegates had still stronger vested interests in sustaining regionalization.

It was above all the managerial discretion granted to the regional directors, in particular over staffing decisions, through which the HFA reform reinforced intra-regional dependencies. As the Board's Programme Committee reported in 1987, the percentage of professional staff recruited from within the regions had risen significantly in all regional offices, and was nowhere below 80 percent (WHO 1987g, p. 6). This trend fuelled a system of regional patronage, with regional directors having well-nigh unchecked authority over the careers of their staff that they could freely assign to positions throughout the region. Especially in poor countries where well-paid jobs outside the WHO were hardly available, this administrative discretion bred strong dependencies for regional WHO staff (Godlee 1994a, p. 1567). Likewise, delegates of member states had strong incentives to be loyal to their regional directors given that this was the most likely potential employer for the time following the national service. This dependence was even stronger for members of the Executive Board than for delegates to the regional committees, given that Board members were usually junior in rank compared to regional delegates. Thus, while regional committees were usually attended by high-level delegations from national ministries of health, Executive Board members were lower in their countries' political hierarchy—a constellation that counteracted the Board's formal super-ordination over the regional subunits (Godlee 1994a, p. 1567, 1995a, p. 584).

Consequently, efforts undertaken at the Executive Board to reassert centralized authority over the regions faced insurmountable resistance. Several such efforts were undertaken in reaction to Mahler's accusation and the ensuing reports on regional inefficiency. Like in the 1950s and 1960s, the practice of regional self-governance came under attack at the Executive Board. Ironically, this time the leading critics were from the Americas, the historical originators of the WHO's regionalized structure (see Chapter 3): Together with the representative of Guyana, the US member of the Executive Board proposed to recentralize organizational power in the hands of the DG. Regional directors should be appointed upon suggestion by the DG, and centralized administrative control should be reinforced as well (WHO 1987c, p. 6). This suggestion had special weight as it came from the greatest net contributor to the WHO's budget (Vaughan et al. 1996, p. 236).[16] Moreover, due to Ronald Reagan's policy to radically cut regular contributions to the UN, US contributions to the WHO were almost entirely paid as conditional, extra-budgetary funds (WHO 1987b, p. 9). At a time of budgetary strain, where it was expected that at least 10 percent of the WHO's program would not be carried out due to lack of funds (WHO 1986, p. xii), such donor pressure was indeed threatening for the organization.

[16] An evaluation of the WHO's funding schemes found that by 1994, the US contributed twice as much as any other country to the WHO's extra-budgetary funds (Vaughan et al. 1996, p. 236).

However, it was impossible to reach agreement on the proposal. Several Board members criticized that the draft resolution left loopholes for the Pan American Health Organization (PAHO), meaning that centralization would only apply to PAHO once it was fully integrated into WHO as required by Article 54 of the Constitution. As long as PAHO remained legally independent, it would continue to appoint a director who then automatically served as WHO's regional director in the Americas. For many Board members, this was an unacceptable exception. Yet even without American exception, many Board members strictly opposed any infringement on regional self-governance (WHO 1987c, pp. 6–11).

As in previous attempts at curbing regional self-governance, the proposals were watered down in a process of successive concessions. In a sub-committee of the Board, a compromise was proposed by which regional committees would submit a ranked shortlist of three candidates from which the Board could select a regional director. The DG would be systematically involved in the search for candidates (WHO 1987g, p. 9). However, this proposal was—more or less diplomatically—rejected by all regional committees (WHO 1987e, pp. 7–8), and the Board failed to reach an agreement on it, too (WHO 1987f). A still weaker centralization proposal was made by the DG, who suggested the introduction of regional search committees that would base their suggestions on no less than twenty-four criteria the candidates would have to fulfill.[17] Yet these criteria were criticized as being too restrictive. Likewise, the search committee procedure was considered inappropriate and impracticable for many countries. In the end, no consensus on revised appointment procedures was reached and the US initiative died a death (WHO 1988, 1989).

Attacks on regionalization would continue over the 1990s. Mahler's successor in office, Hiroshi Nakajima (1988–98), would display a far more critical attitude toward regional autonomy (Godlee 1995a), like many of his colleagues at headquarters (see Siddiqi 1995, pp. 67, fn. 37; Peabody 1995, p. 740). Under his incumbency, another review of the WHO's constitution was sanctioned, and again the proposal was made that the DG should henceforth appoint the regional directors (Godlee 1995a). The renewed centralization proposals were again submitted to the regional committees, which all rejected centralized infringements on their selection procedures and also refused to report on their choices and criteria (WHO 1994, pp. 69–73, 1997, p. 11).[18] Instead, referring to the constitutional prerogative of the regional

---

[17] Among the enumerated qualifications were age restrictions (no older than fifty-five), the "ability to withstand possible pressures from his or her government," "emotional and moral involvement in the goal of health for all by the year 2000," "broad epidemiological experience," as well as the preparedness to "accept criticism" (WHO 1987a, pp. 1–2).

[18] The Board could only agree to limit the term of office of regional directors to a maximum of two five-year terms (WHO 1998a).

organizations to determine their own rules of procedure (Art. 49), the defendants of regionalization consistently blocked any procedural revisions that would have constrained their appointment practices.

With regional self-governance preserved, the new budgetary competencies of the regions also remained unchallenged. Quite the contrary, the managerial response to the implementation gap again reinforced regional autonomization: The delegation of evaluation and audit activities in the 1980s contributed to a development by which each region won all-out operative autonomy. Planning, budgeting, evaluation, and staffing with the exception of the highest professional category (D1) were now controlled by the regions, with headquarters only exerting superficial managerial oversight (WHO 1993, p. 3). This made it well-nigh impossible to hold the regional units accountable to the central governing bodies (see also Sridhar and Gostin 2011, pp. 1585–6).

4.5 Conclusion: From Reform Euphoria to Legitimacy Crisis

The WHO's regional offices controlled resources that were vital for the PHC agenda: A privileged access to national policy-makers through the regional committees, and a strategic filter position in the WHO's budgeting process. They had acquired this position after protracted power struggles during the WHO's founding moment, and maintained it as states henceforth oriented their distributional claims to the regional offices (see Chapter 3). This constellation amounted to a path dependent constraint for the Geneva-based reformers who needed to get the regional offices on board for implementing PHC policies in target countries. Hoping for an organization-wide enactment of the Health for All reform, the DG strengthened the regions' capacities to such an extent that the regional offices became practically autonomous in managerial terms. The historical advantage of the regional offices thus yielded increasing returns to them over the WHO's first major round of reform. Their operational autonomy has been protected ever since. The PHC case suggests that scholars should look beyond the immediate policy goals when assessing the outcomes of IO reform. Even reforms which do not attain their ("primary") policy goals and may therefore seem inconsequential can have lasting ("secondary") effects at the organizational level.

The record of the PHC reform demonstrates how power-driven path dependence (PDPD) plays out on reform processes in IOs: Attempts at reproducing an IO in the face of novel challenges feed into and reinforce the historical power structures that shape the organization. This path dependent dynamic is fragmenting where an asymmetry in favor of the subunits—in the WHO case: Of the regional offices—already exists. In this constellation, mobilizing for reform comes at the price of moving the organization deeper into the fragmentation trap. Nevertheless, it must also be stressed that the PHC agenda was particularly prone to produce a fragmenting "reform design" in the WHO. A developmental agenda with a strong commitment to country ownership was especially reliant on collaboration by the regional offices, and thus brought them in a favorable power position in the Health for All reform game. An alternative reform agenda, for example one that focused above all on controlling and eradicating infectious diseases, may have engendered a stronger centralization of organizational capacities, including the creation of organizational structures that bypassed the regional level in order to ensure speedy and coherent activities. Hence, what was at the time the exceptional design of the Smallpox Eradication Programme (Henderson 2009) could have become the blueprint for a rather different reform. Similarly, a reform agenda like the PHC reform need not produce the same fragmenting effect on IOs that start from a more hierarchical structure. This aspect will be discussed in more depth in Chapter 6 that discusses varieties of territorial decentralization in two other UN organizations: The more hierarchical International Labour Office (ILO), and the UN Educational, Scientific and Cultural Organization (UNESCO) where the thematic sectors are the main drivers of fragmentation.

It must also be stressed that regionalization may have complicated the implementation of PHC, but that is was far from being the sole or even main cause for policy failure in this case. Regional gatekeeping certainly inhibited the implementation of PHC measures in WHO member states (see Section 4.4). Still, the regional filter was only one factor determining the fate of the Health for All revolution, which failed due to a multitude of historical causes. Insufficient funds were one of these factors. Despite all assertions that PHC could be smart and cheap and did not require much financial investment (see Section 4.3), resource shortages were a main impediment to a policy shift that also depended on a favorable socioeconomic development (see Burci and Vignes 2004, p. 164). In this connection, the "neoliberal turn" of the 1980s additionally drained public capacities for health systems development (Thomas and Weber 2004). Concomitantly, already by the late 1970s Primary Health Care went out of fashion in the global health community, which instead turned to the strategy of Selective Primary Health Care (SPHC)—an agenda promoted by the Rockefeller Foundation in collaboration with the World Bank and other main development funders (Chorev 2012, pp. 80–1; see Chapter 5). Finally, the resistance of physicians and public health professionals to accept the de-professionalizing and social medicine aspects of Primary Health Care also played an important part. The PHC reform challenged the medico-professional jurisdiction over health matters by relying on neighboring policy sectors such as education or agriculture as well as on simply trained health staff next to doctors and nurses. It was accordingly attacked by professionals for referring health to "second-category" personnel (Burci and

Vignes 2004, p. 164), and raised suspicion in developing countries that PHC may be a means to offer them second class medicine. Also at the WHO headquarters, Health for All was far from commonsensical, and "mocked by senior-level staff, who counted the number of days remaining until the end of the century" (Litsios 2002, p. 725; and see Peabody 1995, p. 735). Hence, not all WHO staff were PHC "believers" in the first place. Against this backdrop, regionalization was one of many obstacles in the reform process, but above all it was a lasting by-product of what in bureaucratic terms were revolutionary times at the WHO.

The failure of HFA was followed by another legitimacy crisis. The central themes in the aftermath of the reform were no longer policy dysfunctions, but more and more the criticism centered on organizational pathologies: Bureaucratic inertia, dysfunctional regionalization and ineffective field activities. When Mahler decided not to run for a fourth term in 1988, internal conflicts dominated the WHO's work and undermined its reputation. This was particularly felt with the fate of its Global Programme on AIDS that provoked significant opposition in particular by WHO regions (Hanrieder 2014b). The weak standing of Mahler's successor Nakajima, who was elected in 1988 against the will of the WHO's Western donors, did little to alleviate this situation (Godlee 1994d). On the contrary, the dictum of the 1990s was: "The WHO: Change or die" (Smith 1995). Thus, when in 1998 Nakajima was succeeded by the former Norwegian Prime Minister Gro Harlem Brundtland, a novel attempt at engineering organizational unity and strategy was launched at the WHO. The ambitions and outcomes of the sweeping Brundtland reforms will be examined in the following chapter.

5

One WHO

New Managerialism, Old Structures, and the Simulation of Corporate Agency

> The WHO: Change or die
>
> (Smith 1995)
>
> Change at last
>
> (Godlee 1998)

The article titles quoted above indicate the climate of emergency within which Gro Harlem Brundtland, former prime minister of Norway, was elected the World Health Organization's (WHO's) fifth director-general (DG) in 1998. Her arrival at the WHO was heralded as the badly needed renewal of a moribund organization after a decade of decline. After Halfdan Mahler's frustrated "Health for All" reform, the WHO faced recurrent charges of bureaucratic pathology (see Chapter 4). Its regional organizations were criticized as sites of cronyism and patronage that were effectively decoupled from the central organization (Godlee 1994a). But also the Geneva secretariat had lost much of its legitimacy under Mahler's successor Hiroshi Nakajima (1988–98), a DG who lacked the support of the WHO's main donors and faced vivid accusations of mismanagement and corruption (Yamey 2002b, p. 1107). Other organizations like the World Bank began to rival the WHO's leadership in the international health field. And the most publicized international health challenge of the 1980s and 1990s, the HIV/AIDS pandemic, was no longer governed by the WHO, but by the newly created Joint United Nations Programme on HIV/AIDS (UNAIDS, established in 1995/6). In this atmosphere of decline, commentators presented leadership change as the last chance for the WHO to regain legitimacy and international support (Smith 1995).

Brundtland, a trained physician but otherwise an outsider to the WHO, was therefore welcomed as a much needed reformer "cut from the same cloth as Mahler—a Scandinavian with deep moral convictions and a capacity to bring together broad constituencies" (Lee 2009, p. 104). Her international prestige as the former leader of the "Brundtland Commission" on sustainable development and her high-ranking political connections as a former prime minister made her the highest-profile DG in the WHO's history. The new DG used this political clout to prepare an encompassing reorganization of the WHO, with the help of a "transition team" that was instituted several months before she took over as the WHO's head. Tellingly, the reformers gave priority to the task of reintegrating a "non-aligned Organization" during the first phase of reform, a task that was presented as the precondition for the WHO to be able to make an impact at all (Brundtland 1999a). Hence, while in the Health for All reform of the 1970s and 1980s had mainly been about preparing a *policy* shift toward Primary Health Care, by the late 1990s the WHO's very organizational *structure* had become the focus of reform.

Forging organizational unity out of the WHO's historical fragmentation should be achieved through the "One WHO" process. Its guiding vision was that of a coherent organization capable of strategic priority setting and coordinated action. With the help of a massive relocation of staff, state-of-the-art managerial methods, a results-oriented budget, and sophisticated techniques for priority-setting, the Brundtland reform heralded the era of a new and strategic WHO that was to replace a discredited bureaucracy. "Determined and fast change" was pronounced so as to reintegrate the regional offices and bring all WHO funds and activities under one centralized program budget, the "One Budget for One WHO."

And yet, when Brundtland left the organization in 2003, after only one term in office, not much was left of the One WHO ambition. While her support for global health initiatives such as the Global Fund to Fight AIDS, Tuberculosis and Malaria was much applauded, it was also clear that her internal reform goals had not been realized (Andresen 2002; Yamey 2002b). Quite the contrary, the WHO had moved onwards on the pathway to fragmentation: From *deepened* regionalization toward a fragmentation that was *widened* to the myriad special programs founded during the Brundtland years. In the subsequent years, the WHO's fragmentation reached such a point that in 2011 DG Margaret Chan publicly warned that the WHO was not functioning and—again, or still—in need of a historical reform (see Chapter 1).

As I will argue in the present chapter, this legacy of the Brundtland reform is not the outcome of managerial mistakes or fatal choices, but a consequence of the eminent structural constraints with which Brundtland's reform team was confronted when it set out to reinvent the WHO. In the end, these constraints made the One WHO reform a fragmenting rather than a unifying move.

The One WHO reform can be read as a real-world experiment in engineering agency in fragmenting organizations. It illustrates the compromises which reformers have to make in the face of entrenched internal deadlock, and it shows how these compromises reinforce the fragmentation trap. Regarding the WHO's fragmentation pathway, the Brundtland reform has not been a turning point, but catalyzed and brought into sharp relief the WHO's reform dilemma: On the one hand, Brundtland's efforts at recentralizing authority— by reintegrating the regions and enhancing corporate control over the WHO's income—were swiftly frustrated. While the fragmentation pathway could not be reversed, it was easily reinforced through what became the dominant strategy of change, namely the layering of new units on the WHO. New units were grafted onto existing structures and granted considerable auton-omy, which allowed them to bypass internal vetoes but also prevented that they were aligned with organizational priorities. While the special programs emerged strengthened from this mobilization, the corporate prize of this bypassing strategy has been that the WHO's fragmentation has been *widened* to new organizational layers. Attempts to correct this fragmentation through managerial regulations have at best diverted from this dilemma; and they created zones of informality that further undermined corporate agency.

The One WHO reform will be analyzed in six main steps. Section 5.1 introduces the legitimacy crisis and reform pressures that the WHO faced at the turn of the millennium. Section 5.2 outlines Brundtland's reform ambi-tion to create an integrated and strategic organization marked by economic rationality. Section 5.3 investigates the organizational obstacles which the reformers faced in their integration effort: An irreversible regionalization and a steady decline in regular budgetary contributions. Section 5.4 retraces how these constraints channeled the reform efforts in the direction of change by layering, and Section 5.5 shows that the outcome of this strategy counter-acted the One WHO ambition. The concluding Section 5.6 reconsiders the differences and commonalities between the One WHO experience and the preceding Health for All reform.

5.1 The Pressure for Reform

At Brundtland's arrival in 1998, the WHO appeared ripe for change. As we have seen in the previous chapter, the WHO's legitimacy crisis had already begun in the 1980s, when the failure of the Health for All reform became plain and (futile) attempts were made to curb regional autonomies. Beginning in the 1980s, donors put a halt to the WHO's regular budget growth and turned to extra-budgetary contributions instead, thus showing their lack of confi-dence in what was viewed as a dysfunctional bureaucracy (see Section 5.3).

The perceived need for change had several sources: A decade of leadership crisis under DG Nakajima, growing competition in the international health sector, and the reform impetus created by Kofi Annan's takeover as Secretary-General of the United Nations (UN) in 1997.

First, throughout the 1990s the WHO was confronted with calls for leadership change and massive attacks on its DG. Hiroshi Nakajima's election (in 1988) and re-election (in 1993) had been overshadowed by public charges of vote buying against the Japanese government (Lee 2009, p. 83). In Western media and public health journals, the DG was criticized for his poor (English) communication skills and accused of mismanagement and nepotism, not only from the outside, but also by WHO staff members (Godlee 1993b, 1993a). The impression was that Nakajima's WHO was a "fossilized bureaucracy" (Yamey 2002c) that suffered from a wasteful bureaucratic overhead, had no vision for international health policy and produced insufficient output (Lee 2009, pp. 83–4). A multitude of evaluations were published by academics and development institutes that came to very harsh conclusions: "WHO is unable to meet new challenges and needs reform" (Daes and Daoudy 1993; see Danida 1991; Forss et al. 1996, p. 138; Tollison and Wagner 1993; Vaughan et al. 1996). The most prominent of these attacks was mounted by the editors of the influential *British Medical Journal*, where a whole series of articles about all aspects of the WHO's work and structure was published (see Godlee 1994b, c,d,e, 1995b,c). Calls to replace Nakajima as soon as possible (Godlee 1995a; Smith 1995) were followed by a WHA resolution in 1996 which limited the service of WHO DGs to two (five-year) terms, which was a novelty in the UN system (Godlee 1996). Although this resolution did not apply to Nakajima as the current officeholder, he was sufficiently discredited by 1998 to pave the way for Brundtland's election—the first female WHO leader, and the first DG recruited from outside the organization. The desire to break with the past was obvious.

Second, a new start also seemed imperative as the WHO found itself under growing competitive pressure. The 1980s and 1990s had seen the influx of ever more organizations into the international health sector who were challenging the WHO's status as the lead agency in the field (Hanrieder forthcoming 2015). The United Nations Children's Fund (UNICEF), the WHO's traditional partner for implementing technical cooperation programs, was acquiring its own health expertise and working much more independently from the WHO than in the first decades of its existence. The World Bank had begun to fund health-specific projects in the 1980s (Ruger 2005, pp. 64–5) and by the 1990s became the dominant IO for health development—both ideationally, through its agenda-setting 1993 report *Investing in Health*, and materially, through its superior funding capacities (Lee et al. 1996, pp. 303–4). But also other UN organizations such as the UN Development Programme

(UNDP, created in 1965) and the UN Population Fund (UNFPA, established in 1969) were very active in the health sector (Lee et al. 1996, pp. 303–4). Non-governmental health work was also on the rise. Not only the number of non-governmental organizations primarily concerned with health was constantly increasing (Inoue and Drori 2006, pp. 205–7), but also influential new donors such as the philanthropic Bill and Melinda Gates Foundation, founded in 1999, became major players in the international health field (Lee 2009, p. 99).

The WHO's standing in this crowded environment seemed increasingly precarious. In particular, its loss of leadership in the combat of HIV/AIDS was perceived as a sign of historic decline. While since the mid-1980s, the WHO's Global Programme on AIDS had guided the multilateral response to this new and devastating disease, in the 1990s its activities were transferred to a newly created umbrella organization UNAIDS, which was established in 1995/6. The creation of UNAIDS should signal the urgency and multi-sectoral nature of the pandemic, but also downgrade the WHO's role in whose leadership donors had little confidence. Henceforth, the WHO had to confine itself to the status of a co-sponsoring agency and by the end of the 1990s practically dismantled its capacities in a domain that was regarded as one of the most pressing health challenges in the late twentiethth century (Slutkin 2000; Soni 1998). The impression of the 1990s was that the WHO risked drifting into irrelevance.

Finally, the blueprint for an organizational revival was already being developed at the UN headquarters in New York, at a time when supranational administration was put into question as an outdated form of bureaucracy. The neoliberal suspicion of public bureaucracy that had already unleashed a wave of "New Public Management" reforms in industrialized countries (Brunsson and Sahlin-Andersson 2000; Hood 1995; Kettl 2000) had now also reached the UN that were often seen as an eminent example of red tape, inertia, and undue politicization (Siddiqi 1995). To counter such criticism and regain the confidence of powerful donor states, first and foremost the United States (US), the UN's new Secretary-General Kofi Annan (1997–2006) announced a fundamental "rationalization" and "modernization" of the UN secretariat. This implied above all the adoption of more business-like styles of administration and governance.

With Annan's arrival, a "new leadership culture and management structure at the UN" (Annan 1998, p. 128) was promoted that should replace traditional bureaucratic with more entrepreneurial structures and thus make the UN more effective and efficient (Alesani et al. 2007). This implied cuts in administration and overhead, in order to free more resources for operative tasks. To make the secretariat more goal-oriented and effective, Annan announced a shift from "input based" to "results-based" budgeting, and established a "Strategic Planning Unit" to develop corporate policies (UN General Assembly

1997, pp. 17, 19). Furthermore, Annan embraced the "global governance" agenda and promoted the participation of non-governmental actors in the delivery of global public goods, and thus a shift toward less hierarchical but more inclusive modes of inter- and transnational cooperation. New partnerships with civil society and business actors were encouraged as a means to make the UN fit for a post-Cold War environment that was marked by economic global-ization and the rising importance of transnational actors (Annan 1998, pp. 133–5). This managerial modernization should serve as an example for reforms in other UN programs and specialized agencies as well. The impulse was willingly endorsed by Brundtland who would also borrow private sector techniques to regain organizational legitimacy. Such techniques seemed par-ticularly apt to infuse agency and strategy into a fragmented bureaucracy.

5.2 An Economic Paradigm for Change

Brundtland's fresh start should be truly strategic and based on rational analysis. Upon her nomination by the Board in January 1998, the future DG installed a five-person "transition team" to prepare her takeover six months later in mid-July. Financed by a so-called "Renewal Fund" that was mostly paid by the Norwegian government, the transition team reviewed the WHO's policies and strategies and developed proposals for an encompassing reform. The group mainly consisted of internationally renowned academics, the ideal-typical "disinterested professionalized others" embodying the modern principles of rationality and detached expertise (Meyer and Jepperson 2000, pp. 113–16). The reformers further demonstrated their independence through their physical location outside the WHO building, in a nearby ecumenical center.[1] Programs were scrutinized, staff interviewed, and new objectives and job positions devised for a radically renewed WHO (Lerer and Matzopoulos 2001, pp. 429–30). The message conferred by this renewal strategy was clear, namely "that the past was irrelevant and that the organization had turned over a new leaf" (Lerer and Matzopoulos 2001, p. 429), and intentional agency was asserted in a commit-ment to all-out organizational change (Brundtland 1998b):

> Yes there will be change. A change in focus. A change in the way we organize our work. A change in the way we do things. A change in the way we work as a team.

The objective of this change strategy was to infuse the WHO with economic rationality at the policy as well as organizational levels. Its policies should be

---

[1] This independence was later put into question when many members of the transition team were appointed to senior positions and could thus personally exploit the insights that staff members had disclosed in the interviews (Lerer and Matzopoulos 2001, p. 430).

guided by a utilitarian approach based on macroeconomic reasoning. And through drastic reorganization, the secretariat should be transformed into a collective homo oeconomicus that is capable of intentional change.

The Turn to Health Utilitarianism

Brundtland's team heralded a new approach to international health policy that has been labelled "health economism" due to its reliance on macroeconomic thinking (Lee 2009, pp. 111–15). Taking up ideas from the above-mentioned World Bank report *Investing in Health* (1993), the WHO's new policy paradigm was spelled out in the 1999 World Health Report *Making a Difference* (WHO 1999f) and the report by the WHO Commission in Macroeconomics and Health that was headed by the US economist Jeffrey Sachs (WHO Commission on Macroeconomics and Health 2001). This approach entailed both an economic justification for the provision of health services and an economic rationale for choosing the right policy measures.

First, a macroeconomic rationale was given for making health an international priority: Investments into the health sector, so the message conferred by Brundtland's team, would pay in terms of socioeconomic development. Health, while being and end in itself, was thus also a means to reduce poverty and foster economic growth (WHO Commission on Macroeconomics and Health 2001, p. 1). Good health ensured a productive workforce, and it freed resources for economic investments that would otherwise be needed for curing or treating illness. The Sachs Commission therefore argued that health should occupy a central place on the global development agenda and predicted that such global investments would pay economically (WHO Commission on Macroeconomics and Health 2001, pp. 9–12). Brundtland drew on these arguments (and her political clout) in her international campaigning for health which, different from established WHO practice, was not only targeted at national health ministers but also prime ministers and ministers of finance (Chorev 2012, pp. 166–8). And indeed, health was given a priority in the new millennium. According to one estimate, health assistance funds rose from US$5.6 billion in 1990 to US$21.8 billion in 2007 (Ravishankar et al. 2009). Likewise, the United Nations Millennium Development Goals that the UN General Assembly announced in 2000 made health a core topic of development. Three out of eight goals referred directly to health: Goal 4 to reduce child mortality, Goal 5 to improve maternal health, and Goal 6 to combat HIV/AIDS, malaria, and other diseases.[2]

---

[2] See <http://www.un.org/millenniumgoals/> (accessed August 13, 2014).

Second, the macroeconomic approach not only served to place health high on the development agenda, but also shaped how health policies were formulated. It provided policy tools for selecting health measures according to their relative effectiveness per dollar invested, thus aiming to make the most of notoriously limited public health resources. Thus, rather than aiming for all-out health systems change as under Halfdan Mahler's Primary Health Care (PHC) paradigm, Brundtland's team sided with the philosophy of Selective Primary Health Care (SPHC) that had emerged by the late 1970s, also in reaction to PHC (Magnussen et al. 2004, see Section 4.5). The strategic choice of policy priorities should be made possible by an economic analysis of which interventions could produce the maximum impact on public health. The focus of the WHO therefore shifted to targeted high-impact interventions, mostly disease-specific campaigns, which should be chosen on the basis of overall cost-effectiveness (Lerer and Matzopoulos 2001, p. 431).

The method for choosing the right priorities was a calculation of the so-called "burden of disease," which had first been developed in a joint World Bank/WHO project in 1990 (Murray et al. 1994). Burden of disease is measured with the help of the "disability-adjusted life year," shortened to DALY. DALYs quantify the loss in healthy life years caused by diseases and injuries and thus include both premature mortality and time lived with disability (WHO 1998b, p. 5). They can be used to select the most cost-effective interventions with a given health budget: The more DALYs an intervention is capable to save per dollar invested, the more worthwhile is the intervention (Anand and Hanson 1998, pp. 307–8).

DALY calculations should henceforth be the basis for priority setting not only in the WHO. According to Brundtland's WHO, this economic approach to health policy should as well become the basis of a "new universalism" for national health systems. It was emphasized that this philosophy did not necessarily entail the privatization of health services. Public health services were deemed indispensable for equitable and efficient health systems, but they needed to be based on scientific analysis to target interventions to where most health value for scarce public money was to be obtained (WHO 1999f, pp. 31–46). At the WHO, this analysis was performed by the newly created Evidence for Information and Policy Cluster which helped select a range of corporate priority projects and was to improve the WHO's analytical and strategic capacities (Brundtland 1998b; WHO 1999f, pp. 31–2).[3]

This emphasis on rational planning echoed earlier reforms such as Mahler's reliance on systems analysis as a rational tool for decision making (see Section 4.3). Nevertheless and despite all similarities between both public

---

[3] An important share of the unit's staff was recruited from the authors of the 1993 World Bank report *Investing in Health* (Chorev 2012, p. 175).

Table 5.1. From "Health for All" to "Making a Difference"

Primary Health Care	Selective Primary Health Care
Health conditioned by socioeconomic development and social justice	Health as a precondition for socioeconomic development
Priority on the poor at the periphery → Distributive egalitarianism	Priority on overall cost-effectiveness → Distributive utilitarianism
Empowering communities through, e.g. • primary health worker • prevention and education • fighting poverty	Targeting the major killers through, e.g. • immunization • oral re-hydration • drug generation and supply

health philosophies, it is worth carving out the major differences between the PHC and the SPHC paradigms, differences which are summarized in Table 5.1. First, the respective emphasis with regard to the health-development nexus differs. While PHC advocates have much emphasized the importance of socio-economic equity as a precondition for improving health, the SPHC approach puts more emphasis on the reverse relationship: The role that health plays for hindering or fuelling socioeconomic development and growth. Second, both approaches are based on different underlying visions of just distribution. PHC heralds the *egalitarian* principle of giving priority to the poorest at the periphery, whose empowerment shall come first in public health policy making. By contrast, the rationale of *Making a Difference* (so the title of the 1999 World Health Report WHO 1999f) is to increase aggregate utility and thus to avoid wasting public health resources. It is held that the "most cost-effective services in a given setting should be provided first" (WHO 1999f, p. 33). SPHC is thus based on the *utilitarian* principle of serving the greatest number, rather than taking the disadvantaged as a starting point (critically Anand and Hanson 1998).[4] Finally, the policy ambitions of both approaches differ. While PHC aims at long-term transformative change through community empowerment and health system development, the SPHC approach favors pragmatically targeted measures with visible and measurable short-term effects. This economic rationality should also inform the restructuration of the WHO so as to make it ready for the reform effort.

---

[4] In political theory terms, "utilitarian" approaches to just distribution seek to maximize the common good. The central normative standard for just institutions is that they produce optimal collective welfare. Egalitarian approaches, by contrast, are primarily concerned with equal distribution and stress that the individual welfare of the weakest may not be sacrificed for the collective good, but has to serve as the yardstick for distributional justice. This distinction between utilitarianism and egalitarianism has been prominently established by the philosopher John Rawls in his *Theory of Justice* (cf. Rawls 1999, pp. 3–46).

The WHO as Homo Oeconomicus

The strategic selectivity that the WHO promoted for global health policy should also be applied to the organization itself, which should be recalibrated according to its comparative advantage vis-à-vis other organizations. The WHO was to focus on activities through which a maximum value-added could be attained for global health governance (Lerer and Matzopoulos 2001, p. 415). Brundtland therefore stressed that the WHO needed a corporate strategy and clear-cut priorities to "make a difference" on the international health landscape (WHO 1998b, p. 3):

> I wish to concentrate our resources in a way which enables us to do fully what we decide to do—and to let go what we decide not to do—either because others do it better or because we simply can't do all.

To turn the WHO into a strategic actor, several managerial changes were implemented. First of all, a rationalized organizational chart should more clearly communicate the WHO's priorities (see Andresen 2002, p. 15): The secretariat was restructured into nine thematic clusters comprising altogether thirty-five—instead of previously fifty—programs: (1) Sustainable Development and Healthy Environments, (2) Family and Health Services, (3) Social Change and Mental Health, (4) Communicable Diseases, (5) Non-Communicable Diseases, (6) Evidence and Information for Policy, (7) Health Technology and Pharmaceuticals, (8) External Relations and Governing Bodies, and (9) General Management. This structure should make plain to both staff and observers what "business" the WHO was "in" (Brundtland 1998b).[5]

Furthermore, to substitute new ideas for established routines at the level of workforce, a rapid turnover of staff was set into motion. Within three months until November 1998, the headquarters were completely restructured. Quasi all top staff were replaced with new appointees—many of them recruited from the transition team (see Footnote 1)—and the tasks were redefined. The positions of "politically appointed" assistant directors-general (ADGs), usually

---

[5] The core of the WHO's priorities and foci is nevertheless hard to pin down, given that these were presented in various guises at different occasions. Change and the number "four" were among the few constants in the organization's strategy formulation. To give a few examples of the evolving conceptualizations: In her speech to the 1998 Assembly as DG elect, Brundtland named four "areas of concern": communicable diseases, non-communicable diseases, health systems (with special emphasis on mother and child health), and health advocacy (WHO 1998b, p. 3). At the January 1999 Executive Board, four "strategic themes" were introduced: effective work with countries, better and more equitable health outcomes, effective support of health sector development, and innovation through influential health partnerships (WHO 1999g, p. 6). In the "corporate strategy" prepared for the January 2000 Executive Board, Brundtland named, again, four "strategic directions" that also informed the preparation of the 2002–3 budget: reducing excess mortality, morbidity and disability, promoting healthy lifestyles and reducing risk factors, developing better health systems, and improving the institutional environment in the health sector (WHO 1999a, p. 3, 2001c).

representatives of the WHO's most powerful member states (meaning the permanent members of the UN Security Council), were abolished and the office holders were asked to resign (Lerer and Matzopoulos 2001, p. 416). Instead, a new managerial team—called the "cabinet"—was recruited, with an eye to ensuring gender balance and a balance between officers from developed and developing countries (Brundtland 1998b).[6] Most cabinet members, now called "executive directors," were newcomers to the WHO and had outstanding academic credentials—which created the impression that now Harvard and the World Bank were to tell national and international health officials how development worked (Yamey 2002b, p. 1110).

In addition, 750 (out of about 1200) headquarters staff were rotated to new assignments, including a massive physical reshuffling between offices (Lerer and Matzopoulos 2001, p. 429).[7] Timely retirement was encouraged to build a younger workforce,[8] and human resource development was made a cabinet priority, with special emphasis being laid on encouraging staff mobility between locations and assignments (Brundtland 1999a). The extra costs created by this turnover were shouldered with the help of an additional US$2.5 million "Global Health Leadership Fund" donated by the Rockefeller Foundation (Dove 1998).

Finally, deliberate change was not only to be facilitated by restructuring the secretariat, but also through the introduction of new working methods. In particular, the shift from "resource-based management" to "results-based management" that was also part of Annan's United Nations reform (see Section 5.1) was emulated at the WHO. This meant that the WHO's budget was no longer to be structured according to resource input, but formulated in terms of strategic objectives to which the required resources—in terms of staff and money—would be assigned only in a second step (WHO 2001c, p. 9). In line with the new public management philosophy, results-based budgeting envisaged a shift from bureaucratic and procedural control to a system of output-based accountability, in order to make the organization more responsible and goal-oriented (Brunsson and Sahlin-Andersson 2000; cf. Hood 1995). This accountability was to be ensured through improved monitoring and evaluation based on newly developed performance indicators

---

[6] This cabinet format was similar to the UN's Senior Management Group introduced at the UN secretariat in 1997 (Annan 1998, p. 129).

[7] In 1999, out of 3,452 total staff, 1,261 were working at headquarters (WHO 1999d, p. 4).

[8] With a UN retirement age of only sixty, the WHO had developed a practice of further employing retired staff as consultants—a practice that the staff association regularly indicts as a source of nepotism (e.g. WHO 2000a, pp. 3–4). Critical of this practice and emphasizing meritocratic principles, the Brundtland team lowered the average age of senior management staff from fifty-nine to forty-nine (Brundtland 1999a). Still, complaints that due process was still not observed by the new leadership were brought forward by the WHO staff association on several occasions (see, for example WHO 2001d).

(WHO 2000b, p. 2).[9] The new budgeting technique was thus a further means to break with bureaucratic habit and craft a truly goal-oriented organization. Yet, this project of deliberate renewal also had to confront old structural obstacles—obstacles that Brundtland sought to overcome through the One WHO agenda.

5.3 Fragmentation and the Limits to Corporate Control

Staff turnover and new analytical methods notwithstanding, the reform agenda could not be implemented on a clean slate, but had to be realized within preexisting structures. This was well acknowledged by the transition team whose analysis had identified the WHO's fragmentation as a central structural challenge. Brundtland summarized the team's findings as follows (Brundtland 1999a):

> People spoke of more than 50 WHOs—meaning the more than 50 individual programmes at Headquarters. They spoke of 7 WHOs, meaning Geneva and the six Regional Offices. They spoke about 2 WHOs, meaning the one financed by the regular budget and the one financed by extra-budgetary contributions.

The reformers' goal was to forge a unified WHO out of this compartmental-ization and to develop a more "holistic" approach to planning, resource mobilization, and performance assessment (WHO 1999a, p. 1). To integrate the WHO's activities on a day-to-day basis, internal exchange and communi-cation were much encouraged. Staff rotation and mobility were made prior-ities of human resource development, and meetings at all organizational levels were institutionalized to ensure ongoing communication. Moreover, to better connect headquarter and regional activities, a tele- and video-network was installed between Geneva and the six regional offices (Brundtland 1999a). These measures should encourage a "culture of information sharing" to create synergies between the WHO's different programs and units (Brundtland 1998b).[10]

The main instrument to create One WHO, however, was the idea of devel-oping One Budget for One WHO. The WHO's biennial program budget is the official document that determines the organization's funding and priorities. It is prepared at many levels: At the regional offices, at the Geneva headquarters,

---

[9] The WHO's new managerial professionalism was also demonstrated by presenting the budget in power-point format instead of using the traditional format of information documents (see WHO 2001c).
[10] The technological integration of the WHO also involved the introduction of new management software in 2006 in order to connect the regional offices to the headquarters and track income and expenditure across the WHO—although according to many interviewees, this technological change proved difficult to implement and involved many delays.

and at the Executive Board. It is also bindingly endorsed by the World Health Assembly. This central authorization notwithstanding, programming was a highly decentralized process at Brundtland's arrival, reflective of the WHO's fragmented organizational structure. First, because the regional organizations determined their share quasi independently of headquarters. And secondly, because the growing share of extra-budgetary funds was not included in the regular program budget.

Regional Resistance to Centralized Authority

Like her predecessors, Brundtland faced the challenge of how to obtain the cooperation of the regional directors (see Chapters 3 4). Regional collaboration had even been described as the "big test" of her reform (Robbins 1999, p. 36; see Godlee 1998). Following the example of previous DGs, Brundtland held consultations with all regional directors and put those meetings on a regular basis in the so-called "Global Cabinet" (Brundtland 1999a).[11] Still, such consultative practices could not change the fact that regional collaboration was practically voluntary in a system where the heads of the regional offices were independently elected and monopolized the control over the WHO's country-level activities. The new DG attempted to circumvent such regional authorities through her "country focus initiative," whereby the headquarters should become involved in appointing country representatives—an intrusion that was strongly resented by the regional offices (Andresen 2002, p. 18). As interviewees at WHO headquarters bequeathed to me, rumors were spreading in the wake of the reform that the new DG was gathering support for abandoning the elections of regional directors—a change that would indeed have reverted a decades-old practice. Yet, the sole tangible effect of such re-centralization plans was to provoke regional distrust and resistance toward the reform process. Instead, the regional offices rather delayed reorganization measures that would align them with the new cluster structure at headquarters, for example the One Budget for One WHO initiative.

The integrated budget should break with a practice that had made the regional offices so powerful in the first place (see Section 3.5): Their competence to put together the budgets for the regions that would then be included within the overall program budget. In the One Budget process, however, headquarter clusters and their regional counterparts should jointly produce a coordinated program (Brundtland 1998a; WHO 1999f, p. xix). Thus the 2002–3 budget, the first one entirely drafted by Brundtland's team, was

---

[11] She also reached out to the WHO's country representatives, who usually report to the regional directors, by organizing the first global meetings of WHO representatives in Geneva in 1999 and 2001 (Brundtland 1999a, 2001).

prepared in a multi-stage consultation process between the headquarters and the regional offices (WHO 2001c, p. 3). The new method should align global and regional objectives and define expected results for the WHO as a whole (Joint Inspection Unit 2001, p. 17).

However, this coordination process went far from smoothly and met fierce regional resistance, meaning that integrated budgeting barely exceeded window-dressing. Most regions resented these coordination efforts and rejected them as "top-down governance," with the result that no agreement on priorities was reached between headquarters and the regions (see Joint Inspection Unit 2001, p. 17). In the African region, for example, pre-established operational plans remained totally unaffected by the new corporate program budget (Yamey 2002c, p. 1171). Thus, debates continued to be preoccupied with the share of regular and extra-budgetary funds allocated to the regional level, and with their distribution between individual regions—not with the definition or implementation of corporate objectives (Joint Inspection Unit 2001, p. 17).

Brundtland thus had to realize that governing the regions was only formally part of her job description. The recalcitrance of regionalization was also felt in one of her flagship or "cabinet projects," Roll Back Malaria (RBM). RBM, a health partnership with the aim of cohering global efforts in the prevention and treatment of malaria infections, quickly became the object of much criticism as it was seen to produce insufficient output (Schäferhoff 2009; Yamey 2002b, p. 1109). A self-evaluation of the initiative reported in 2002 that ongoing frictions between WHO headquarters and the regions considerably hindered RBM's work and made policy formulation often impossible (Roll Back Malaria and World Health Organization 2002, p. 59).[12] It was highlighted that one could hardly speak of "One" WHO, given that communication and coordination functioned neither vertically across organizational levels, nor horizontally between the different regions (Roll Back Malaria and World Health Organization 2002, p. 59). As a reaction, donors and partners of the WHO lamented the problems involved in working through the WHO's (or UNICEF's) regional structures and were looking for alternatives, for example the GAVI Alliance for Vaccines and Immunization that was more independent from the WHO (Schäferhoff 2009, p. 226; see Section 5.4). The RBM example illustrates that even for a priority project that was directly launched by the DG's office, hierarchical control was limited. It also underscores the legitimacy costs that regionalization entails vis-à-vis outside

---

[12] As most of the time, the African region was singled out as particularly problematic and uncooperative (Roll Back Malaria and World Health Organization 2002, p. 59; Yamey 2002a, p. 1238).

supporters. Yet, regionalization was not the sole obstacle to corporate control over the WHO's program and budget.

How to Strategize with Special Funds

Integrating the WHO's budget was also difficult for a second reason, namely the fact that an increasing number of organizational activities was getting dissociated from the regular programming process. This tendency had already begun in the 1980s with the establishment of so-called "special programmes" such as the already mentioned Global Programme on AIDS. Different from the WHO's regular activities, special programs were operated from headquarters and strived to evade regional control—much to the outrage of the regional offices (Godlee 1995c). Ironically, this new method of organizing the WHO's work had been established during Mahler's incumbency, who in the 1970s had taken numerous steps to make the regions the operational centers of the WHO's development work (Litsios 2002, pp. 730–1).

Mahler's frustration with regional collaboration for Primary Health Care has been laid out in the previous Chapter 4. The PHC experience had shown how collective policies could be blocked at the regional level. Avoiding regional blockades through special programs not only became a popular method for "vertical" programs, that is, concerted efforts to combat single diseases such as diarrhea or respiratory diseases (Godlee 1995c). The bypassing strategy was also used for pursuing controversial activities such as birth control that many resented for religious reasons, but that headquarters pursued in a research program on human reproduction (WHO 2008b, pp. 94–6). Similarly, the WHO's HIV/AIDS program was seen critically in some regions such as the African region, where many governments feared racist undertones and reacted with hostility to Western AIDS policies (Int. 6; Knight 2008, pp. 10, 14). The program evaded such opposition by simply circumventing the regional administrations (Chin 2007, pp. 200–1; Hanrieder 2014b).

Such bypassing was made possible by the fact that special WHO programs raised their own, independent funds, so-called extra-budgetary contributions that were controlled by the program leaders at headquarters. By the mid-1990s, about ten such special programs existed in the WHO, and extra-budgetary funds made up half of its operating budget (Godlee 1995c; Walt 1993, pp. 128–9).[13] The advantage of these funds was that they allowed donors and program leaders to "layer" new initiatives on all-too inert structures. The

[13] The main source of extra-budgetary funding for the WHO was the official development assistance provided by member states, which in 2000 made up about 60 percent of the WHO's voluntary funds. The other major donors were the UN and other international organizations and large private foundations such as the Rockefeller Foundation, the Rotary Foundation or the Bill and Melinda Gates Foundation (Minelli 2002).

WHO could thereby grow even though donors were no longer prepared to increase their assessed contributions, suspicious of an organization that since the 1980s was under constant fire for being too bureaucratic (Godlee 1995c). Donors, in return, could continue to use the WHO, but without funding its regular structures and programs. Their policy of zero real growth since the 1980s (whereby the budget was merely adjusted to inflation) and zero nominal growth since the mid-1990s (whereby the regular budget was shrunk) was thus counterbalanced by an ongoing increase in extra-budgetary funds (Lee 2009, pp. 38–9; see also Figure 1.2).

Regarding the goal of unifying the WHO behind a corporate strategy, however, the increase of extra-budgetary funds posed considerable problems. Brundtland therefore criticized that the WHO's independently funded projects were not operating in a coordinated manner, if not at cross-purposes (Brundtland 1999a; and see Godlee 1995c; Vaughan et al. 1996):

> All too often WHO—like far too many agencies—delivered dispersed advice, without matching closely the real needs of our Member States. All too often a WHO staff member met a colleague at the airport or at the doorstep of the same donor agency—without knowing in advance that the other was expected at the same place at the same time.

In addition to this lack of horizontal coordination, the reliance on extra-budgetary contributions undermined corporate planning and thus Brundtland's vision of the strategic organization. Voluntary contributions were barely paid on a regular basis, and they were inflexible due to their earmarking for specific purposes. Using them for organizational priorities thus was extremely difficult.[14] To alleviate this situation, Brundtland made a pledge at her first Executive Board meeting in January 1999 that member states augment their regular contributions to the WHO and return to a policy of zero real growth (WHO 1999g, pp. 13–14). This motion unleashed a vivid debate at the Board that continued up until the May 1999 Assembly. Yet apart from the French delegation, the donor states represented at the Board were not prepared to increase their assessed contributions (WHO 1999c, pp. 63–76). Instead, the Assembly called on the secretariat to compensate its declining income through budgetary discipline, efficiency savings and a shift of resources from "low" to "high priority" areas (Brundtland 1999b). The request to strengthen centralized control by regularizing payments, however, was denied.

---

[14] Moreover, with an overhead charge of 13 percent that the WHO can deduct from voluntary contributions, the various short-term donations and staff contracts can hardly be administered. For this reason, donors came to an ad hoc agreement in 2006 that permitted the WHO to reallocate earmarked funds to core administrative expenses (Lee 2009, p. 106).

Brundtland's team sought to produce an integrated program budget in spite of these obstacles, and to use results-based budgeting as a means to achieve this objective. Henceforth, the program budget should not only cover those activities funded by regular contributions, but also include the anticipated income from voluntary contributions. This should facilitate the move from planning by resources to planning by results that was the rationale of the new budgeting technique: Goals should be formulated first and be endorsed by the WHO's governing bodies, and subsequently funds would be raised to finance the planned activities—with the hope that donors would base their pledges on defined priorities (WHO 1999e, p. 6). Thereby, the lamented budgetary split should be overcome, while donors could be confident that targeted fund-raising rather than bureaucratic process was guiding the WHO's work.[15]

5.4 Mobilization by Delegation

In spite of all these obstacles, Brundtland's goal for the WHO was to create visible impact through targeted high profile initiatives. In this effort, she could make use of her international prestige and diplomatic connections to donor governments and potential partners such as the Bill and Melinda Gates Foundation (Naím and Brundtland 2002, p. 27). Yet, as this subsection will demonstrate, to win cooperation for new WHO projects she also had to sever organizational control—both at the headquarters where she strengthened subunit autonomy, and with regard to the health partnerships initiated by the WHO.

First, the Brundtland reform involved a further empowerment of the WHO's thematic units at the headquarters. Given her ambitious budgetary projections—for the 2002–3 budget, a 15 percent rise in voluntary funds was envisaged, and the 2004–5 budget even set the target of a 23 percent increase (Minelli 2002, pp. 160–7)—Brundtland acknowledged that this goal could only be attained through decentralized fundraising: "We should not artificially centralize our fundraising efforts. Donors expect to see first class expertise and hands-on experience before they allocate extra resources" (Brundtland 1998b). Therefore, it was first and foremost the clusters and their executive heads that were made responsible for bringing in the necessary funds, and they were empowered to do so through new managerial competencies. Communication services were decentralized to the clusters, allowing them to better

---

[15] Several donor states such as Switzerland and the Scandinavian countries voiced concern over the "imbalance" between core and voluntary funds. Yet most WHO members, and in particular the US as a major contributor of extra-budgetary funds, lauded the new budgetary approach and encouraged further budgetary discipline to keep regular contributions at bay (WHO 2001b, pp. 9–13).

market their activities. Furthermore, the clusters were granted considerable operative discretion, including authority over staffing decisions which had previously been centralized in the DG's office. Their administrative autonomy was also reinforced by establishing so-called "Management Support Units" (MSUs). Replacing the preexisting centralized system of administrative support, MSUs enabled the clusters to manage contracts and expenses independently. Likewise, those administrative support functions previously located in individual programs—mostly those earning lots of extra-budgetary income—were integrated into the MSUs (WHO 1999b). With these managerial competencies, executive directors took the role of the modern "accountable manager" who is held responsible by results but freed from administrative interference (see Brunsson and Sahlin-Andersson 2000, p. 728)—or like ministers in a national cabinet: They could negotiate with donors, strike funding agreements, hire staff and administer their income without passing through the DG's Office.

In addition, to mobilize support for global health initiatives, the WHO made systematic usage of the partnership mode of governance whereby authority was shared with other health agencies including private actors. The dozens of health partnerships launched at the time usually focused on circumscribed activities such as delivering vaccines or developing drugs for neglected diseases (Buse and Waxman 2001).[16] They are not governed through old bureaucratic and multilateral processes, but by their own governing bodies where the relevant stake- and shareholders should have a say. The Global Fund to Fight AIDS, Malaria and Tuberculosis, a foundation dedicated to raising funds for the treatment of these three major diseases, is exemplary in this regard. The voting members at its Board consist of eight donor representatives, seven developing country representatives (one from each WHO region and one additional from Africa), and five civil society/business representatives. The WHO and UNAIDS, by contrast, participate only as non-voting members.[17]

The turn to partnerships allowed the WHO to bring in new powerful funders such as the Gates Foundation that was a central driver behind the establishment of many partnerships such as the GAVI Alliance, which was jumpstarted with a US$750 grant from the Gates Foundation. It reasserted, among others, the goal of polio eradication (Andresen 2002, p. 24; Schäferhoff

---

[16] In 2007, between eighty and a hundred international public–private partnerships for health were counted, depending on their definition. Most partnerships were established after 1996, with a peak of new creations between 1999 and 2001 (Bull and McNeill 2007, p. 66). Available data suggest that the WHO is a partner in most of these partnerships, but not always represented on their boards (see Buse and Harmer 2007, p. 260; People's Health Movement et al. 2008, p. 213).

[17] Governance structure as determined in the 2011 version of the Fund's bylaws (The Global Fund to Fight AIDS, Tuberculosis and Malaria 2011). Previously, the World Bank was also represented as a non-voting member of the Board (People's Health Movement et al. 2008, p. 262).

2009, pp. 223–6).[18] Functioning as the modernized version of WHO special programs, these and many smaller partnerships are governed outside the WHO's established bureaucratic structures. They differ with regard to their degree of integration into the WHO. Many are *layered* upon the WHO's bureaucratic structures as semi-independent programs with separate donor agreements and reporting lines. For example, Roll Back Malaria was jointly initiated with other IOs and private actors in 1998, but is operated from the WHO's Cluster on Communicable Diseases since 2000. Others such as the Global Fund were initially hosted by the WHO, but subsequently moved out of WHO headquarters to set up their proper administration—thus evolving into emanations (Shanks et al. 1996). In any case, partnerships, just like special programs, escape the control of the WHO's directorate and strike their own bargains with donors and partners.

In summary, while Mahler's WHO had still sought to implement his Health for All reform from within, by empowering the regional organizations (see Chapter 4), Brundtland strived to circumvent the WHO's recalcitrant bureaucratic structures. Her strategy to delegate authority to issue-specific programs greatly lifted the WHO's profile in the media and among major donors (Lee 2009, pp. 106–8). It also helped to boost the WHO's extra-budgetary income: In 2000 alone, voluntary contributions to the WHO increased by 40 percent (WHO 2001a, p. 5). Yet the flipside of successful mobilization for special programs and partnerships was that it widened the WHO's fragmentation to new, issue-specific centers of authority.

5.5 The Aftermath of the One WHO Reform: Growing More Fragmented

What these mobilization strategies did not achieve, however, was to make the WHO "One." As noted above, the centralization efforts by the new team were resisted by discontent staff members. Not only did the drastic managerial changes introduced by the transition team provoke dissatisfaction and resistance among WHO staff (Lerer and Matzopoulos 2001), but in particular attempts at reintegrating the regions were effectively averted. This regional resistance was seen by many to have (among other reasons) motivated Brundtland's departure from the WHO after only one term in office (Yamey 2002b, pp. 1110–11).[19] On the other hand, the empowerment of the special programs

---

[18] An overview of public–private partnerships for health is provided in People's Health Movement et al. (2008, pp. 210–23); for some exemplary portraits see Bull and McNeill (2007, pp. 76–82).
[19] Officially, she did not seek re-election for reasons of age and personal health. Another reason for her early departure is seen in the protest and criticism she received for the 2000 World Health

was reinforced through the internal competition that it stirred as well as through the positive feedback that it received from the WHO's donors.

First, the strategy of decentralized fundraising exacerbated the competition between the units, further inciting them to strive for exclusive ties with external supporters. Since the units had to bring in a large share of the projected funds by themselves, and given that resources were notoriously scarce, they strived to outcompete each other (Lee 2009, p. 106). Many interviewees described the clusters as "silos" that were marked by distrust and rivalry. Given that promotions also hinged on successful fundraising, the competition for extra-budgetary funds was a strong disincentive to information sharing across the units—in spite of the incantation of flat hierarchies and horizontal communication at all organizational levels. Special relations with donors were an asset in this competition, yet risked to produce a duplication of efforts so that the wheel was reinvented in different parts of the organization. The competitive climate was reinforced by the rising job insecurity within the organization, given that the surge in project-specific funding also implied a growing share of short-term contracts for WHO staff members (Lee 2009, p. 106; Yamey 2002c, p. 1171; see Section 7.1).[20]

Second, the donor's strategies have equally reinforced the WHO's fragmentation into separate programs. Certainly, several donors acknowledged that the WHO's funding situation was unsustainable and pledged to provide more flexible and less earmarked funds (HM Government 2009). The directorate continued to ask for more flexible funds as well to win discretion over the budget (WHO 2011b, pp. 9–15). Still, in 2006–7, about 83 percent of all voluntary contributions received by the WHO were closely tied to specific purposes: 10 percent were tied to broader organizational objectives, and only 1–7 percent were donated as flexible funds (WHO 2009, p. 14 and see WHO 2010). While prestigious and visible programs such as polio eradication or HIV/AIDS attracted disproportionate funding, less fashionable activities such as health systems development are less successful in raising the necessary funds. Meanwhile, even core normative activities risked to be discontinued due to lack of funds (Horton 2006, p. 1794; Levine 2006, pp. 1015–17), while other, more popular programs were "overbudgeting," as one WHO program director expressed it. Yet, for member states, unearmarking would amount to paying the overhead for projects that other states can then take the

---

Report, which contained a much contested ranking of national health systems (Yamey 2002b, p. 1111).

[20] Catherine Weaver reports a similar trend toward intra-organizational competition that resulted from the World Bank's introduction of internal contracting schemes, in a so-called "matrix management system" (Weaver 2008, pp. 161–2).

credit for—an option far less attractive than investing in high-profile campaigns.

This decentralized reinforcement of the WHO's programmatic fragmentation proved difficult to reverse with managerial measures. Evidently, it is decentralized alliances and not the directorate that select between competing programs, so that a control mechanism in the sense of "divide and rule" is not available. Furthermore, the technique of results-based budgeting cannot do away with the fact that resources are often tied, and thus cannot be aligned according to results. Lacking its basic precondition—the control over resources—results-oriented management remains a vain aspiration (see Section 7.1).

Brundtland's successors have made further attempts at integrating the programs. One attempt was a beginning recentralization of the administrative competencies that had been devolved to the clusters' management support units. In the eyes of the staff members that I talked to, this undertaking has created overlapping and unclear responsibilities within the secretariat—and a climate of reform fatigue. In addition, to gain more control over the budget Margaret Chan, the WHO's DG since 2006, introduced the tool of budgetary "ceilings" as an antidote to "overbudgeting." These ceilings defined the maximum resources to be spent per program, as well as the maximum number of staff that a particular program may hire. My interviewees emphasized that those programs that are raising more funds than agreed can seek to raise their ceiling in a multi-stage negotiation with the directorate, but otherwise have to renounce at contributions exceeding their ceiling—or pass them on to the central management. Several WHO officers have also pointed out that their programs bypass their respective ceilings by channeling funds through the regional and country offices. For the units, this is preferable to the option of passing unspecified funds "to the seventh floor"—the WHO's senior management located on top of the main headquarters building. Hence from the viewpoint of the WHO officers whom I interviewed, the ceilings were relatively toothless instruments.

Additionally, in the context of the post-2010 WHO reform, a new consultative method shall better integrate the WHO's funding. This is the so-called Financing Dialogue between the WHO secretariat, member states, and crucial private donors. The forum first met in June 2013 after the 2013 World Health Assembly. The dialogue's aim was to sensitize the donors to the WHO's financial dilemma and thereby guide their funding behavior. The participants of the Financing Dialogue endorsed six general aspirations with regard to financing the WHO's work, namely "alignment," "predictability," "flexibility," "broadening the contributors' base," "transparency," and "continuing the discussion." A second Financing Dialogue took place in November 2013, and a web portal was installed that should enhance the flow of information on financial flows.[21] The external evaluation of this consultation tool concluded that the Financing Dialogue was well received by the participants, but that it did not constitute a form of pledging conference. It was a nonbinding mechanism whose main function consisted in raising awareness of the budgetary fragmentation and how it jeopardized the WHO's work (Pricewater-houseCoopers SA 2014). It seems unlikely that this soft mechanism will significantly curb the autonomy of the special programs.

But it is not only the thematic programs that have consolidated their position in the aftermath of the One WHO reform. The regional offices, too, have been further strengthened. After Brundtland's failed attempt at curbing the region's budgetary autonomy, no further assaults on their powers have been made. To the contrary, Brundtland's successor Jong-Wook Lee (2003–5) has decided to devolve WHO funds to the regional level on the basis of a 70/30 principle for the WHO budget: 70 percent of the budget should be spent in the regional and country offices, and 30 percent be left for the Geneva headquarters (see Lee 2003). Although according to the WHO's financial reports the 70/30 principle is not fully implemented, it is affirmed as a budgetary aspiration and supports the regional offices' claim to their control of the main part of the WHO budget. But also at the managerial level, the competencies of the regional directors have been further strengthened in the post-Brundtland era. According to my interviewees, DG Chan has meanwhile delegated the authority to appoint senior staff to the highest director category (D1) to the regional directors—while previously it was only up to D2.

Hence, the WHO's fragmentation along regional and along programmatic lines has been perpetuated in the aftermath of the One WHO endeavor. The result is a complex organizational set-up which is obscure to observers and participants alike. The headquarter-based thematic programs receive the main share of their funding through extra-budgetary channels, funding comes in irregularly and on short-term notice only. For program leaders, the flipside of earning their proper earmarked funds is that earmarking sometimes is so tight that the funds raised cannot even be spent. Many departments are "sitting on unspent money" that is, for example, on funding specified for drug delivery that cannot be used because funding for the required personnel is lacking. Program leaders at the WHO headquarters therefore bemoaned that staff had to be fired despite the existence of unspent funds. These varied constraints and zones of informality have led to the situation described in the introductory Chapter 1, with a DG alerting to her organization's dysfunctions and calling for "far reaching reforms" (WHO 2011c).

---

[21] See <http://www.who.int/about/resources_planning/financing_dialogue/en/> (accessed August 13, 2014).

5.6 Summary: WHO Reform in the Fragmentation Trap

The hope for change that accompanied Brundtland's election as the WHO's DG was justified in many respects. Health became a central concern of national governments and a host of new health initiatives such as GAVI or the Global Fund were jumpstarted with the help of the WHO. Brundtland's political clout was also crucial for negotiating the WHO Framework Convention on Tobacco Control (2003), which was concluded in spite of fierce industry opposition; and her determined leadership during the 2002/3 SARS crisis boosted the WHO's authority in disease surveillance and control (Hanrieder and Kreuder-Sonnen 2014; Lee 2009, pp. 100–9).

However, Brundtland's attempt to change the WHO structure and thereby halt its organizational fragmentation was less successful. Her One WHO strategy was launched as a major attempt at recentralizing agency in the WHO by aligning its regional and functional subunits with the corporate strategy. For this purpose, Brundtland's reform team had devised an encompassing blueprint for the WHO's "rationalization" through managerial changes and the integration of the regions into the budgeting process. This plan, however, was frustrated by the entrenched fragmentation of the WHO. The regional offices participated only superficially in Geneva-based planning strategies, and the thematic units at the headquarters took advantage of the budgetary shift—which Brundtland well-nigh had to reinforce in order to implement her policy goals. Challenging in vain the regions' control of the regional budgets and bidding in vain for more centralized funds from the WHO's donors, Brundtland relied on a mobilization strategy that was again centrifugal: She empowered the thematic subunits—the clusters—to engage in local coalitions with program-specific partners. New health initiatives thus were designed as additional organizational "layers" and granted independent authorities. This reform strategy *widened* the WHO's fragmentation to Geneva-based programs.

The One WHO reform thus perpetuated a history of WHO reform whose centrifugal bias had already become obvious in the Health for All initiative of the 1970s and 1980s. In fact, despite their different philosophies regarding health policy, the Health for All reform and the One WHO reform share the experience of rationalizing ambitions being frustrated by fragmenting tendencies in the WHO. Both initiatives heralded unified IO agency and were concentrated on a strong leading figure, which symbolized the determination to engage in deliberate change. Likewise, both reforms were accompanied by incantations of unity of purpose, the propagation of rational managerial strategies, and manifold measures to mobilize (and physically move) WHO staff for corporate goals (see Section 7.1). Yet, while Mahler's mobilization effort was still concentrated on changing the WHO from within and therefore made the regional offices the central agents of change, Brundtland's main policy initiatives were realized by circumventing established structures and creating new layers. Hence, whereas Mahler delegated power to the regional offices in the hope that they would follow the Primary Health Care flag, Brundtland delegated authority to issue-specific clusters in the hope that they would bring in the required funds for the WHO's program. Both strategies revealed the limits to steering fragmented organizations and showed that their mobilization for reform comes at the price of reinforcing centrifugal tendencies.

Still, like the Mahler reform, the outcome of the Brundtland reform was not all-out determined. Even though the discussion is this chapter has made plain that she faced powerful incentives to move further along the fragmentation pathway, a different reform input may have had less fragmenting consequences. For example, had Brundtland managed to persuade the WHO's major donors to grant their contributions on an unconditional basis, these donations could have been used as centralized funds managed by the directorate. Hence, had her initial bid for a greater share of regular funds been successful, the One WHO agenda might have been as well. That this bid was declined at her first Executive Board (see Section 5.3) can thus be seen as a decisive co-determinant for the fragmenting outcomes of the reform. Fragmentation was an absorbing state in the WHO that Brundtland sought to unify, but it was not an iron law.

Likewise, it needs to be emphasized that both the Mahler and the Brundtland reforms were not turning points, but rather, climaxes within long-term processes of organizational adaptation and reform. The Brundtland years and their enormous fundraising successes only accelerated a budgetary shift that had already started in the 1980s, and the regionalization steps initiated by Mahler confirmed a strategic position that the regional offices had built up since their very creation. The two reforms brought these tendencies into sharper relief, and thus reinforced the fragmentation pathway that the WHO has followed since the installment of its uniquely powerful regional subunits. The following chapter discusses in how far centrifugal dynamics are at play in international organizations that are not marked by the WHO's extent of regional autonomy.

6

Decentralization and Fragmentation in the United Nations

Comparing ILO and UNESCO

The World Health Organization's (WHO's) fragmentation trap (analyzed in Chapters 3–5) has entrenched a regionalized structure that is peculiar within the United Nations (UN). While nowadays most UN organizations entertain field presences, they do not feature a comparable extent of regional autonomy. This will be shown in the present chapter, which analyzes *varieties of territorial decentralization in the UN system*. I argue that on the one hand, the decentralization of IO activities to the country and regional levels is a broader trend in the United Nations. However, the extent to which territorial decentralization produces a fragmenting effect on individual IOs is path dependent on the organizations' initial (more or less fragmented) structure.

   The chapter compares varieties of decentralization in two UN agencies, which differ with respect to their initial fragmentation: the United Nations Educational, Scientific and Cultural Organization (UNESCO), and the International Labour Organization (ILO). While the ILO has embarked on decentralization as a rather hierarchical and centralized standard setter, the UNESCO's starting point was one of functional fragmentation into highly autonomous thematic "sectors." Due to these different starting conditions, the ILO's expansion of field activities has remained subject to centralized control, whereas in UNESCO it reinforced fragmentation along the organization's thematic sectors. In this latter case, *deepening* fragmentation occurred as UNESCO's sectors extended their authority to theme-specific field offices, which served as exclusive branches of the responsible "parent" sector rather than UNESCO as a whole. In addition, *widening* fragmentation occurred as reformers sought to initiate change with the help of additional "inter-sectoral" programs that created additional layers of authority within the organization.

Thereby, the UNESCO case exemplifies the wider applicability of the fragmentation trap. Different from the WHO example, UNESCO's fragmentation is not driven by the regional organizations, but by the thematic sectors. Yet, the reinforcement mechanisms of deepening and widening fragmentation unfold in its sector-based structure as well.

The juxtaposition of these two trajectories underlines the relevance of path dependence in the process of UN reform. It illustrates that the UN's global decentralization trend—the establishment and strengthening of field presences across the UN family—is not per se a fragmentation process. Rather, the comparison rather shows that the historical condition of the fragmentation trap—subunit authority—shapes how decentralization is enacted in IOs. The path dependent nature of decentralization trajectories also raises important questions for UN-wide reform efforts such as the ongoing "Delivering as One" agenda. Through these efforts, different IOs shall be better coordinated at the country level. This requires, however, that the field offices of individual IOs enjoy sufficient discretion to collaborate on the ground. As a consequence, the cohesion of single IOs can at the same time lead to inter-agency fragmentation.

The short case studies presented herein are plausibility probes that provide a preliminary assessment of the fragmentation trap's wider analytical utility (George and Bennett 2005, pp. 75–6). They are based on organizational documents and evaluation reports as well as secondary sources. This analysis serves to bring out major differences in the organizations' overtime patterns of decentralization. While reflecting on the ways in which these pathways interacted with organizational reform agendas, the chapter does not provide in-depth investigations of individual reform efforts and their implementation (cf. Section 2.4). It shall provide, though, the basis for more detailed assessments of the intended and unintended mechanisms through which both IOs have been reproduced and transformed since their creation.

In the following, I will first provide an overview of territorial decentralization in the UN (see Section 6.1). I next examine the ILO's trajectory of decentralization, using its flagship program against the worst forms of child labor as an illustration (see Section 6.2). In Section 6.3, I retrace UNESCO's decentralization pathway that reinforced its sectoral fragmentation. Finally, I discuss the implications of IO decentralization pathways for the UN's Delivering as One reform (see Section 6.4).

6.1 The Field Presences of UN Organizations

Most UN programs and specialized agencies have started from small and centralized beginnings, with most staff operating from a European or an

Table 6.1. Country and regional offices in UN agencies and programs[a]

Organization	Headquarters	Country Offices	Regional and Sub-regional Offices
ILO	Geneva	21 Country Offices	5 Regional Offices 13 Decent Work Teams 28 Other Offices
WHO	Geneva	150 Country Offices	6 Regional Offices
UNESCO	Paris	27 National Offices	13 Regional Bureaus 4 Liaison Offices 17 Cluster Offices
FAO	Rome	142 Country Offices	5 Regional Offices 9 Sub-regional Offices 5 Liaison Offices
World Bank	Washington D.C.	>120 Country Offices in 6 regions	
IMF	Washington D.C.	87 Local and Resident Representative Offices	4 Regional Offices 2 Europe Offices 1 Technical Assistance Office
UNHCR	Geneva	84 Field Offices 83 Branch Offices 49 Sub-Offices 16 Field Unit Offices 7 Chief of Mission Offices 5 National Offices	20 Regional Offices 12 Liaison Offices 3 "Specialized" Headquarters
UNICEF	New York City	>200 Field Offices in 156 countries	7 Regional Offices
UNDP	New York City	135 Country and Territory Offices	5 Regional Bureaus 7 Liaison Offices

[a] Information derived from IO websites (for WHO: <http://who.int/about/structure/en/>, accessed May 16, 2014; for UNESCO: <http://www.unesco.org/new/en/bfc/all-offices/>, accessed January 30, 2014, for FAO: <http://www.fao.org/about/who-we-are/worldwide-offices/en/>, accessed May 16, 2014; for IMF: <http://www.imf.org/external/country/ResRep/index.aspx>, accessed January 30, 2014; for UNICEF: <http://www.unicef.org/about/structure/index_field.html>, accessed January 30, 2014, for UNDP: <http://www.undp.org/content/undp/en/home/operations/contact-us>, accessed January 30, 2014) and reports (International Labour Office 2013: 56; WB Annual Report 2013, <http://https://openknowledge.worldbank.org/bitstream/handle/10986/16091/9780821399378.pdf?sequence=1>, accessed January 30, 2014, p. 23, Fahamu Refugee Program: UNHCR Country Office List, available from <http://www.refugeelegalaidinformation.org/sites/default/files/uploads/UNHCROffices_addresses_contact%20details.pdf>, accessed January 30, 2014).

American headquarters. Yet, as the organizations consolidated themselves and took on more tasks and activities, most of them also established field presences in addition to their central offices. They strengthened their country presences and regional or sub-regional offices that serve as intermediaries between the headquarter and the country level and that are differently defined and delineated in each organization.

Table 6.1 lists the number and variety of country and field offices presently entertained by nine major UN organizations that engage in technical cooperation.[1] The table shows that each organization entertains both country

---

[1] The first six entities—ILO, WHO, UNESCO, the Food and Agriculture Organization of the UN (FAO), World Bank and the International Monetary Fund (IMF)—are specialized agencies that are formally more autonomous than the UN High Commissioner for Refugees (UNHCR), UNICEF, and the UN Development Programme (UNDP). The information about country and regional offices has

offices—in the case of United Nations International Children's Emergency Fund (UNICEF), several offices in one country—and inter-country offices that are defined as regional, sub-regional, or multi-country liaison offices. The number of country and regional offices varies between the organizations, which delineate geographic areas differently and endow their field offices with different types of tasks and competencies. Hence, there is no UN-wide blueprint for the shape of regional subunits. Yet, at the same time, an overall pattern of federalism can be observed across the organizations. Their bureaucracies increasingly rely on offices that are placed outside the Western headquarters.

Two major concerns have encouraged the expansion of territorial units within UN organizations. First, an enlarged membership, mostly due to decolonization, considerably extended the organizations' territorial reach beyond the original Western metropolises. Since the 1960s, the growing representation and assertiveness of the Third World altered the activities of many IOs, and in particular technical cooperation became more central to the work of many UN entities (Müller 2010, p. 6). The World Bank's development turn in the era of Robert McNamara (1968–81), for example, centrally involved the buildup of country-level capacities and offices. Similarly, the Food and Agriculture Organization of the United Nations (FAO) launched a Technical Cooperation Programme for food aid delivery in 1976, which led to the establishment of over seventy country offices engaging in food aid activities (Beigbeder 1997, p. 63). In a similar vein, the International Telecommunication Union (ITU) began to create regional and area offices in the 1980s in an attempt to enhance communication assistance to developing states (Posta and Terzi 2009).

Second, decentralization has often been undertaken to (re-)legitimate UN bureaucracies. It serves as a promise to make the UN's organizations and agencies more efficient and effective. UN-wide institutional reform agendas almost routinely entail calls for decentralization. In the face of recurrent criticisms that the UN is a conglomerate of top-heavy and self-serving bureaucracies, many pledges were made to devolve activities from headquarters to field offices. Territorial decentralization here promises to create a more visible impact of UN work at the country level. In many reform contexts, it also became part of efforts to maximize "efficiency savings"—which is a constant aspiration, given ongoing funding shortages and recurrent cuts in contributions by dissatisfied donor states.[2]

---

been retrieved from the websites of the organizations and their regional bodies on January 30, 2014.

[2] See, for example, debates about the resource shortages at the FAO (Food and Agricultural Organization of the United Nations 2007).

Thus, for example, at the end of the Cold War when the UN repositioned itself in the emerging system of global governance, the UN General Assembly (UNGA) issued several resolutions calling for a more decentralized UN system. In a 1989 resolution, the UNGA called for a "more decentralized and strengthened capacity of the United Nations system at the country level" (United Nations General Assembly 1989). The goal of such restructuration was both to decentralize the structures of individual IOs, and to integrate their activities at the country level, under the auspices of the UN resident coordinator. IO decentralization thereby served as a means to improve inter-agency cooperation (see also Joint Inspection Unit 1992). This reform ambition has been kept alive until today. It has been reiterated in the Delivering as One initiative, which was launched in 2005 under Secretary-General Kofi Annan, and which is carried out by the UN Development Group, an umbrella organization for more than thirty UN organizations working on development issues. Restating the goal of bundling the field-level activities of UN agencies, the reform seeks to strengthen the UN resident coordinators, who shall be in charge of a single UN office, program and budget for all UN organizations in a particular country (UN 2006). The reform, which has entered a pilot phase in eight countries, re-emphasizes the importance of the field level for legitimating the UN.[3]

Meanwhile, the pressure to scale up field-level activities is felt by practically all organizations of the UN system. However, their adoption of decentralization impulses has been diverse, as we can see from the comparative snapshot presented in Table 6.1. In the following sections, we shall take a dynamic perspective and compare different pathways of decentralization in the UN. The contrasting trajectories of the ILO and UNESCO highlight path dependent variation within the overall decentralization trend. They thereby also provide insight into the prospects for UN-wide reform.

6.2 The ILO: Capacity Building from Above

The ILO is the oldest of the organizations listed in Table 6.1. Together with the League of Nations, it was established through the 1919 Treaty of Versailles to serve as a global legislator for labor policy. After some rather minor modifications of its constitution in the wake of World War II, the ILO became the first UN specialized agency in May 1946. From the outset, the ILO was a very active standard setter producing numerous recommendations and conventions. Yet, faced with the relative ineffectiveness and low ratification rates of most of its standards, in the 1990s the organization undertook a major readjustment of

---

[3] See <http://www.undg.org/?P=7> (accessed April 16, 2014).

its governance approach, turning from formal standard setting to soft law and capacity building strategies. This also involved a push toward decentralizing the International Labour Office's activities to its federal units. In this section, I turn to the field level, focusing in particular on one of the ILO's largest technical cooperation programs—the International Programme on the Elimination of Child Labour (IPEC)—which prominently illustrates the ILO's approach to technical cooperation. The ILO/IPEC case shows how a historically centralized organization can implement decentralization as a hierarchical enterprise.

I will roughly distinguish three phases in the ILO's development. I first introduce the ILO's initial set-up and decentralization practice until the mid-1990s, then present its post-Cold War policy shift toward soft law and technical cooperation, and finally, examine how this shift is implemented in the ILO's federal offices.

The ILO's Origins as a Centralized Standard Setter

The ILO was created to regulate labor policy at the international level. Its design was chiefly shaped by social reformers and trade unionists from France and the United Kingdom (UK), at a time when organized labor had grown strong in Europe. During the war, new social policies had been widely adopted to accommodate and mobilize trade unions, which became a vocal party to the ensuing negotiation of the postwar settlement (Ghebali 1989, pp. 6–8). Their position was strengthened not the least by the specter of the Russian Revolution, so that the ILO was built to function as a European alternative to bolshevism.[4] Its central task was to issue labor standards in the form of international conventions and recommendations, whereby it should counter a race to the bottom in European social policy while at the same time containing revolutionary sentiment in postwar Europe.

The ILO's main outputs are international labor conventions, which become legally binding upon national ratification, and recommendations that are legally non-binding. Many of these ILO standards are general and universal, referring, for example, to the freedom of association and collective bargaining, employment, and working conditions, the elimination of forced labor and child labor, or social security and workplace health. Additionally, country-specific standards are tailored to diverse national conditions, and industry-specific standards make detailed technical prescriptions for different industrial domains. Since its creation, the ILO's normative output has been

---

[4] The United States (US) only joined the ILO in 1934 after the election of Franklin D. Roosevelt (Hughes and Haworth 2011, p. 11). It withdrew from the ILO from 1977 to 1980, at a time of intense policy controversies over labor and market regulation (see Standing 2010).

extensive, averaging two conventions per year in the period between 1960 and the late 1980s (Baccaro and Mele 2012, p. 198). All in all, by the end of 2013, the ILO had adopted 189 conventions and 202 recommendations.[5] Its ambitious legislative output won it the Nobel Peace Prize in 1969 (Helfer 2006, p. 653).

This output is produced through a governance structure that is mostly known for its tripartite composition of the governing organs—a unique historical bargain between governments, unions, and employers. Both in its plenary body, the International Labour Conference (ILC), and in its executive organ called the Governing Body, governments, employers and union delegates are represented at a respective 2–1–1 ratio.[6] Although formally the delegations are nationally appointed, the social partners usually form separate groups in the ILO's principal organs and tend to vote with their respective groups rather than with their governments (Helfer 2006, p. 651).

Yet, not due the least to the diversity of preferences among these groups, it was above all the pro active engagement of the International Labour Office, the ILO's bureaucratic organ, that allowed the ILO to produce its extensive normative output. As specified in Article 396 of Part XIII of the Treaty of Versailles and subsequently in Article 10 of the ILO constitution, the Office's main task is policy-advisory. It shall collect and distribute information on social and labor concerns with a special view to preparing and proposing issues for international conventions (International Labour Office 1923, p. 335, 2010, p. 10). This task was actively interpreted by the Office's directors-general (DGs), especially Albert Thomas, the ILO's first DG, between 1919 and 1932, who laid the grounds for the ILO's centralized bureaucratic structure. Thomas reached out to labor representatives to promote labor standards, and he assumed a strategic role as an agenda-setter and a policy broker. Hence, capitalizing on the directorate's central position amidst the ILO's tripartite constituency, Thomas, as well as later DGs, managed to expand the Office's authority in the policy process by way of, for example, facilitating treaty ratification and introducing monitoring tools (Cox 1973, p. 120; Helfer 2006, pp. 681–9).

Emphasizing the directorate's independent "political role" (Ghebali 1989, p. 12), the DGs also took care to maintain a strong position within the bureaucratic hierarchy (Cox 1973, p. 120). Rather than working through intermediate organizational layers, the founding DG Thomas established direct and "quasi-personal" ties with staff to ensure bureaucratic loyalty—a model that was perpetuated by his successors (Ghebali 1989, p. 12). This

---

[5] See <http://www.ilo.org/dyn/normlex/en/f?p=NORMLEXPUB:1:0::NO:::> (accessed December 29, 2013).

[6] In the Governing Body, ten of the government seats are permanently held by countries of so-called "chief industrial importance," which are presently Brazil, China, France, Germany, India, Italy, Japan, the Russian Federation, the UK, and the US (Hughes and Haworth 2011, p. 23).

leadership model that is based on the centrality of the DG's position and thus the direct interaction with, and control of, subordinate units has also shaped the ILO's early decentralizing moves.[7] In the ILO, first field presences were established between 1950 and 1952 in Asia, America, and the Middle East to provide technical and policy advice to unions and governmental actors (Alcock 1971, pp. 139–48; Helfer 2006, p. 681). As the ILO gradually extended its technical cooperation activities over the 1960s, the growing number of field offices were grouped together in four regional offices in Africa, Asia, Latin America, the Middle East, and a European Regional office seated at the Geneva headquarters, each one presided over by a regional advisor (Alcock 1971, pp. 239–40; Beigbeder 1997, pp. 65–6). This regional setup was again reorganized in response to the above-mentioned GA resolution of 1989, which called for a strengthened field presence of UN organizations (see Section 6.1). To meet this request, in 1992 DG Michel Hansenne (1989–99) initiated the creation of so-called multi-disciplinary teams which replaced the regional advisors. The teams were instructed to deliver services to countries in collaboration with ILO regional offices. Yet the DG also made sure that these regional bodies acquired no independent policy-making authority (International Labour Office 1993, p. 1), and that the directorate remained the central port of call for all offices: All regional units of the ILO were asked to seek headquarter guidance and, if necessary, contact the DG directly to resolve problematic issues (International Labour Office 1993, p. 2).

The centralized control of field activities would also be maintained through the 1990s, as the ILO shifted its focus from lawmaking to capacity building.

From Legislation to Capacity Building

The mid-1990s saw a major change in the ILO's regulatory approach. It was launched by DG Hansenne with his 1994 report at the occasion of the ILO's seventy-fifth birthday (International Labour Office 1994). In the report, Hansenne responded to the criticism that despite the ILO's sizeable normative output, the organization was deemed a rather ineffective, if not irrelevant, regulator of late twentieth-century labor conditions. Its weakness was both due to flaws in the ILO's normative output, as well as changes in the globalized world of labor.

---

[7] Due to the centrality of the ILO's DG, who entertained direct ties to all constituent groups and organizational levels, Robert Cox portrayed the organization's structure as "monarchic," resembling the organization of a royal court (Cox 1973). In network theoretical terms, the direct access of the DG to the ILO's units (and vice versa) can be described as the DG's "closeness centrality," i.e. the maintenance of short communication and decision paths between the directorate and the ILO's subunits (cf. Hafner-Burton et al. 2009, p. 564).

First, the sizeable body of ILO conventions and recommendations had grown incoherent and poorly ratified. Many ILO conventions and recommendations were not complementary, but contradictory, given that there was no procedure for harmonizing rules or for replacing old standards with updated versions. Old and new, general and specific standards coexisted without their interrelationship being clarified (Helfer 2006, pp. 698–9). In addition, ILO standards suffered from a growing gap between treaty making and treaty ratification. Although this gap had always been considerable,[8] the ratification rates for ILO standards declined further over time. Hence, between the 1960s and the 1980s, the average number of ratifications per convention was merely thirteen (Baccaro and Mele 2012, p. 198). The incoherence and deficient ratification of ILO standards thus undermined the impact of ILO treaty making.

Second, the changes in worldwide working conditions associated with globalization also challenged the relevance of ILO standards (Hughes and Haworth 2011, pp. 36–7). These were tailored to industrial workplaces structured around salaried (full-time) employees with benefits and pensions—a reality that was eroded by the ongoing economic liberalization. The concomitant rise of part-time and self-employed, and often informal work even in Western welfare states questioned the established corporatist model. Likewise, the growing transnational workforce escaped the reach of social legislation (Helfer 2006, pp. 705–7). Hence, the "policy drift" that Jacob Hacker has conceptualized for the United States (US) welfare state could also be observed at the global level: Established labor regulations persisted, but nevertheless their impact changed or eroded due to changing socioeconomic conditions (see Hacker 2004).

In the light of the ILO's deteriorating normative output together with its declining impact, Hansenne shifted the ILO's governance approach from hard legislation to "soft law" sustained by local capacity building (International Labour Office 1994, p. 49). To consolidate ILO law, he initiated the weeding out and concentration of existing ILO law. Dated treaties were separated from up-to-date standards, and a list of eight fundamental labor conventions was compiled, for which the office launched a universal ratification campaign. These eight norms indeed attained ninety percent of all possible ratifications (Helfer 2006, pp. 707–17). Apart from this concentration and contraction of hard ILO law, the organization turned to soft law as a means to generate universal adherence to international labor norms. With the 1998 Declaration on Fundamental Rights at Work, four core international labor norms were asserted as universally valid: The freedom of association and right to collective

---

[8] In the 1920s and 1930s, ILO standards on average attained about twenty-five percent of all possible ratifications (Helfer 2006, pp. 684–5).

bargaining, the elimination of forced labor, the abolition of child labor, and the elimination of workplace discrimination.[9] Following the "single under-taking" model of the World Trade Organization (created in 1994), the so-called core labor standards affirmed in the Declaration reflect a normative bargain that shall oblige all members of the ILO, even though it is not legally binding. The Declaration comes with distinct review mechanisms, such as a special annual report, but its main focus is on capacity building in the countries.

To realize the Declaration's aims, the ILO relies on managerial rather than enforcement techniques; that is, it provides technical support to countries to enable them to guarantee labor rights (International Labour Office 1994, p. 61; Liese 2005). Hence, several technical cooperation programs have been established under the Declaration, which combine advisory services and local capacity building (Thomann 2008, pp. 74–5). The biggest and most prominent of these programs is the IPEC (see International Labour Office 1994, p. 61). Its implementation illustrates how a hierarchical IO can run decentralized activities without fragmenting its authority structures.

Capacity Building from Above

The ILO estimates that there exist about 215 million child laborers (aged 5–17) worldwide, and that about 115 million of them are doing hazardous work in diverse sectors such as mining, service, manufacturing or agriculture (International Programme on the Elimination of Child Labour 2011). Preventing or terminating in particular these types of work is the focus of the IPEC that was initiated in 1992, and has become the ILO's largest technical cooperation program with an annual budget of about US$60 million and projects carried out in more than eighty countries. Although the IPEC's aim is to eliminate all forms of child labor eventually, the program gives priority to combating the worst forms of child labor as defined in ILO convention no. 182; the 1999 Convention against the Worst Forms of Child Labour (Mielke 2009, p. 183). The convention—the most successful convention in the ILO's history in terms of ratifications (Baccaro and Mele 2012, p. 198)[10]—defines the "worst forms of child labor" as comprising child slavery or slavery-like prac-tices, prostitution, and pornography involving children, the involvement of children in illicit activities such as the sale of drugs, and "hazardous" work; that is, work that harms the "health, safety or morals" of children. Hazardous

[9] See <http://www.ilo.org/declaration/thedeclaration/textdeclaration/lang–en/index.htm> (accessed December 29, 2013).

[10] The convention received 150 ratifications within only five years (Baccaro and Mele 2012, p. 198). The number rose to 179 by January 2015. See <http://www.ilo.org/dyn/normlex/en/f?p= NORMLEXPUB:11300:0::NO::P11300_INSTRUMENT_ID:312327> (accessed January 12, 2015).

work exemplifies the limitations of a law-based, corporatist approach to labor policy. It is mostly informal and, according to the ILO's policy approach, requires empowerment and capacity building rather than hard regulation to be curbed and eventually eliminated. This is reflected in the IPEC's working methods.

The program's genesis illustrates the organization's gradual turn to capacity building strategies: An initial legislative focus on child laborer protection, based on treaties such as the 1919 and 1973 Minimum Age Conventions, was succeeded in the 1970s by a stronger emphasis on research and campaigning, and from the 1990s by the IPEC's capacity building approach (Mielke 2009, p. 183). While also engaging in global normative activities such as research and campaigning, the program's operational focus is on local empowerment. Therefore, the IPEC is designed as a "highly decentralized" program, with about 90 percent its staff working outside ILO headquarters (International Programme on the Elimination of Child Labour 2010, p. 4). IPEC projects support education and training for child laborers, capacity building for ILO constituents, and social mobilization. Today the main types of IPEC projects are the so-called time-bound programs (TBPs) that are based on the principle of local ownership, and last for a period of five to ten years. TBPs are designed at the national level in collaboration with IPEC staff. They usually involve a plenitude of non-governmental actors who ensure access to target groups such as informal or self-employed child laborers and their families.

Yet, although the projects are designed and carried out at the local level, the ultimate say is not with project managers or the heads of field offices. Rather, the ILO headquarter exercises managerial and policy control through various techniques. The headquarters takes the lead in campaigning and fundraising for IPEC projects, and it filters proposals through centralized application procedures. Thus, to receive IPEC support, TBPs have to follow detailed guidelines that specify principles for the design of projects, the formulation of targets, project implementation, and evaluation.[11] Once established, IPEC projects are monitored and evaluated through centralized procedures, too (see International Programme on the Elimination of Child Labour 2013, p. 33). With the help of these techniques, ILO headquarters assert policy leadership as well as managerial control over its flagship program.

The IPEC is not an exception in this regard. It represents a top-down capacity building approach in the ILO that has been noted in several reviews

---

[11] See <http://www.ilo.org/ipec/lang–en/index.htm> (accessed December 30, 2013), and Liese (2005, pp. 70–3).

of the organization's federal design. The reviews by the Joint Inspection Unit have noted a tight dependence of ILO field offices on headquarters for administrative decisions. In this vein, a 1999 review notes that staff recruitment authorities have only been devolved to area offices and directors of multidisciplinary teams on paper, and that staff profiles are centrally determined (Joint Inspection Unit 1999, pp. 22–3). With regard to the execution of country-level programs, regional and sub-regional capacities are deemed too circumscribed to allow for a meaningful participation in program development and implementation (Ortiz et al. 2005, p. 10). A report by an internal review team that was published in 2013 again highlighted that country offices were lacking capacities and that the delegation of authorities to field offices was diffuse and allowed for multiple interventions by the headquarters; for example, Geneva-based fundraisers or outcome coordinators (International Labour Organization 2013, pp. 13, 24–5, 42). Technical cooperation was criticized for being too general and supply-driven and the review further noted that headquarter priorities rather than country strategies determined the work plan (International Labour Organization 2013, pp. 9, 20). The report therefore stated that, although not foreseen by the official division of labor between the ILO's bureaucratic levels, the direct interference of headquarters in field operations was common practice in the ILO (International Labour Organization 2013, p. 45). These are noteworthy observations given that the report was directly addressed to the DG. They suggest that the ILO's centralist tradition continues, although the turn to capacity building has given rise to a more extensive and complex multi-level design of its work.

In summary, the ILO's legacy as a centralized and "policy-based" (Ortiz et al. 2005, p. 10) organization has definitely shaped its turn to soft law and the implementation of capacity building that culminated in the reforms of the 1990s. The organization has expanded its field presence as technical cooperation became more important in programs such as IPEC. Yet, due to the strong position of the headquarters and the DG, its decentralization of activities has been managed from above. The ILO's centralized decision making, budgeting, fundraising, and monitoring has been criticized for being too rigorous (Ortiz et al. 2005), and the inefficiencies and confusion coming with centralized interferences into field activities have been noted and brought to the attention of the DG (International Labour Organization 2013). The ILO case supports the path dependent nature of IO fragmentation. It shows that the decentralization of IO activities to the field does not automatically trigger a fragmentation trap, as long as the IO starts from a hierarchical authority structure. A contrasting case is provided by UNESCO, which started from a completely different mandate and set-up from the ILO.

6.3 Sectoral Fragmentation in UNESCO

Unlike the ILO with its focused lawmaking mandate, UNESCO was "born plural" (Sewell 1975, p. 135). The twenty country delegates who signed the UNESCO constitution in November 1945 in London agreed on an encompassing mandate for this specialized agency which, in the broadest sense, should foster peace through the promotion of humanist ideals and the Enlightenment values of tolerance, culture and education, and science-based progress (Singh 2011, pp. 1–5). UNESCO not only mobilizes international support for the preservation of cultural heritage, the activity it is best known for; it also promotes scientific and cultural exchange, supports the development of school textbooks, facilitates research for the world's oceans, or launches initiatives to bridge the digital divide. The variety of policy domains covered by these activities is also reflected in UNESCO's internal organization. In addition to the domains specified in the organization's name—education, science (which is organizationally split up into "natural sciences" and "social sciences and humanities") and culture—communication and media constitutes a distinct "thematic field" or, as they are more commonly referred to, "sector" (Singh 2011, p. 35).

UNESCO's plural mandate has thus contributed to a bureaucratic structure that has been fragmented not into territorial units—like the WHO's regions—but into functional subunits, the thematic sectors. Still, we will see in this section that UNESCO's sectoral fragmentation has given rise to comparable self-enforcing dynamics. Fragmentation was *deepened* as the sectors acquired more authorities over time, and it was *widened* as new inter-sectoral programs were layered on top of UNESCO's fragmented bureaucracy. Furthermore, the section shows that decentralizing moves were integral parts of these fragmentation dynamics, especially through the practice of "parent sectors" whereby field offices are assigned to individual sectors and thus perpetuate sectoralism within federalism. In the following, I will first examine the origins of UNESCO's sector structure, then reconstruct the gradual deepening of sectoral power, and finally turn to the inter-sectoral initiatives which widened UNESCO's fragmentation to new organizational layers.

Departments of Humanism: The Formation and Lock-in of Sectors in UNESCO

The organization of UNESCO's thematic sectors has two main historical sources: Disagreement among its founders concerning the UNESCO mandate, and the "academic" managerial approach of its first executive head. Regarding the first component, UNESCO's structure was shaped by the heterogeneity of preferences among its constituents, meaning both state and non-state actors.

UNESCO was designed at the series of Conferences of Allied Ministers in Education (CAME) that were convened by the British government between 1942 and 1945.[12] The participating government representatives held diverging views about the future organization's domain of work and settled on a cumulative bargain: It contained a focus on Culture that was mostly promoted by France, an "E" for education that was mainly heralded by the UK and the US, and a commitment to the topic of mass communication that, although heavily opposed by the Soviet states and not reflected in the organization's name, is laid down in the constitution (Art. 2 I a) (Sewell 1973, p. 142).

But non-state actors, which had previously been organized at the Paris-based International Institute for Intellectual Cooperation,[13] also had an important say at UNESCO's founding conferences. Structure-wise, the academics, scientists and artists involved in the founding meetings successfully rallied for civil society organs within the new agency. While governments are UNESCO's primary principals who govern the IO through its plenary body, the General Conference, and the Executive Board, civil society actors also have a formal status within the organization. They are represented in UNESCO's National Commissions,[14] and formally attached to UNESCO's work as advisors and operational collaborators (Singh 2011, pp. 28–45). Topic-wise, civil society actors were critical in adding another policy domain to UNESCO's mandate, namely science. The inclusion of "S" for science as a distinct organizational pillar in November 1945 was in part due to the horrors of science that had become apparent with the bombing of Hiroshima (Sewell 1973, p. 142). Yet, it was also based on the lobbying of scientific associations such as the International Science Cooperation Service, who argued that the German dominance in the sciences needed to be broken in the postwar order (Sewell 1975, pp. 48–52; Singh 2011, pp. 13–14; Valderrama 1995, pp. 22–3). The outcome was a constitution comprising the preferred themes of varied constituencies, which also bore the seeds of its institutional fragmentation.

These seeds bore fruit also due to a second historical cause, namely, the managerial style of its first leader, Julian Huxley. Huxley, a British biologist and a writer,[15] became UNESCO's first DG in 1946. He was a controversial leader because of his eccentric moral and political views, which he labeled "scientific, evolutionary humanism," an atheistic utopia that also endorsed eugenics (Huxley 1946). Although from the outset Huxley only bid for a

---

[12] The CAME meetings were attended by European state representatives and observers from, among others, the US, the Soviet Union, and China (Sewell 1973, pp. 141–2).

[13] UNESCO's other main predecessor was an intergovernmental organization, the Bureau of International Education that was seated in Geneva (Singh 2011, pp. 12–13).

[14] These commissions are attended by national non-governmental organizations and civil society representatives, and advise or sometimes even supplant governmental delegations to UNESCO (Singh 2011, pp. 28–45).

[15] Julian Huxley was the older brother of the more widely-known writer Aldous Huxley.

two-year term as DG,[16] he left an important imprint on UNESCO's structure by modelling it after the organizational form of the university. As Huxley explained in a *Nature Medicine* article in 1945, "equivalent divisions" for thematic fields should be headed by assistant directors-general (ADGs) who controlled their own budgetary share and worked autonomously within the general guidelines established by UNESCO's governing bodies (Huxley 1945, p. 554; cf. Sewell 1975, p. 90). They should be run like university faculties. As mentioned above, UNESCO was divided into "themes," which were soon consolidated and referred to as "sectors": Apart from the "reconstruction sector" that was operational in the immediate postwar (Valderrama 1995, p. 40), UNESCO henceforth harbored an education, a natural sciences, a social sciences and humanities, a culture, and a communication and information sector (Singh 2011, p. 35). At first, several sectors were overseen by one ADG, yet over time each sector was assigned a proper ADG (Singh 2011, p. 34).

The sectoral structure was locked in through the positive feedback it received from member states. Depending on their preferences, different states assigned different lead ministries in charge of guiding their UNESCO delegations. These were mostly education, but also foreign affairs, culture, or development ministries (Singh 2011, pp. 29–30). These delegates forged relatively stable coalitions with their priority sectors (Sewell 1975, pp. 141, 158). State representatives thereby demarcated discrete spheres of influence and alliances with bureaucrats. This allowed them, more or less formally, to influence subunit programming and budgeting to an extent that exceeded their overall standing within the organization (Hoggart 1978, p. 121; Sewell 1975, p. 173). Such "local" gains from states' sectoral alliances help to lock in a fragmented outcome such as UNESCO's sectoralism (see Proposition 1 in Section 2.3) What is more, UNESCO's organizational development has been marked by the deepening and widening of its fragmentation. The field offices played a central part in this development.

Deepening Sectoral Power through Decentralization

Like other UN agencies, UNESCO has established field presences in many countries, and it has used decentralization as a legitimation strategy in the face of outside pressure to reform. The implementation of UNESCO's decentralization, however, did not transcend but reinforced its sectoral structure.

From the beginning, nearly all field offices established by UNESCO were created by, and attached to, individual "parent" sectors. UNESCO's first

---

[16] After a rather controversial nomination process, the Executive nominated Huxley in December 1946 on the condition that he accepted the "explicit understanding that in two years he would need to return to private life," which Huxley accepted (Sewell 1975, p. 107).

decentralized offices were the science cooperation centers that were established between 1947 and 1951 for Latin America, the Middle East, the Far East, South-East Asia, and South Asia. They were followed by regional offices specializing in education, and a regional office in Havana that was created in 1950 and became a regional office for culture for Latin America and the Caribbean (UNESCO 1991, p. 5). Their territorial delineation and functional scope differed greatly, yet what most of the offices shared was a strict subordination under one parent sector. In addition, the managerial reports cited in a 1991 UNESCO report on decentralization critically noted the unwillingness of UNESCO staff to work outside Paris, and thus an organizational structure marked by "centralism and sectoralism" at the same time—that is, it was the headquarter-based sectors that dominated the work of the field offices and determined their (very circumscribed) staff and administrative decisions (UNESCO 1991, pp. 6–10; similarly, Hoggart 1978). Hence, reinforcing UNESCO's initial fragmentation into sectors, the earliest field presences yielded increasing returns to sectoral power rather than devolving authority to the territorial units of UNESCO.

With the growing politicization of UNESCO since the 1970s, again pledges were made to decentralize the organization and bring it closer to its constituency. Such reform moves responded to the growing legitimation pressure that UNESCO faced at a time of intense political conflict. One political conflict shaking UNESCO at the time was the Arab-Israeli dispute for which UNESCO became a major arena. A series of anti-Israel resolutions in the 1970s—for example, requests that the DG take over the educational system in occupied Arab territories—upset important donor states such as the US (Kennedy 2006, p. 174). The second main conflict was fuelled by the movement for a New World Information and Communication Order (NWICO) of the 1970s and 1980s, whose main proponents were developing and socialist countries. The NWICO movement attacked the Western dominance over global media communication that they deemed responsible for negative and one-sided representations of the developing world. Next to calls for technical assistance and self-reliant communication infrastructures, the NWICO agenda also entailed the promotion of national regulations for journalists and the media. This demand was strongly opposed by Western countries, above all the US and the UK, who rejected the NWICO as an assault on the freedom of the press (Singh 2011, pp. 112–20).

In addition to these political conflicts, UNESCO's management became a target of criticism. Allegations of mismanagement and patronage appointments, mostly attributed to the leadership of DG Amadou-Mahtar M'Bow (1974–87), discredited the organization. The allegations even led to a series of extraordinary managerial investigations performed by the US General Accounting Office (GAO). The GAO presented altogether three reports on

UNESCO's management in the 1980s and 1990s. The reports criticized, among other things, that UNESCO was too centralized and that about 80 percent of its staff was working in Paris rather than in developing countries (Kennedy 2006, p. 175; see Hoggart 1978).

M'Bow made some attempts to counter such allegations and declared a "new policy of decentralization" in the mid-1970s. Following a survey among member states regarding their views on decentralization, the DG initiated the establishment of all-purpose (rather than sectoral) regional offices. Between the late 1970s and late 1980s, so-called regional coordinators were entrusted to represent the DG in the regions. Yet their authority remained merely symbolic, while "[r]eal decision-making power continued to rest with the different sectors at Headquarters" (UNESCO 1991, p. 10). In fact, UNESCO's legitimacy crisis escalated during M'Bow's tenure, which saw the withdrawal of important donor states. In particular the US and the UK were dissatisfied with the organization's management and the politics of the NWICO, and formally quit the organization in 1984 and 1985, respectively. Their exit implied a drastic budgetary shortfall of about 30 percent (Beigbeder 1987, pp. 2–38; Singh 2011, pp. 32–3).

M'Bow's successor, Frederico Mayor (1987–99), therefore launched an encompassing organizational reform to win back donor support. This reform entailed as a central pillar the decentralization of UNESCO (Beigbeder 1997, pp. 60–3, 79–82).[17] A Bureau for the Coordination of Field Units was established to support the transfer of staff and resources to the varied categories of UNESCO's territorial units, which around the 1990s included both sectoral and integrated offices at the regional and sub-regional level, and posts for advisors at the regional, sub-regional and country level (Joint Inspection Unit 1992, p. 9; UNESCO 1991, p. 15). Over the 1990s, the number of field offices nearly doubled from thirty-eight to more than sixty (Joint Inspection Unit 2000, p. 14), whereas in the new millennium several offices were again closed so that according to one count, the number was down to fifty-three in 2004 (UNESCO Executive Board 2004, p. 1). While the territorial office structure has remained in constant flux, the devolution of staff to the field offices has been accelerated in the new millennium, so that the share of UNESCO staff working outside headquarters rose from a quarter in 1999 to about one half a decade later (Joint Inspection Unit 2000, p. 16; Singh 2011, p. 134).

Nevertheless, recent reviews of UNESCO's structure continue to stress that decentralization is implemented along sectoral lines. Despite attempts to the

---

[17] This attempt was not successful right away. The UK only returned to UNESCO in 1997, the US followed in 2003 (Singh 2011, p. 11). Political conflicts again escalated in 2011, when the US and Israel stopped their financial contributions to UNESCO in reaction to the accession of Palestine as a full member of the organization. Two years later, UNESCO therefore suspended US and Israeli voting rights (BBC 2013).

contrary, the "parent sector approach" has been maintained, so that field offices report to sector leaders rather than the DG (Joint Inspection Unit 2000, pp. 15–16; Roman-Morey and Zahran 2011, pp. 22–3). For example, the above-mentioned Havana office for culture in Latin America and the Caribbean has been formally designated to serve as a "cluster office," but it continues to prioritize the cultural sector (Roman-Morey and Zahran 2011, pp. 21–2). The "many small UNESCOs" (Roman-Morey and Zahran 2011, p. 22) existing today are mostly managed through the sectors, also because of a recent delegation of human resource competencies to the sector heads (Roman-Morey and Zahran 2011, p. 27). Apparently, the sectors have managed to defend their position throughout the reorganization of field-level activities. UNESCO's decentralization has not undermined, but reinforced the sectors, which could capitalize on their historical advantage and extend their authority to parented field offices.

Inter-sectoral Initiatives and the Widening of UNESCO's Fragmentation

But also beyond decentralization, reform initiatives in UNESCO are confronted with the fact that the sectors have turned into the organization's main hubs of activity. To name a few of these sectoral activities (for overviews, see Hoggart 1978, pp. 31–7; Singh 2011, pp. 18–28): The cultural sector launched programs for the protection of minorities and their languages, for the preservation of cultural monuments such as the Nile region of Nubia, or for the recording of oral cultural heritage and history. UNESCO's biggest sector, education, has established and even operated schools, and issued guidelines for politically charged contents in school textbooks. The science sectors have become most profiled in the fields of natural resources and sustainability research and scientific and bioethics. The communication sector presently engages in the promotion of e-government and measures to bridge the worldwide "digital divide." These activities are carried out in collaboration with field offices and adjunct institutions such as the International Council of Museums, the Intergovernmental Oceanographic Commission, the International Bioethics Committee, or the International Centre for Technical and Vocational Education and Training.

By contrast, policy initiatives undertaken by the DGs have traditionally aimed to span across the sectors and integrate activities with the help of overarching programs, programs that should strengthen the organization's corporate identity within the UN (Evans 1963, pp. 80–1; see Sewell 1973, p. 160). Beginning in the 1950s, UNESCO has regularly launched inter-sectoral flagship programs that should bundle the organization's resources toward thematically or regionally focused policy goals. Also called "major programs," these projects assumed tasks as diverse as enhancing the productivity of arid zones, fostering East–West dialogue or providing primary education to children in Latin America (Evans 1963, p. 80). In the past three to four decades, every five-year budget cycle entailed two such major programs that are aimed to shape the priorities of all of UNESCO's thematic sectors (Singh 2011, p. 26). For example, the priority topics of the 2008–13 medium-term strategy were "Africa" and "gender."

In practice, however, fights for sectoral leadership and organizational resources have inhibited the implementation of UNESCO-wide policies (Singh 2011, pp. 26, 40; see Joint Inspection Unit 2000, p. 2 and Roman-Morey and Zahran 2011, p. 40). Similar to the recalcitrant regional organizations in the WHO (see Chapters 4 and 5), UNESCO's sectors proved reluctant to implement corporate reform agendas. To circumvent such sectoral opposition, reformers have repeatedly turned to the layering strategy and created additional subunits, such as, for the 2008–13 priorities, a gender and an Africa department (Roman-Morey and Zahran 2011, p. 50; see UNESCO 2008). They have thereby effected a *widening* of UNESCO's fragmentation from sectoral to inter-sectoral units. As a managerial inspection team noted in 2000 (Joint Inspection Unit 2000, p. 2):

> more than half of the units, bureaus or offices not linked to programme sectors were attached to the Directorate. It appears that one of the reasons why so many were placed directly under the responsibility of the Director-General, was that cooperation and coordination between sectors often proved very poor.

UNESCO's double fragmentation into sectors with locked-in authorities plus a plethora of inter-sectoral units has further contributed to its legitimacy crisis. Although the US and the UK have meanwhile rejoined the organization,[18] reform pressure is high. An external evaluation commissioned by UNESCO's Executive Board concluded that UNESCO's sectoral and inter-sectoral subunits attained very high "autonomy scores" (Independent External Evaluation Team 2010, p. 39). Hence, tellingly for the robustness of the sectors, a recent attempt at bringing the number of sectors down from five to three—made by DG Irina Bokova in 2012—was unsuccessful (Hüfner 2013, p. 38, see Footnote 16). At the same time, most countries and donors express dissatisfaction with what they deem an ineffective and overly fragmented organization. This is also reflected in the organization's shrinking resources. In contrast to its UN peers, UNESCO has to cope with declining extra-budgetary funds, and therefore a shrinking total budget, which also implies a very thinly spread workforce across its diverse offices (Roman-Morey and Zahran 2011, pp. 28, 42–4). This funding crisis is exacerbated by the US's withholding of contributions since 2011, in protest against Palestine's accession to the organization (Hüfner 2013). As the record

---

[18] See Footnote 16.

of UNESCO's institutional development since the 1940s demonstrates, such a contraction of resources need not lead to a concentration and (re-)centralization of organizational authority. Its sectoral legacy has moved UNESCO into its own variety of the fragmentation trap.

6.4 Conclusion: IO Decentralization Pathways and the Prospects for UN-wide Reform

Decentralization is a broad trend in the UN system, yet its enactment and implementation vary considerably between different IOs. The two organizational trajectories presented in this chapter show that preexisting institutional structures condition the extent to which decentralization benefits an IO's central leadership or subunits instead. The ILO here is a case of initial bureaucratic hierarchy that allows the directorate to maintain channels of centralized control over its growing field-level activities. Throughout its decentralization agenda, the ILO has retained direct communication and reporting lines from headquarter to field offices. The UNESCO case, by contrast, demonstrates how an IO's initial fragmentation is reinforced through decentralization: The thematic sectors here extended their authority beyond Paris by erecting their own field offices, offices that that reported to the sector heads rather than the directorate.

The fact that IOs enact decentralization in path dependent ways also matters for the UN-wide reform ambitions that accompany decentralization agendas. As noted in Section 6.1, calls for decentralization in the UN are usually tied to calls for more coherence among agencies in the field. The Delivering as One agenda here is the most recent example. It aims at developing coherent technical cooperation programs that in each country follow a single national development strategy. Each IO active in the country shall contribute to this singular strategy. Under the auspices of the UN Development Programme (UNDP), the so-called "four Ones"—one leader, one budget, one programme, and one office—shall be implemented through an empowered resident coordinator. This approach shall avoid that multiple reporting lines and fund raising requirements create overlaps and burdensome overhead in the countries, and thereby reduce duplication and create synergies among agencies.[19]

However, the coherence and hierarchy that may facilitate reforms within an IO can at the same time become an impediment to efforts at reducing

---

[19] See <http://www.undg.org/?P=7> (accessed June 6, 2014). As of March 2014, thirty-seven UN member states have requested the UN to adopt the Delivering as One strategy in their countries (see <http://www.undg.org/docs/13413/Delivering%20as%20One%20countries_March%202014.pdf>, accessed June 6, 2014).

fragmentation within the UN system. Weak territorial units lack the discretion to collaborate with the UNDP on the ground, and thus, rather follow the directives from their headquarters than UNDP-led development strategies at the country level. The ILO case exemplifies this obstacle to UN reform. Its field offices simply lack the agency that would allow them to collaborate with other organizations active in the same country (Joint Inspection Unit 1999, p. 22). Without "increasing the level of delegated authority" (Ortiz et al. 2005, p. 10)—as requested by UN reviewers—the ILO will remain a centralized organization that resists system-wide harmonization and integration efforts.

For UN reformers, this points to a trade-off between IO-level and system-level coordination. It also implies that path dependencies in IOs are a major factor shaping the development and implementation of inter-agency projects. Allies for such projects may be found at different levels of an organization, depending on the IO's bureaucratic structure and internal power games. This is a considerable challenge given the complexity and age of the UN system, which has gone through many waves of reform already. Reforms that aim for policy coherence must not only take into account the particulars of circumstances in the target countries. They must also be tailored to the different preconditions of specific institutional trajectories within the UN. "One size fits all," thus, is not only an inadequate recipe for IO policy reforms (Barnett and Finnemore 2004). Likewise, blueprints for organizational reform must be sensitive to the historical pathways they confront in different IOs.

7

Implications

Reform and Fragmentation in Global Governance

> So reforms are facilitated not by learning but by forgetfulness, by mechanisms that cause the organization to forget previous reforms or at least those of a similar content.
>
> (Brunsson and Olsen 1993, p. 41)

Since the United Nations system was established in the 1940s, the system of global governance has changed in many respects. International organizations (IOs) have not only grown bigger but also more numerous, now spinning a complex network of public authorities beyond the state. Decolonization and the rise of new powers have challenged the hierarchies within the member state constituencies of IOs. Private authorities such as business associations or non-governmental organizations (NGOs) have gained in importance, and their style of work challenges the model of public bureaucracy embodied by supranational secretariats. Still, amidst all this novelty, IOs continue to be deeply affected by historical legacies. The trajectories of the World Health Organization (WHO), of the International Labour Organization (ILO), and of the United Nations Educational, Scientific and Cultural Organization (UNESCO) illustrate the role that path dependence plays for IO change. Decisions made during their founding moments still impact on the way in which these IOs enact reforms, govern their field activities, and respond to UN reform.

This book has shown how path dependence has circumscribed the WHO's development since its creation (Chapters 3–5). By integrating the Pan American Sanitary Bureau (PASB) into its foundational design, the WHO embarked on a self-reinforcing fragmentation pathway. The reformers of the WHO have either reinforced the regional offices or bypassed them at the price of adding new power centers to the organization. They have deepened and widened, but failed to reverse the WHO's fragmentation. Path dependence also sheds light on the federal systems of the ILO and UNESCO, whose trajectories were compared in Chapter 6. The ILO was created as a hierarchical standard setter, and its centralized origins also shaped how the Office later on governed its territorial offices. While the ILO still exerts a significant amount of centralized control over its field offices, this is not the case in UNESCO. The federal system of this organization was implemented in an already sectoral structure, because UNESCO was historically partitioned into thematic units. As UNESCO's sectors created their own, theme-specific field offices, the decentralization agenda has further deepened its sectoral structure. Reformers who strived to overcome inter-sectoral blockades grafted new "inter-sectoral" units on UNESCO's structure, thereby widening its fragmentation to additional organizational layers. These IO pathways demonstrate the lasting impact of historical bargains on subsequent organizational developments, and they illustrate the variety of fragmentation traps that can be triggered by the thematic and territorial subunits of IOs.

The studies presented in this book are based on the approach of power driven path dependence (PDPD), which combines a bureaucratic politics view of IOs with historical institutionalist insights. This approach adds to a growing body of research about the temporal dynamics that underpin global governance (Fioretos 2011) and sheds a new light on the determinants of organizational design and change. Yet, beyond this contribution to the literatures on IO design and change that I have outlined in Chapter 2, the book also has implications for wider debates in IO research. Two debates in particular shall be taken up in this concluding chapter: The "constructivist" debate about bureaucratic cultures, and the "rationalist" debate about forum shopping and regime complexes in global governance.

In the following, I will reconsider the insights of this book with a view to these debates, with the aim to point out areas of cross-fertilization and avenues for future research. Drawing on the WHO and other IO examples, I will first summarize the main elements of the "culture of reform," which is based on specific bureaucratic technologies that shall construct agency in IOs. These technologies of agency are designed to counter allegations of red tape and inertia, and are thus pitched against the very model of bureaucracy which is at the center of constructivist theories of bureaucratic culture (see Section 7.1). Second, I will discuss how IO fragmentation pathways are affected by the wider trend toward institutional complexity and forum shopping in global governance. I here argue that fragmentation at the inter-organization level is likely to reinforce fragmentation within individual IOs (see Section 7.2). Finally, the chapter draws some historical lessons for ongoing and future reform attempts in the United Nations (see Section 7.3).

7.1 The Culture of Agency

Reform has become a constant in international organizations. Proofs of change are demanded by all groups of stakeholders. Member states and private donors want to see value for their money and evidence of organizational impact. Increasingly, civil society actors demand public justification of IO practices as well (Zürn et al. 2012). Not the least, the civil servants working for IOs expect that their employers demonstrate leadership and promote change when dysfunctions arise. In order to comply with these expectations, IOs have become "reforming organizations" that are constantly emphasizing their capacity to change (Brunsson and Olsen 1993).

By embracing reform, IOs respond to a "rationalization" imperative that IO scholars have long identified as a normative script for global bureaucracies. Specifically, theorists of "bureaucratic culture" emphasize that IOs function like Weberian bureaucracies in that impartial procedures and impersonal rule are highly valued. Bureaucratic rules imbue IOs with "rational-legal" authority, and they predispose IO staff to act in accordance with organizational values (Barnett and Finnemore 1999, 2004). These rules are usually interpreted as recipes for continuity and stability, and thus as impediments to change (see Section 1.3). By contrast, this section highlights the technologies of change that are equally enshrined in modern IO cultures, and that are endorsed as outright challenges to the red tape and inertia associated with "bureaucracy." Especially since the 1980s, with the spread of business-style managerial techniques from the Anglo-Saxon world, the actorhood of public organizations has become a main currency of organizational legitimacy (see Brunsson and Sahlin-Andersson 2000). This can also be observed in IOs. Technologies of agency target both organizational structures and IO staff. They illustrate the tensions inherent in contemporary bureaucratic cultures.

Engineering Intentionality in IO Structures and Procedures

IO reforms are accompanied by pledges to "rationalize" global bureaucracies and thus to make them more goal-oriented. This ambition pertains to many dimensions of IO structures and procedures. First, reforms usually entail the reorganization of organizational charts to make them reflective of the organization's strategy—or, in the words of former WHO DG Gro Harlem Brundtland: To show what "business" the organization is "in" (Brundtland 1998b). The organizational charts of UN agencies and programs indeed seem to be under constant reconstruction. Programs are renamed and regrouped into new units to create synergy, and to signal the ongoing adaptation of organizational goals. Furthermore, reorganization can prove a commitment to lean and efficient management. Brundtland's invention of the "cluster" structure for the WHO at the turn of the millennium exemplifies this quest for coherence. The nine clusters communicated to WHO staff and to outside observers that the organization had clearly ordered aims and priorities, brief: A corporate strategy (Lerer and Matzopoulos 2001).

Second, the "rationalization" of IO structures also implies that efficiency is enhanced through the reduction of overhead costs. Announcements of "efficiency savings" are omnipresent in IO works plans, which stress that resources will not be "wasted" on bureaucracy but will be used to create policy impact. In the terminology of a recent evaluation of the UN Food and Agricultural Organization (FAO), a reduction of "heavy bureaucracy" (FAO 2007, p. 13) is to boost the organization's "flexibility" and "agility" (FAO 2007, p. 12). The proclaimed efficiency savings can be attained by downsizing or closing down administrative units. They may also be attained via outsourcing general service functions. In this vein, the WHO has engaged a private contractor in Malaysia, where computer problems and staff contracts are handled at lower cost due to moderate wages (WHO 2005, p. 7). By seeking to minimize administrative expenses, the organization responds to the reluctance of donors to fund core running costs (see Lee 2009, p. 106).

Third, the rationalization ambition also involves IO procedures and practices. This entails, on the one hand, a scientization of the decision-making methods in IOs. Through formalized techniques of program formulation and assessment, reformers seek to assert that their priorities are based on rational, objective criteria. They here draw on up-to-date technologies of rational choice and computation. We have seen in Chapter 4 how in the 1970s, WHO DG Halfdan Mahler introduced systems analysis techniques and computer-aided methods of policy planning, in order to implement a scientific policy making style for Primary Health Care reforms (Litsios 2002, p. 717). Likewise, in the 1990s, the WHO and the World Bank developed the measure of the "disability-adjusted life-years" (DALYs) that are saved by targeted public health interventions. DALY calculations served to rationalize the selection of policy priorities for Brundtland's reform strategy and thereby should guarantee the WHO's maximum possible effectiveness (WHO 1999f).

On the other hand, the goal-orientation of organizational processes shall be ensured through adequate managerial technologies. As I have discussed in Chapter 5, the UN nowadays promotes a system-wide shift from "resource-based" to "results-based" management techniques. Spearheaded by Kofi Annan's managerial reform that was launched in the late 1990s, results-based budgeting has become the model for all UN agencies and programs. Its implementation is monitored by the UN Joint Inspection Unit (JIU) through its regular investigations of individual organizations or of overarching managerial problems (e.g. González and Mezzalama 2002, p. v; Joint Inspection Unit 1999, p. 3). Results-based budgeting postulates that programs are not designed on the basis of the funds that are allotted to IO units, but on the basis of the goals to be attained. In this vein, the WHO's program budgets are nowadays structured along "strategic objectives," which indicate strategic priorities, not the least for funders who can dedicate their contributions to selected objectives. The WHO management constantly develops the operationalization of these objectives, introduces new evaluation tools and more powerful software to monitor the organization's goal attainment (WHO 2011b, pp. 32–3, 2011a). Thereby, the output of the IO shall become measureable—and the humans working in it shall be educated to adopt a goal-oriented working style.

Personifying Corporate Agency

The culture of IO agency also manifests itself at the level of "human resources." More than any depersonalized procedure, humans are expected to embody the agentic quality of organizations. Nowadays, the Weberian ideal type of the impersonal expert who is effaced behind universal rules (Barnett 2002, pp. 106–7) has long been superseded with a new, more entrepreneurial role for modern bureaucrats. This role is based on the expectation that humans work proactively toward corporate goals, and that they become the central carriers of organizational change. Personal agency is meant to be enacted both by the ordinary staff and by the leaders of international organizations.

The mobilization of "ordinary staff" was a central component of the two big reforms in the WHO, which comprised measures to foster professional and physical staff mobility. For example, physical staff rotation was integral to the Health for All reform of the 1970s. To mobilize the headquarter and the field office staff for Primary Health Care, DG Mahler propagated a practice of staff rotation between Geneva and the regions and among the different regions. Likewise, the Brundtland reform encompassed the reassignment of WHO staff to new tasks and new offices. More than half of the bureaucrats at the WHO headquarters were requested to move to different offices in the course of the Brundtland reform (Lerer and Matzopoulos 2001, p. 429). Staff rotation continues to be a central aspiration in the WHO. Asked about current challenges, an officer from the human resource department stressed to me that above all inter-regional mobility was deficient and needed to be improved.

Next to encouraging territorial rotation schemes, WHO reformers have strived to enhance the professional mobility of their staff, so as to counter the IO's compartmentalization into specialized units. Critical of the parochialism that is part of bureaucratic specialization, Mahler and Brundtland were keen promoters of generalist skills among their staff. For example, in his effort to spread the PHC message across the organization, Mahler stressed that "a new type of WHO staff member" was needed, one that could see the bigger picture and guide an inter-sectoral approach to health policy (Mahler 1975b, p. 45). Inter-disciplinary thinking and the holistic vision of the generalist were prioritized over technical expertise, which was suspected of being self-referential and forgetful of public health's political context (Mahler 1976). Similarly, the Brundtland reform entailed the reassignment of WHO staff members to new tasks in which they had no specialization or prior experience (see WHO 2001d). What is more, for the leading posts in her technical clusters she appointed externally recruited academics from the economic professions. Their specialization thus consisted of general change management skills rather than of public health-specific training (Lerer and Matzopoulos 2001).

The bureaucratic culture that such measures aim to develop is one of entre-preneurship and initiative. Especially since the turn of the millennium, WHO staff members are urged to raise funds and initiate partnerships with donors, and communication and public relations have gained in prestige and rele-vance within the WHO. Visibility and demonstrated impact are highly valued in the increasingly crowded organizational environment that the WHO navi-gates. Its competition for project money also entails, more or less voluntarily, a growing reliance on short-term employees. Partially due to the short time horizons of extra-budgetary funds on which many staff members are employed, a cut in lifetime positions also signals a commitment to strategic recruitment, and to the idea that employees have to prove their usefulness for the IO in order to get new contracts. Staff turnover and redeployments to new assignments are accompanied by calls that the WHO "must create an organ-izational culture not driven by bureaucratic rules but one that promotes performance and results" (Brundtland 1998b). Though performance pressure and job uncertainty have also engendered protest and even a strike at the WHO,[1] the entrepreneurial ideal has become imperative for its bureaucrats.

On top of the general mobilization of workforce, it is leaders who personify organizational agency. The heads of international organizations are faced with high expectations with regard to their leadership and ability to transform IOs. Member states elect IO heads with the expectation that they implement requested reforms, and staff members expect them to solve internal organi-zational problems as well. In fact, many of my interviewees at the WHO

---

[1] The demoralization of WHO staff has become a main theme of WHO reform debates (Lee 2009, p. 106; People's Health Movement et al. 2005, pp. 282–3). The management's tensions with the staff association escalated in 2005, when several hundred WHO staff members participated in a one-hour work stoppage—the first such protest in the WHO's history. The protesters bemoaned deteriorating conditions of work and, in the words of one employee, a system of "authoritarian and highly discretionary staff management" that was seen to undermine the officer's technical independence (Katz 2008, p. 162). The staff association also commissioned a WHO staff survey to assess the level of workplace harassment and mobbing within the organization. The study, which was conducted by a team of organization psychologists from the University of Frankfurt in 2003, concluded that harassment in the WHO was extreme and mostly attributed to harassment by superiors (Zapf 2004).

headquarters expressed their conviction that good leadership was what the WHO most needed. Many were nostalgic of the charismatic Mahler years— irrespective of whether they had experienced this legendary epoch them- selves. UN secretary-generals as well as the heads of other UN organizations must be super-individuals who are able to transcend petty bureaucratic con- flicts, work for the common good and unite the IO behind greater goals such as peace, health, or development. Their prominent role responds to the wide- spread impulse to ascribe organizational behavior to individual agency (see Pfeffer and Salancik 2003, pp. 6–10), and therefore requires that they demon- strate resolve and their personal accountability for the IO's output. The per- sonality, professional credentials, and integrity of IO leaders are eagerly scrutinized by their employees and by external observers—and may be mas- sively attacked by those dissatisfied with the IO's performance.

The public pressure on IO leaders is illustrated by the criticism of the WHO's fourth DG Nakajima (1988–98) and the concomitant calls for leadership change (see Chapter 5). Recurrent headlines such as "New leader, new hope for WHO" (Yamey and Abbasi 2003) testify to the high premium placed on good leadership (similarly People's Health Movement et al. 2005, p. 228, 2008, p. 221; Smith 1995). Leadership shall make the IO more effective, even under difficult circumstances, since "just as healthy behavior can often counteract genetic predispositions to disease, strong leadership can compensate in part for the institutional DNA" (Levine 2006, p. 1015). It seems that the more IOs are confronted with institutional inertia, the stronger grows the hope for heroic agency.

The Bureaucratic Culture of Change

The *homo oeconomicus* is not only an assumption of rational choice theory. It is a cultural imperative for modern IOs, whose legitimacy hinges on the capacity to change. The diffusion of the bureaucratic "culture of change" can be observed at all levels of IO reform, ranging from program formulation to human resource management. Obviously, the organizational technologies through which IOs aim to replace routines with initiative, continuity with flexibility, and rules with results, are themselves highly formalized. The irony of the culture of change is that the very measures that shall agentify IOs do at the same time bureaucratize them. Reorganizations shall streamline and sim- plify IO structures, but they are usually accompanied by simultaneous add- itions to the bureaucratic machinery. Just like Annan's United Nations reform implied the creation of a Strategic Planning Unit alongside cuts in administra- tion (UN General Assembly 1997, pp. 17–19), so Brundtland's reorganization for One WHO entailed the creation of an Evidence and Information for Policy cluster as the organization's new strategic center. Observers claim that the

One WHO reform did not lead to a reduction, but to an increase in headquarter posts, short term as well as permanent (Yamey 2002c, p. 1170).

Similarly, results-based management is no less, if not more, formalized than a resource-based budgeting procedure. It engenders new technologies for conceptualizing strategic goals and outcome indicators, evaluation and reporting techniques, and computerized monitoring systems. Strategy-making entails bureaucracy-making (see Büttner 2012, pp. 98–9, 194–5). The structures arising from previous reforms thus can become the targets of new rounds of rationalization. Or, in the words of Nils Brunsson and Johan Olsen, "reforms tend to generate reforms" (Brunsson and Olsen 1993, p. 33).

It seems that elaborate technologies of change and ingrained path dependencies are two sides of the same coin. The more reform obstacles IO leaders face, the more they seem to invest in symbols of organizational agency and change. This may be an instance of successful "organized hypocrisy:" IOs legitimate themselves at the level of managerial "talk," even though at the level of "action" there is very little change (Weaver 2008). In addition, however, future studies should explore in how far reform cultures are themselves path dependent. How do earlier blueprints reappear in later reforms? Do reform technologies generate their own constituencies and vested interests? What makes (which aspects of) reform beliefs survive despite all frustrations with models such as results-based management (see Chapter 5)? Such questions at the intersection between historical institutionalist and social constructivist IO studies promise to generate important insights into the interplay of IO inertia and change.

7.2 The Organizational Environment of Fragmentation

The insights of this book can also be extended to debates about inter-organizational competition in global governance. Nowadays, a growing body of literature asserts that IOs should not be studied in isolation, because they are embedded in ever denser "complexes" of international regimes and organizations. Hence, it is not only individual IOs that are fragmenting, but entire organizational fields are becoming more fragmented. As international institutions are growing in both size and number, their jurisdictions increasingly overlap and are in conflict with each other (Alter and Meunier 2009; Raustiala and Victor 2004). Institutional complexity characterizes a multitude of policy areas such as, for example, climate change (Keohane and Victor 2011), election monitoring (Kelley 2009), refugee protection (Betts 2009)—or international health (Fidler 2007). In a world marked by regime complexity, states can often choose between different institutions when pursuing specific aims, and IOs must take into account the activities of rival organizations (Cooley and Ron 2002; Faude 2015).

The regime complexity literature with its focus on system-wide fragmentation invites cross-fertilization with the fragmentation trap account offered in this book. Extending the line of reasoning in Chapter 2, I suggest in this section that inter-organizational competition is unlikely to "weed out" IO fragmentation, but on the contrary reinforces it. First, because trans-organizational networks further strengthen IO subunits. Second, because exit opportunities allow states to selectively draw on rather than reform fragmented IOs.

Trans-organizational Networks

IO environments are not monolithic markets with one dominant selection mechanism. Rather, they offer many potential allies for the units within the organizations. IO units network with a multitude of external peers, entertaining distinct coalitions with departments of national governments, other IO or NGOs. Thus, what may be a competitor from one unit's perspective can be an ally from the viewpoint of other units (Jönsson 1986; Koch 2009). Denser, more "competitive" organizational environments thus multiply the menu of available ties for IO subunits, rivaling the directorate's external relations with states and other organizations.

Hence, competitive IO environments should be sources of positive feedback for IO fragmentation. They facilitate the emergence of *trans-organizational* networks between IOs: Networks that are spun between lower-level units such as theme-specific departments or federal layers of IOs, and that bypass the organizations' respective directorates. Such relations have been studied in the context of *trans-governmental* networks that are entertained by the departments of national governments. For example, Anne-Marie Slaughter argues that interstate cooperation increasingly takes place at lower bureaucratic levels, often without the involvement of government heads (Slaughter 2004). But also IO departments work through trans-organizational channels. They collaborate with "their" governmental departments such as the ministries of health and development in the WHO case, or the ministry of labor in the ILO case. IOs like UNESCO have partners in various governmental departments—science, culture, and/or education—and are thus prone to reproduce their fragmentation through these various ties (see Chapter 6). Furthermore, the availability of ever more IO and NGO peers should provide additional opportunities for forging trans-IO coalitions across formal organizational boundaries. This invites a further exploration of trans-organization theory for IO studies.

Evidently, the suggestions that external and internal fragmentation are mutually reinforcing needs to be further investigated. In this connection, the extent to which trans-organizational networks nowadays structure IO activities could be examined with the help of network analysis, a research tool that is increasingly used by IR scholars.[2] From a network analytical perspective, the amount of regular contacts or ties across IO boundaries would be an indicator of the importance of trans-organizational relations for the structure of global governance. If lower-level IO units gained in centrality in such networks, this would be a strong sign of interlocking fragmentation across IOs (see Hafner-Burton et al. 2009, pp. 563–5; Thurner and Binder 2009). Certainly, measuring the networks between bureaucratic units—and potentially also their evolution over time—is a laborious undertaking. Yet such research promises to add important insights for the ontology of IOs and their agency in global governance.

The Choice for Fragmentation

But also from the perspective of institutional choice theory, we have reason to expect that an IO's fragmentation is facilitated rather than threatened by external competition. This may at first sight appear counterintuitive. Where states have plenty of occasions to play IOs against each other, why should they stick with organizations that resist all efforts at reform? Could they not switch to other IOs or bilateral programs or, in the extreme case, create a new IO, as it was the case with the establishment of UNAIDS in the 1990s (see Hanrieder 2014b)? I have discussed in Chapter 2 why the member states' opportunity to shop among IOs has at most ambiguous implications for the fragmentation trap. States that are dissatisfied with an IO may indeed use their outside options as bargaining chips and thereby seek to push for organizational reform (see Section 2.3). Conversely, the availability of "exit" can also diffuse the need to invest in "voice," that is, organizational change (Hirschman 1970).

Where states have organizational alternatives at their disposal, the need to reform a given IO according to their needs and wishes becomes less pressing. States can choose among several strategies that have been distinguished by theorists of institutional choice, without binding themselves to one dominant strategy. Sometimes they may find it more attractive to "use" or "change" and IO, while in other cases they prefer to "select" or even "create" a different IO (Jupille et al. 2013). Such selectivity is facilitated by fragmented IO structures. We have seen how in the WHO case earmarked contributions allow states to

---

[2] An analysis of the worldwide IO network, measured in overlaps among state memberships, has been carried out by Jason Beckfield, who found out that the field of international organizations has become less cohesive and is increasingly centered around regional nodes (Beckfield 2010).

support only those programs that they deem beneficial, while disregarding those that do not meet their interests (see Chapter 5).

It is therefore questionable whether reform pressure increases with the proliferation of outside options, even if an IO's fragmentation is seen to be highly dysfunctional. On the contrary, we can suspect that fragmentation itself makes IOs attractive for states, that is, states may use them *because*, rather than *in spite of* their fragmentation. One advantage here is the relative intransparency of fragmented IOs. In organizations such as the WHO or the UN Refugee Agency UNHCR that are marked by ad hoc and earmarked funding, the official program budget is only a rough predictor for what the IO actually does, and actual budgetary flows and channels of influence are hard to penetrate for outside observers. This makes it easier for donors to support activities that would otherwise be criticized as selfish or parochial, for example, because the policies favor a country's economic or security interests. Fragmented IOs hence allow states to shift accountability for unpopular policies to a broadly multilateral setting where capture may go unnoticed (see Stone 2011). Accordingly, where programs turn out to be dysfunctional, the blame can be shifted to "the" IO. Among the numerous concerns that may drive states' choices among competing organizations, opportunities for capture and blame shifting may speak in favor of fragmented IOs. Regarding the continuum of institutional choice options theorized by Joseph Jupille and colleagues (2013), IO fragmentation should thus push states toward the continued "use" rather than the novel "creation" of international organizations.

Beyond "factoring in" fragmentation into studies IO of choice, a next step must, of course, consist of disaggregating the "choosing state" as well—in line with the research on trans-governmental networks outlined above. Which parts of the state (ministries, governing organs) are involved in choosing which part of an IO—and do their local ties create parallel systems of IO use, choice and change? How do these systems interact? And do precedents in one domain create path dependent constraints for other domains? Hence, the fragmented state of global governance does not mean that path dependence, sequence, and timing become irrelevant (see Farrell and Newman 2010). Rather, it relocates questions about institutional reform and change to new units of analysis below the unitary IO, or state.

7.3 The Future of Reform

It remains to be asked what a historical analysis of path dependent fragmentation implies for present political action. Past experiences often shed a skeptical light on the prospects for change. There may be plenty of reasons to expect that reform projects will not be implemented or generate undesired effects. Worse still, one might conclude that reforms notoriously create more problems than they solve, and thus refrain from any political demand for change. Still, the arguments presented in this book should not lead to the "reactionary" conclusion that all efforts at change are doomed or even counterproductive (Hirschman 1991). Inaction is not an alternative in any case; and renouncing reform can be as fatal as engaging in the "wrong" reform. In fact, hardly any reform ever fails completely. Some goals will be attained, some will not, and some side-effects will be generated that reformers may have anticipated or not. Experience may warn against certain projects, but only hindsight can reveal whether they have been worth undertaking.

An understanding of the path dependent constraints on reform thus cannot compensate for the historical decisions and the situated judgments of knowledgeable actors. It can only point out patterns that typically mark the reform process in IOs, and make researchers and practitioners aware of the types of feedback that IO pathways generate on reform initiatives. With this caveat in mind, two broader lessons with regard to the prospects of reform, both in the WHO and in the UN at large, shall be highlighted in this concluding section. These lessons concern the risk of goal displacement in IO reform, and the trade-off between UN-level and IO-level reform goals.

Reform Goals and Goal Displacement

Facing reform pressure on the one hand and reform blockades on the other, reformers tend to overpromise. I have highlighted in this chapter how the promise of all-out change accompanies IO reform. IOs invest heavily in the performance of agency and the respective bureaucratic technologies. This also implies the formulation of reform-specific organizational goals—for example, the goal of shifting to results-based budgeting techniques, or the goal of specifying strategic objectives and respective indicators for each organizational activity. The advantage of such intermediate (or "meta-level") goals is not only that they signal an IO's compliance with the modern agency imperative. Equally important is that their attainment can be documented and measured. The organization fabricates domains of activity where it can deliver, and where it can deliver more immediately than with regard to more intricate challenges. The attainment of managerial goals is closely monitored in the current UN system, and new goals are constantly developed in rounds of reform.

Yet, focusing on such intermediate reform goals also bears a classic organizational risk, which is often referred to as goal displacement (March and Olsen 1998, pp. 966–8). Where underlying conflicts cannot be resolved, it is tempting to focus on lower hanging fruits. The mechanism of goal displacement is illustrated by the ongoing WHO reform, which set out to reintegrate the finances of the organization, but soon shifted the debate to the terrain of managerial processes (Shashikant 2011; WHO 2010, 2014). Such diversion is a tempting strategy for IO leaders but also for state delegates, who strive to produce tangible outputs and be able to report on their successful implementation. Its downside is that means come to be taken for ends. Where secondary goals take on a life of their own and de facto move to the center of the reform endeavor, attention is diverted from the underlying distributional conflicts and badly needed compromises between conflicting parties. Such conflicts tend to disappear behind calls for rationalization, and the failure to implement organizational policies is cured with new strategizing techniques rather than exposed.

Given the time horizons of political decision makers, a focus on "easy" short term goals is certainly not surprising. To counter such goal displacement dynamics, researchers, policy makers, and societal actors must make sure that they do not to lose sight of the "elephants in the room" (see Chapter 1), whatever these elephants may be in a given context. Ultimately, this also requires a stronger public awareness of and societal debate about global governance problems (see Zürn et al. 2012), so that historical lessons are kept alive and acted upon in the politics of IO reform.

Reforming the UN Together with its Agencies

Finally, it should be borne in mind that IO-level and system-level reforms are interlinked and can come with trade-offs. This is an important linkage given the ongoing efforts to harmonize the broader global governance architecture, for example through the UN's Delivering as One agenda. This reform shall ensure that the various UN activities in developing countries are integrated through single national focal points and guided by the principle of national ownership. As we have seen in Chapter 6, country-level UN coordinators are installed with the aim that different organizations do not duplicate or undermine each other's work, but contribute to the realization of one national development strategy. Likewise, the member states of the Organization for Economic Cooperation and Development (OECD) are pledging to improve inter-agency coordination. In two successive OECD declarations, the 2005 Paris Declaration on Aid Effectiveness and the 2008 Accra Agenda for Action, donor states have called for an integration of development funding.[3] And also the post-2015 development agenda, which is to replace the UN Millennium Development Goals after 2015, reiterates the need to overcome inter-agency

---

[3] Cf. <http://www.oecd.org/dac/effectiveness/parisdeclarationandaccraagendaforaction.htm> (accessed August 9, 2014).

fragmentation (UN 2013, p. 21). Hence, inter-agency coordination is high on the global governance agenda.

This book has not only underlined that such global reform endeavors will always be circumscribed by the path dependencies of individual IOs. IO trajectories are difficult to change, and thus need to be taken into account when designing inter-agency programs. As in any broader reform agenda, one size fits all is not an option. What is more, even successful harmonization efforts are likely to come at a price. Integrating the work of different IOs within one country demands that each organization provides for compatible field level structures. Those IOs that grant autonomy to their field offices can therefore better collaborate with UN coordinators on the ground than more hierarchical IOs. This tension between IO-level integration and inter-agency coordination exemplifies the inevitable trade-offs that reformers confront in an ageing UN system.

APPENDIX 1

Ratifications of the WHO constitution by April 7, 1948[a]

1	China*	July 22, 1946
2	United Kingdom*	July 22, 1946
3	Canada*	August 29, 1946
4	Iran*	November 23, 1946
5	New Zealand*	December 10, 1946
6	Syria*	December 18, 1946
7	Liberia*	March 14, 1947
	Switzerland	March 26, 1947
	Transjordan***	April 7, 1947
8	Ethiopia*	April 11, 1947
	Italy	April 11, 1947
9	Netherlands*	April 29, 1947
	Albania	May 26, 1947
10	Saudi Arabia*	May 26, 1947
	Austria	June 30, 1947
11	Union of South Africa*	August 7, 1947
12	Haiti*	August 12, 1947
13	Norway*	August 18, 1947
14	Sweden*	August 28, 1947
15	Iraq*	September 23, 1947
16	Siam***	September 26, 1947
	Finland	October 7, 1947
	Ireland	October 20, 1947
17	Yugoslavia*	November 19, 1947
18	Egypt*	December 16, 1947
19	Turkey*	January 2, 1948
20	India*	January 12, 1948
21	Australia*	February 2, 1948
	Portugal	February 13, 1948
22	Czechoslovakia*	March 1, 1948
23	Greece*	March 12, 1948
24	USSR*	March 24, 1948
25	Ukraine*	April 3, 1948
26	Byelorussia*	April 7, 1948
27	Mexico*	April 7, 1948

* UN member state
** renamed Thailand in 1949
*** renamed Jordan in 1950

[a] Source: WHO (1948c, p. 86). Only UN member states are counted, because twenty-six UN member state ratifications were required for the entry into force of the constitution (see Chapter 3).

APPENDIX 2

The WHO's geographical areas and regional offices by 1951[b]

Area	Countries	Regional Office
Eastern Mediterranean	Egypt, Saudi Arabia, Iraq, Syria, Lebanon, Palestine, Transjordan, Yemen, Iran, Turkey, Pakistan, Greece, Ethiopia, Eritrea, Tripolitania, Dodecanese Islands, British Somaliland, French Somaliland, Aden, Cyprus, (Israel)	Alexandria (1949)*
Western Pacific	Australia, China, Indochina, Indonesia, Japan, Korea, the Philippines, New Zealand, Malaysia	Manila (1951)
South-East Asia	Burma, Siam, Ceylon, Afghanistan, India	New Delhi (1949)
Europe	Comprising the whole of Europe	Geneva (1949: special office for Europe; 1951: regional organization for Europe)**
Africa	South of the 20 degree N parallel of latitude to the western border of the Anglo-Egyptian Sudan to its junction with the northern border with the Belgian Congo; thence eastwards along the northern borders of Uganda and Kenya; thence southwards along the eastern border of Kenya to the Indian Ocean	Brazzaville (1951)
Americas	Comprising the Americas	Washington D.C.

* Transferred to Cairo in 2000.
** Transferred to Copenhagen in 1957.

[b] Regional boundaries and memberships (second column) are taken from the 1948 WHA decision (WHO 1948a, pp. 330–1). On regional office sites cf. Goodman (1971, pp. 214–17). Several country memberships have been changed later on. For example, Greece (in 1949) and Turkey (in 1952) transferred from the Eastern Mediterranean to the European region (Goodman 1971, pp. 214–17).

References

Abbott, K.W. and Snidal, D. (1998). "Why States Act through Formal International Organizations." *The Journal of Conflict Resolution* 42 (1): pp. 3–32.

Alcock, A. (1971). *History of the International Labor Organization.* New York: Octagon Books.

Alesani, D., Liguori, M., and Steccolini, I. (2007). "Strengthening United Nations Accountability: Between Managerial Reform and Search for Legitimacy." In: *Management Reforms in International Organizations,* edited by Michael W. Bauer and Christoph Knill, pp. 97–115. Baden-Baden: Nomos.

Allen, C.T. (1950). "World Health and World Politics." *International Organization* 4 (1): pp. 27–43.

Alter, K.J. and Meunier, S. (2009). "The Politics of International Regime Complexity." *Perspectives on Politics* 7 (1): pp. 13–24.

Anand, S. and Hanson, K. (1998). "DALYs: Efficiency Versus Equity." *World Development* 26 (2): pp. 307–10.

Andresen, S. (2002). *Leadership Change in the World Health Organization: Potential for Increased Effectiveness?* FNI Report 8/2002. Lysaker: The Fridtjof Nansen Institute.

Annan, K. (1998). "The Quiet Revolution." *Global Governance* 4 (2): pp. 123–38.

Ascher, C.S. (1952). "Current Problems in the World Health Organization's Program." *International Organization* 6 (2): pp. 27–50.

Baccaro, L. and Valentina, M. (2012). "Pathology of Path Dependency? The ILO and the Challenge of New Governance." *Industrial and Labor Relations Review* 65 (2): pp. 195–224.

Bachrach, P. and Baratz, M.S. (1962). "Two Faces of Power." *American Political Science Review* 56 (4): pp. 947–52.

Barnes, B. (2001). "Practice as Collective Action." In: *The Practice Turn in Contemporary Theory,* edited by Theodore R. Schatzki, Karin Knorr Cetina, and Eike von Savigny, pp. 25–35. London, New York: Routledge.

Barnett, M. (2002). "Historical Sociology and Constructivism: An Estranged Past, a Federated Future?" In: *Historical Sociology of International Relations,* edited by Stephen Hobden and John M. Hobson, pp. 99–119. Cambridge: Cambridge University Press.

Barnett, M. and Duvall, R., eds. (2005). *Power in Global Governance.* Cambridge: Cambridge University Press.

Barnett, M. and Finnemore, M. (1999). "The Politics, Power, and Pathologies of International Organizations." *International Organization* 53 (4): pp. 699–732.

References

Barnett, M. and Finnemore, M. (2004). *Rules for the World: International Organizations in Global Politics*, Ithaca: Cornell University Press.

BBC (2013). *US Loses UNESCO Voting Rights After Failing to Pay Its Dues.* British Broadcasting Corporation, November 11, available at: <http://www.bbc.com/news/world-us-canada-24871100>.

Beckfield, J. (2010). "The Social Structure of the World Polity." *American Journal of Sociology* 115 (4): pp. 1018–68.

Beigbeder, Y. (1987). *Management Problems in United Nations Organizations: Reform or Decline?* New York: St. Martin's Press.

Beigbeder, Y. (1997). *The Internal Management of United Nations Organizations: The Long Quest for Reform.* New York: St. Martin's Press.

Benvenisti, E. and G.W. Downs (2007). "The Empire's New Clothes: Political Economy and the Fragmentation of International Law." *Stanford Law Review* 60 (2): pp. 595–632.

Berkov, R. (1957). *The World Health Organization: A Study in Decentralized International Administration.* Geneva: Droz.

Betts, A. (2009). "Institutional Proliferation and the Global Refugee Regime." *Perspectives on Politics* 7 (1): pp. 53–8.

Broome, A. and Seabrooke, L. (2012). "Seeing Like an International Organization." *New Political Economy* 17 (1): pp. 1–16.

Brundtland, G.H. (1998a). *Address to Permanent Missions in Geneva: WHO, Headquarters, 18 November 1998.* Geneva: WHO, copy with author.

Brundtland, G.H. (1998b). *Address to WHO Staff. Geneva, 21 July 1998.* Geneva, available at: http://www.who.int/director-general/speeches/1998/english/19980721_hq_staff.html (accessed March 15, 2012).

Brundtland, G.H. (1999a). *Address to the Geneva Group—UN Directors. Change at WHO.* Geneva: WHO, copy with author.

Brundtland, G.H. (1999b). *Looking Back at 1999: Monthly Briefing for Missions.* Geneva: WHO, copy with author.

Brundtland, G.H. (2001). *Global Meeting of WHO Representatives and Liaison Officers. WHO, Geneva, 26 March 2001.* Geneva: WHO. Copy with author.

Brunsson, N. (2006). *The Organization of Hypocrisy: Talk, Decisions and Actions in Organizations.* Oslo: Liber.

Brunsson, N. and Olsen, J.P. (1993). *The Reforming Organization.* London, New York: Routledge.

Brunsson, N. and Sahlin-Andersson, K. (2000). "Constructing Organizations: The Example of Public Sector Reform." *Organization Studies* 21 (4): pp. 721–46.

Bryant, J. (1969). *Health and the Developing World.* New York, London: Cornell University Press.

Bull, B. and McNeill, D. (2007). *Development Issues in Global Governance: Public-Private Partnerships and Market Multilateralism.* New York: Routledge.

Burci, G.L. and Vignes, C.-H. (2004). *World Health Organization.* The Hague: Kluwer Law International.

Buse, K. and Harmer, A. (2007). "Seven Habits of Highly Effective Global Public–private Health Partnerships: Practice and Potential." *Social Science and Medicine* 64 (2): pp. 259–71.

Buse, K. and Waxman, A. (2001). "Public-private Health Partnerships: A Strategy for WHO." *Bulletin of the World Health Organization* 79 (8): pp. 748–53.

Büthe, T. (2002). "Taking Temporality Seriously: Modeling History and the Use of Narratives as Evidence." *American Political Science Review* 96 (3): pp. 481–93.

Büttner, S. (2012). *Mobilizing Regions, Mobilizing Europe: Expert Knowledge and Scientific Planning in European Regional Development*. London: Routledge.

Calderwood, H.B. (1963). "The World Health Organization and its Regional Organizations." *Temple Law Quarterly* 37 (1): pp. 15–27.

Capoccia, G. and R.D. Kelemen (2007). "The Study of Critical Junctures: Theory, Narrative, and Counterfactuals in Historical Institutionalism." *World Politics* 59 (3): pp. 341–69.

Carr, E.H. (1990). *What is History?*, 2nd edn. London: Penguin Books.

Carr, E.H. (2001). *The Twenty Years' Crisis, 1919–1939: An Introduction to the Study of International Relations*. New York: Perennial.

Checkel, J.T. (2005). *It's the Process Stupid! Process Tracing in the Study of European and International Politics*. ARENA Working Paper No. 26. Oslo: ARENA Centre for European Studies.

Chin, J. (2007). *The AIDS Pandemic: The Collision of Epidemiology with Political Correctness*. Oxford: Radcliffe.

Chorev, N. (2012). *The World Health Organization between North and South*. Ithaca, New York: Cornell University Press.

Chow, J.C. (2010). *Is the WHO Becoming Irrelevant?: Why the World's Premier Public Health Organization Must Change or Die*. Foreign Policy, December 8, available at: <http://www.foreignpolicy.com/articles/2010/12/08/is_the_who_becoming_irrelevant>.

Chwieroth, J.M. (2008). "Organizational change 'from within': Exploring the World Bank's early lending practices." *Review of International Political Economy* 15 (4): pp. 481–505.

Chwieroth, J.M. (2014). "Controlling Capital: The International Monetary Fund and Transformative Incremental Change from Within International Organisations." *New Political Economy* 19 (3): pp. 445–69.

Collins, C. and Green, A. (1994). "Decentralization and Primary Health Care: Some Negative Implications in Developing Countries." *International Journal of Health Services* 24 (3): pp. 459–75.

Cooley, A. and Ron, J. (2002). "The NGO Scramble: Organizational Insecurity and the Political Economy of Transnational Action." *International Security* 27 (1): pp. 5–39.

Copelovitch, M.S. (2010). "Master or Servant? Common Agency and the Political Economy of IMF Lending." *International Studies Quarterly* 54 (1): pp. 49–77.

Cox, R.W. (1973). "ILO: Limited Monarchy." In: *The Anatomy of Influence: Decision Making in International Organizations,* edited by Robert W. Cox and Harold K. Jacobson, pp. 102–38. New Haven: Yale University Press.

Cueto, M. (2004). "The Origins of Primary Health Care and Selective Primary Health Care." *American Journal of Public Health* 94 (11): pp. 1864–74.

Daes, E.-I.A. and Daoudy, A. (1993). *Decentralization of Organizations within the United Nations System: Part III: The World Health Organization.* JIU/REP/93/2. Geneva: Joint Inspection Unit of the United Nations.

Danida (1991). *Effectiveness of Multilateral Agencies at Country Level: WHO in Kenya, Nepal, Sudan and Thailand.* Copenhagen: Danida.

Dannreuther, R. (2011). "Understanding the Middle East Peace Process: A Historical Institutionalist Approach." *European Journal of International Relations* 17 (2): pp. 187–208.

Dingwerth, K. and Jörgens, H. (forthcoming). "Chapter 18: Environmental Risks and the Changing Interface of Domestic and International Governance." In: *The Oxford Handbook of Transformation of the State—Part II Internationalization and the State,* edited by Stephan Leibfried, Frank Nullmeier, Evelyne Huber, Matthew Lange, Jonah Levy, and John Stephens. Oxford: Oxford University Press.

Distler, L.K. (2012). *Institutional Fragmentation: A Means to Obtain Leadership? The World Bank in Global Health.* Paper to be presented to the ISA Annual Convention, 1–4 April 2012, San Diego, CA, USA.

Djukanovic, V. and Mach, E.P., eds. (1975). *Alternative Approaches to Meeting Basic Health Needs in Developing Countries: A Joint UNICEF/WHO Study.* Geneva: World Health Organization.

Dorolle, P. (1976). *WHO Oral History Project.* Interview by Norman Howard-Jones. Geneva.

Dove, A. (1998). "Brundtland Takes Charge and Restructures the WHO." *Nature Medicine* 4 (9): p. 992.

Evans, L.H. (1963). "Some Management Problems of UNESCO." *International Organization* 17 (1): pp. 76–90.

Falkner, G., ed. (2011). *The EU's Decision Traps: Comparing Policies.* Oxford: Oxford University Press.

Farid, M.A. (1980). "The Malaria Programme—from Euphoria to Anarchy." *World Health Forum* 1 (1–2): pp. 8–22.

Farid, M.A. (1998). "The Malaria Campaign—Why not Eradication?" *World Health Forum* 19: pp. 417–27.

Farley, J. (2008). *Brock Chisholm, the World Health Organization, and the Cold War.* Vancouver, Toronto: UBC Press.

Farrell, H. and Newman, A.L. (2010). "Introduction: Making Global Markets: Historical Institutionalism in International Political Economy." *Review of International Political Economy* 17 (4): pp. 609–38.

Faude, B. (forthcoming). "Zur Dynamik inter-organisationaler Beziehungen: Wie aus Konkurrenz Arbeitsteilung entsteht." In: *Internationale Organisationen: PVS Sonderheft 49,* edited by Martin Koch, Andrea Liese, and Eugenia de Conceição-Heldt. Baden-Baden: Nomos.

Fearon, J.D. (1998). "Bargaining, Enforcement, and International Cooperation." *International Organization* 52 (2): pp. 269–305.

Fidler, D.P. (2007). "Architecture amidst Anarchy: Global Health's Quest for Governance." *Global Health Governance* 1 (1): http://ghgj.org/Fidler_1.1_Architecture.htm (accessed January 12, 2014).

Fioretos, O. (2011). "Historical Institutionalism in International Relations." *International Organization* 65 (2): pp. 367–99.

Food and Agricultural Organization of the United Nations (2007). *FAO: The Challenge of Renewal: Report of the Independent External Evaluation of the Food and Agriculture Organization of the United Nations (FAO)*. Rome: FAO.

Forss, K., Stenson, B., and Sterky, G. (1996). "The Future of Global Health Cooperation: Designing a New World Health Organization." *Current Issues in Public Health* 2 (3): pp. 138–42.

Frey, B.S. (2008). "Outside and Inside Competition for International Organizations—From Analysis to Innovations." *Review of International Organizations* 3 (4): pp. 335–50.

Friedberg, E. (1997). *Local Orders: Dynamics of Organized Action*. Greenwich, CT: JAI Press.

Fukuyama, F. (1992). *The End of History and the Last Man*. New York: Free Press.

Furth, W.W. (1977). "WHO's Strategy for Meeting the 60% Technical Cooperation Target." *WHO Chronicle* 31 (9): pp. 348–54.

Gehring, T. (2009). "Die Autonomie Internationaler Organisationen: Lehren aus der systemtheoretischen Organisationstheorie." In: *Die Organisierte Welt: Internationale Beziehungen und Organisationsforschung,* edited by Klaus Dingwerth, Dieter Kerwer, and Andreas Nölke, pp. 60–95. Baden-Baden: Nomos.

Gehring, T. and Faude, B. (2014). "A Theory of Emerging Order within Institutional Complexes: How Competition among Regulatory International Institutions Leads to Institutional Adaptation and Division of Labor." *Review of International Organizations* 9 (4): pp. 471–98.

Genschel, P. (1997). "How Fragmentation Can Improve Co-ordination: Setting Standards in International Telecommunication." *Organization Studies* 18 (4): pp. 603–22.

George, A.L. and Bennett, A. (2005). *Case Studies and Theory Development in the Social Sciences*. Cambridge, MA: MIT Press.

Ghebali, V.-Y. (1989). *The International Labour Organization: A Case Study in the Evolution of U.N. Specialized Agencies*. Dordrecht, Boston, London: Nijhoff.

Gladwell, M. (2001). "The Mosquito Killer." *The New Yorker* (July 2): pp. 42–51.

Godlee, F. (1993a). "Nakajima holds on as WHO's head." *British Medical Journal* 306 (6888): p. 1288.

Godlee, F. (1993b). "WHO's Election Throws Agency into Bitter Turmoil." *British Medical Journal* 306 (6871): p. 161.

Godlee, F. (1994a). "The Regions: Too Much Power, Too Little Effect." *British Medical Journal* 309 (6968): pp. 1566–70.

Godlee, F. (1994b). "The World Health Organization in Africa: Too much politics, too little accountability." *British Medical Journal* 309 (6954).

Godlee, F. (1994c). "WHO at Country Level—a Little Impact, no Strategy." *British Medical Journal* 309 (6969): pp. 1636–9.

Godlee, F. (1994d). "WHO in Crisis." *British Medical Journal* 309 (6966): pp. 1424–8.

Godlee, F. (1994e). "WHO in Retreat: Is It Losing its Influence?" *British Medical Journal* 309 (6967): pp. 1491–5.

Godlee, F. (1995a). "Interview with the Director General." *British Medical Journal* 310 (6979): pp. 583–8.

Godlee, F. (1995b). "WHO in Europe: Does it Have a Role?" *British Medical Journal* 310 (6976): pp. 389–93.

Godlee, F. (1995c). "WHO's Special Programmes: Undermining from Above." *British Medical Journal* 310 (6973): pp. 178–82.

Godlee, F. (1996). "New Hope for WHO?" *British Medical Journal* 312 (7043): p. 1376.

Godlee, F. (1998). "Change at Last in WHO: But Will the Regions Play Ball?" *British Medical Journal* 317 (7154): p. 296.

Goldstone, J.A. (1998). "Initial Conditions, General Laws, Path Dependence, and Explanation in Historical Sociology." *American Journal of Sociology* 104 (3): pp. 829–45.

González, A.D. and Mezzalama, F. (2002). *Review of Management and Administration in the Food and Agriculture Organization of the United Nations (FAO)*. Geneva: Joint Inspection Unit of the United Nations System.

Goodman, N.M. (1971). *International Health Organizations and Their Work*, 2nd edn. Edinburgh: Churchill Livingstone.

Gopakumar, K.M. and Wanis, H. (2011). *WHO: Debate over Proposed Reform Agenda and Priority-setting*. TWN Info Service on Health Issues Nov11/02. Third World Network, available at: <http://www.twnside.org.sg/title2/health.info/2011/health20111102.htm>.

Graham, E. (2014). "International Organizations as Collective Agents: Fragmentation and the Limits of Principal Control at the World Health Organization." *European Journal of International Relations* 20 (2): pp. 366–90.

Greif, A. and Laitin, D.D. (2004). "A Theory of Endogenous Institutional Change." *American Political Science Review* 98 (4): pp. 633–52.

Gruber, L. (2000). *Ruling the World: Power politics and the rise of supranational institutions*. Princeton: Princeton University Press.

Hacker, J.S. (2004). "Privatizing Risk without Privatizing the Welfare State: The Hidden Politics of Social Policy Retrenchment in the United States." *American Political Science Review* 98 (2): pp. 243–60.

Hafner-Burton, E., Kahler, M., and Montgomery, A.H. (2009). "Network Analysis for International Relations." *International Organization* 63 (3): pp. 559–92.

Hall, P.A. and Taylor, R.C.R. (1996). "Political Science and the Three New Institutionalisms." *Political Studies* 44: pp. 936–57.

Hanrieder, T. (2013). *Mahler, Halfdan Theodor*. IO BIO, Biographical Dictionary of Secretaries-General of International Organizations, available at: <http://www.ru.nl/publish/pages/531985/mahler-h-28june2013.pdf>.

Hanrieder, T. (2014a). "Gradual Change in International Organizations: Agency Theory and Historical Institutionalism." *Politics*, 34 (4): pp. 324–33.

Hanrieder, T. (2014b). "Local Orders in International Organizations: The World Health Organization's Global Programme on AIDS." *Journal of International Relations and Development* 17 (2): pp. 220–41.

Hanrieder, T. (forthcoming). "WHO Orchestrates? Coping with Competitors in Global Health." In: *International Organizations as Orchestrators*, edited by Kenneth Abbott,

Philipp Genschel, Duncan Snidal, and Bernhard Zangl. Cambridge: Cambridge University Press.

Hanrieder, T. and Kreuder-Sonnen, C. (2014). "WHO Decides on the Exception? Securitization and Emergency Governance in Global Health." *Security Dialogue* 45 (4): pp. 331–48.

Hasenclever, A., Mayer, P., and Rittberger, V. (2004). "Does Regime Robustness Require a Fair Distribution of the Gains from Cooperation? An Essay on the Methodology of Necessary Conditions as Applied to a Substantive Hypothesis Concerning the 'Staying Power' of International Regimes." In: *Regime Consequences: Methodological Challenges and Research Strategies,* edited by Arild Underdal and Oran Young, pp. 183–216. Dordrecht: Kluwer.

Hawkes, N. (2011). "'Irrelevant' WHO Outpaced by Younger Rivals." *British Medical Journal* 343 (d5012): pp. 1–3.

Hawkins, D.G., Lake, D.A., Nielson, D.L., and Tierney, M.J., eds. (2006a). *Delegation and Agency in International Organizations*. Cambridge: Cambridge University Press.

Hawkins, D.G., Lake, D.A., Nielson, D.L., and Tierney, M.J. (2006b). "Delegation under Anarchy: States, International Organizations, and Principal-agent Theory." In: *Delegation and Agency in International Organizations,* edited by Darren G. Hawkins, David A. Lake, Daniel L. Nielson, and Michael J. Tierney, pp. 3–38. Cambridge: Cambridge University Press.

Helfer, L.R. (2006). "Understanding Change in International Organizations: Globalization and Innovation in the ILO." *Vanderbilt Law Review* 59 (3): pp. 649–726.

Henderson, D.A. (2009). *Smallpox: The Death of a Disease*. Amherst: Prometheus Books.

Hirschman, A.O. (1970). *Exit, Voice and Loyalty: Responses to Decline in Firms, Organizations, and States*. Cambridge, MA: Harvard University Press.

Hirschman, A.O. (1991). *The Rhetoric of Reaction: Perversity, Futility, Jeopardy*. Cambridge, MA, London: Belknap Press of Harvard University Press.

HM Government (2009). *World Health Organization: UK Institutional Strategy 2008–13,* available at: <http://webarchive.nationalarchives.gov.uk/20130107105354/http://www.dh.gov.uk/prod_consum_dh/groups/dh_digitalassets/documents/digitalasset/dh_095295.pdf>.

Hoggart, R. (1978). *An Idea and Its Servants: UNESCO from Within*. London: Chatto & Windus.

Hood, C. (1995). "The 'New Public Management' in the 1980s: Variations on a Theme." *Accounting, Organizations and Society* 20 (2/3): pp. 93–109.

Horton, R. (2006). "WHO: Strengthening the Road to Renewal." *The Lancet* 367 (9525): pp. 1793–5.

Hosli, M.O., Moody, R., O'Donovan, B., Kaniovski, S., and Little, A.C. (2011). "Squaring the Circle? Collective and Distributive Effects of United Nations Security Council Reform." *Review of International Organizations* 6 (2): pp. 163–87.

Howard-Jones, N. (1978). "International Public Health: The Organizational Problems Between the Two World Wars. Epilogue." *WHO Chronicle* 32 (4): pp. 156–66.

Howard-Jones, N. (1981). *The Pan American Health Organization: Origins and Evolution*. Geneva: World Health Organization.

Hüfner, K. (2013). *Wer rettet die UNESCO?* Leipzig: Frank & Timme.

Hughes, S. and Haworth, N. (2011). *The International Labour Organization (ILO): Coming in from the Cold*. London, New York: Routledge.

Hull, C. (1948). *The Memoirs*. New York: Macmillan.

Huxley, J. (1945). "Science and the United Nations." *Nature Medicine* 156 (10 November): pp. 553–6.

Huxley, J. (1946). *UNESCO: Its Purpose and Its Philosophy*, available at: <http://unesdoc.unesco.org/images/0006/000681/068197eo.pdf>.

Illich, I. (1995/1976). *Limits to Medicine. Medical Nemesis: The Expropriation of Health*. London, New York: Marlon Boyars.

Independent External Evaluation Team. (2010). *Independent External Evaluation of UNESCO*. IOS/EVS/PI/107, available at: <http://unesdoc.unesco.org/images/0018/001895/189534e.pdf>.

Ingram, P. and Torfason, M.T. (2010). "Organizing the In-between: The Population Dynamics of Network-weaving Organizations in the Global Interstate Network." *Administrative Science Quarterly* 55 (4): pp. 577–605.

Inoue, K. and Drori, G.S. (2006). "The Global Institutionalization of Health as a Social Concern: Organizational and Discursive Trends." *International Sociology* 21 (2): pp. 199–219.

International Labour Office (1923). *Official Bulletin, Volume I: April 1919–August 1920*. Geneva: ILO.

International Labour Office (1993). *ILO Circular. Active Partnership Policy*. Geneva: ILO.

International Labour Office (1994). *Defending Values, Promoting Change: Social Justice in a Global Economy: An ILO Agenda*. Report of the Director-General to the International Labour Conference, 81st Session 1994. Geneva: ILO.

International Labour Office (2010). *Constitution of the International Labour Organization and Selected Texts*. Geneva: ILO.

International Labour Organization (2013). *ILO Field Operations & Structure and Technical Cooperation Review: Report of the Field Review Team to the Director-General*. Geneva: ILO.

International Programme on the Elimination of Child Labour (2010). *The International Programme on the Elimination of Child Labour (IPEC)—What it is and what it does*. Geneva: International Labour Organization.

International Programme on the Elimination of Child Labour (2011). *Children in Hazardous Work: What We Know. What We Need to Do*. Geneva: International Labour Organization.

International Programme on the Elimination of Child Labour (2013). *IPEC Action Against Child Labour: Highlights 2012*. Geneva: International Labour Organization.

Italian Global Health Watch (2008). "From Alma Ata to the Global Fund: The History of International Health Policy." *Social Medicine* 3 (1): pp. 36–48.

Jacobson, H.K. (1970). "New States and Functional International Organizations: a Preliminary Report." In: *The Politics of International Organizations: Studies in Multilateral Social and Economic Agencies*, edited by Robert W. Cox, pp. 74–97. New York, Washington: Praeger Publishers.

Jacobson, H.K. (1973). "WHO: Medicine, Regionalism, and Managed Politics." In: *The Anatomy of Influence: Decision Making in International Organizations*, edited by Robert W. Cox and Harold K. Jacobson, pp. 175–215. New Haven: Yale University Press.

Joint Inspection Unit (1992). *Decentralization of Organizations within the United Nations System: Part I: Decentralization and Managerial Processes*. JIU/REP/92/6 (Part I). Geneva: JIU.

Joint Inspection Unit (1999). *Review of Management and Administration in the International Labour Office*. JIU/REP/99/4. Geneva: JIU.

Joint Inspection Unit (2000). *Review of Management and Administration in the United Nations Educational, Scientific and Cultural Organization (UNESCO)*. JIU/REP/2000/4. Geneva: JIU.

Joint Inspection Unit (2001). *Review of Management and Administration in the World Health Organization (WHO)*. JIU/REP/2001/5. Geneva: JIU.

Jönsson, C. (1986). "Interorganization Theory and International Organization." *International Studies Quarterly* 30 (1): pp. 39–57.

Jupille, J., Mattli, W., and Snidal, D. (2013). *Institutional Choice in Global Commerce*. Cambridge: Cambridge University Press.

Kahler, M. (1998). "Rationality in International Relations." *International Organization* 52 (4): pp. 919–41.

Kaplan, M.M. (1983). "Dr. M.G. Candau—A Personal Appreciation." *World Health Forum* 4 (1): pp. 3–4.

Katz, A. (2008). "The Independence of International Civil Servants During the Neoliberal Decades: Implications of the Work Stoppage Involving 700 Staff of the World Health Organization in November 2005." *International Journal of Health Services* 38 (1): pp. 161–82.

Kelemen, R.D. and Tarrant, A.D. (2011). "The Political Foundations of the Eurocracy." *West European Politics* 34 (5): pp. 922–47.

Kelley, J. (2009). "The More the Merrier? The Effects of Having Multiple International Election Monitoring Organizations." *Perspectives on Politics* 7 (1): pp. 59–64.

Kennedy, P. (2006). *The Parliament of Man: The Past, Present and Future of the United Nations*. New York: Random House.

Keohane, R.O. and Victor, D.G. (2011). "The Regime Complex for Climate Change." *Perspectives on Politics* 9 (1): pp. 7–23.

Kettl, D.F. (2000). *The Global Public Management Revolution: A Report on the Transformation of Governance*. Washington, DC: Brookings Institution.

Kleine, M. (2013). "Trading Control: National Fiefdoms in International Organizations." *International Theory* 5 (3): pp. 321–46.

Knight, L. (2008). *UNAIDS: The First 10 Years, 1996–2006*. Geneva: Joint United Nations Programme on HIV/AIDS.

Koch, M. (2009). "Autonomization of IGOs." *International Political Sociology* 3 (4): pp. 431–48.

Koremenos, B. (2008). "When, What, and Why do States Choose to Delegate?" *Law and Contemporary Problems* 51 (1): pp. 151–92.

Koremenos, B., Lipson, C., and Snidal, D. (2001a). "The Rational Design of International Institutions." *International Organization* 55 (4): pp. 761–99.

Koremenos, B., Lipson, C., and Snidal, D. (2001b). "Rational Design: Looking Back to Move Forward." *International Organization* 55 (4): pp. 1051–82.

Krasner, S.D. (1984). "Approaches to the State: Alternative Conceptions and Historical Dynamics." *Comparative Politics* 16 (2): pp. 223–46.

Krasner, S.D. (1985). *Structural Conflict: The Third World Against Global Liberalism.* Berkeley: University of California Press.

Krasner, S.D. (1988). "Sovereignty: An Institutional Perspective." *Comparative Political Studies* 21 (1): pp. 66–94.

Lebow, R.N. (2010). *Forbidden Fruit: Counterfactuals and International Relations.* Princeton, NJ: Princeton University Press.

Lee, J.W. (2003). "Resources Should be Decentralised to Countries." *British Medical Journal* 326 (7381): p. 123.

Lee, K. (2009). *World Health Organisation.* London: Routledge.

Lee, K., Collinson, S., Walt, G., and Gilson, L. (1996). "Who Should Be Doing What in International Health: A Confusion of Mandates in the United Nations?" *British Medical Journal* 312 (7026): pp. 302–7.

Lee, S. (1997). "WHO and the Developing World: The Contest for Ideology." In: *Western Medicine as Contested Knowledge,* edited by Andrew Cunningham and Bridie Andrews, pp. 24–45. Manchester, New York: Manchester University Press.

Leiteritz, R.J. (2005). "Explaining Organizational Outcomes: The International Monetary Fund and Capital Account Liberalization." *Journal of International Relations and Development* 8 (1): pp. 1–26.

Lerer, L. and Matzopoulos, R. (2001). "'The Worst of Both Worlds': The Management Reform of the World Health Organization." *International Journal of Health Services* 31 (2): pp. 415–38.

Leuffen, D., Rittberger, B., and Schimmelfennig, F. (2013). *Differentiated Integration: Explaining Variation in the European Union.* Houndsmills, Basingstoke: Palgrave Macmillan.

Levine, R. (2006). "Open Letter to the Incoming Director-General of the World Health Organization: Time to Refocus." *British Medical Journal* 333 (7576): pp. 1015–17.

Liese, A. (2005). "'Capacity Building' als Strategie zur Förderung der Regeleinhaltung. Erfahrungen der ILO bei der Abschaffung von Kinderarbeit." In: *Weltweit geltende Arbeitsstandards trotz Globalisierung. Analysen, Diagnosen und Einblicke,* edited by Eva Senghaas-Knobloch, pp. 63–79. Münster: LIT Verlag.

Lindner, J. and Rittberger, B. (2003). "The Creation, Interpretation and Contestation of Institutions—Rethinking Historical Institutionalism." *Journal of Common Market Studies* 41 (3): pp. 445–73.

Litsios, S. (1975). "Seven Principles of Primary Health Care." In *Eigth Annual Meeting: Paulus-Akademie, 7–11 July 1975,* pp. 17–20. Zurich.

Litsios, S. (1997). "Malaria Control, the Cold War, and the Postwar Reorganization of International Assistance." *Medical Anthropology* 17 (3): pp. 255–78.

Litsios, S. (2002). "The Long and Difficult Road to Alma Ata: A Personal Reflection." *International Journal of Health Services* 32 (4): pp. 709–32.

Litsios, S. (2004). "The Christian Medical Commission and the Development of the World Health Organization's Primary Health Care Approach." *American Journal of Public Health* 94 (11): pp. 1884–93.

Littig, B. (2009). "Interviewing the Elite—Interviewing Experts: Is There a Difference?" In: *Interviewing Experts,* edited by Alexander Bogner, Beate Littig, and Wolfgang Menz, pp. 98–113. Houndmills: Palgrave Macmillan.

Luard, E. (1982). *A History of the United Nations—Volume I: The Years of Western Domination, 1945–1955.* London, Basingstoke: Macmillan.

Magnussen, L., Ehiri, J., and Jolly, P. (2004). "Comprehensive versus Selective Primary Health Care: Lessons for Global Health Policy." *Health Affairs* 23 (1): pp. 167–76.

Mahler, H. (1974a). "An International Health Conscience." *WHO Chronicle* 28 (5): pp. 207–11.

Mahler, H. (1974b). "The Constitutional Mission of the World Health Organization." *WHO Chronicle* 28 (7): pp. 308–11.

Mahler, H. (1975a). "Health for All by the Year 2000." *WHO Chronicle* 29 (12): pp. 457–61.

Mahler, H. (1975b). "New possibilities for WHO." *WHO Chronicle* 29 (2): pp. 43–5.

Mahler, H. (1976). *Director-General's Address on Programme Budget Policy to Meeting of Senior Staff: 8 June 1976.* Geneva: World Health Organization.

Mahler, H. (1977). "Blueprint for Health for All." *WHO Chronicle* 31 (12): pp. 491–8.

Mahler, H. (1980). "The WHO You Want: An Address to WHO Regional Committees." *WHO Chronicle* 34 (1): pp. 3–8.

Mahler, H. (1981). "The Meaning of 'Health for All by the Year 2000'." *World Health Forum* 2 (1): pp. 5–22.

Mahler, H. (1983a). "The Marathon for Health for All." *WHO Chronicle* 37 (6): pp. 187–91.

Mahler, H. (1983b). "WHO's Programme Budget since 1980: Some Lessons for the 1984–85 Biennium." *WHO Chronicle* 37 (2): pp. 43–7.

Mahler, H. (1984). "Voices in Harmony for Health for All." *WHO Chronicle* 38 (4): pp. 155–60.

Mahler, H. (2008). "Primary Health Care Comes Full Circle: An Interview with Dr Halfdan Mahler." *Bulletin of the World Health Organization* 86 (10): pp. 747–8.

Mahoney, J. (2000). "Path Dependence in Historical Sociology." *Theory and Society* 29 (4): pp. 507–48.

Mahoney, J. and Thelen, K., eds. (2010a). *Explaining Institutional Change: Ambiguity, Agency, and Power.* Cambridge: Cambridge University Press.

Mahoney, J. and Thelen, K. (2010b). "A Theory of Gradual Institutional Change." In: *Explaining Institutional Change: Ambiguity, Agency, and Power,* edited by James Mahoney and Kathleen Thelen, pp. 1–37. Cambridge: Cambridge University Press.

March, J.G. and Olsen, J.P. (1998). "The Institutional Dynamics of International Political Orders." *International Organization* 52 (4): pp. 943–69.

Mayntz, R. (2004). "Mechanisms in the Analysis of Social Macro-Phenomena." *Philosophy of the Social Sciences* 34 (2): pp. 237–59.

McGilvray, J.C. (1981). *The Quest for Health and Wholeness.* Tübingen: German Institute for Medical Missions.

McNamara, K.R. and Newman, A.L. (2009). *The European Union as an Institutional Scavenger: International Organization Ecosystems and Institutional Evolution.* Paper Prepared for the 11th Biennial EUSA conference, April 24–26, 2009. Los Angeles, CA.

165

Meyer, J.W. and Jepperson, R.L. (2000). "The 'Actors' of Modern Society: The Cultural Construction of Social Agency." *Sociological Theory* 18 (1): pp. 100–20.

Michels, R. (1989). *Zur Soziologie des Parteiwesens in der modernen Demokratie,* 4th ed. Stuttgart: Kröner.

Mielke, C. (2009). "Die strategische Neuausrichtung der ILO am Beispiel des Verbots von Kinderarbeit—Internationale Normen vs. lokale Realitäten?" In: *Internationale Arbeitsstandards in einer globalisierten Welt,* edited by Ellen Ehmke, Michael Fichter, Nils Simon, and Bodo Zeuner, pp. 172–91. Wiesbaden: VS Verlag für Sozialwissenschaften.

Minelli, E. (2002). "World Health Organization: The Mandate of a Specialised Agency of the United Nations." Milano, available at: <http://www.gfmer.ch/TMCAM/WHO_Minelli/Index.htm>, accessed August 2011.

Mintzberg, H. (1984). "Power and Organization Life Cycles." *Academy of Management Review* 9 (2): pp. 207–24.

Momani, B. (2005). "Limits of Streamlining IMF Conditionality: IMF's Organizational Culture." *Journal of International Relations and Development* 8 (2): pp. 142–63.

Müller, J., ed. (2010). *Reforming the United Nations: The Challenge of Working Together.* Leiden, Boston: Nijhoff.

Murray, C.J., Lopez, A.D., and Jamison, D.T. (1994). "The Global Burden of Disease in 1990: Summary Results, Sensitivity Analysis and Future Directions." *Bulletin of the World Health Organization* 72 (3): pp. 495–509.

Naím, M. and Brundtland, G.H. (2002). "The FP Interview: The Global War for Public Health." *Foreign Policy* 128 (Jan–Feb.): pp. 24–36.

Neumann, I.B. (2007). " 'A Speech That the Entire Ministry May Stand for,' or: Why Diplomats Never Produce Anything New." *International Political Sociology* 1 (2): pp. 183–200.

Newell, K.W., ed. (1975a). *Health by the People.* Geneva: World Health Organization.

Newell, K.W. (1975b). "Health by the People." *WHO Chronicle* 29 (5): pp. 161–7.

Nielson, D.L. and Tierney, M.J. (2003). "Delegation to International Organizations: Agency Theory and World Bank Environmental Reform." *International Organization* 57 (2): pp. 241–76.

Nielson, D.L. and Tierney, M.J. (2005). "Theory, Data, and Hypothesis Testing: World Bank Environmental Reform Redux." *International Organization* 59 (3): pp. 785–800.

Nielson, D.L., Tierney, M.J., and Weaver, C.E. (2006). "Bridging the Rationalist-constructivist Divide: Re-engineering the Culture of the World Bank." *Journal of International Relations and Development* 9 (2): pp. 107–39.

Ortiz, E.F., Gorita, I., and Tadanori, I. (2005). *External Review of the Implementation of Strategic Budgeting within a results-based Management Framework in the International Labour Organization (ILO).* Geneva: International Labour Organization.

Page, S.E. (2006). "Path Dependence." *Quarterly Journal of Political Science* 1 (1): pp. 87–115.

Pan American Health Organization (PAHO) (1992). *Pro Salute Novi Mundi: a History of the Pan American Health Organization.* Washington DC: PAHO.

Park, S. (2005). "Norm Diffusion Within International Organizations: A Case Study of the World Bank." *Journal of International Relations and Development* 8 (2): pp. 111–41.

Peabody, J.W. (1995). "An Organizational Analysis of the World Health Organization: Narrowing the Gap Between Promise and Performance." *Social Science and Medicine* 40 (6): pp. 731–42.

People's Health Movement, Medact, and Global Equity Gauge Alliance (2005). *Global Health Watch 2005–2006: An Alternative World Health Report*. London: Zed Books.

People's Health Movement, Medact, and Global Equity Gauge Alliance (2008). *Global Health Watch 2: An Alternative World Health Report*. London: Zed Books.

Pfeffer, J. and Salancik, G.R. (2003). *The External Control of Organizations: A Resource Dependence Perspective*. Stanford, CA: Stanford University Press.

Pierson, P. (2000). "Increasing Returns, Path Dependence, and the Study of Politics." *American Political Science Review* 94 (2): pp. 251–67.

Pierson, P. (2004). *Politics in Time: History, Institutions, and Social Analysis*. Princeton, NJ: Princeton University Press.

Pierson, P. and Skocpol, T. (2002). "Historical Institutionalism in Contemporary Political Science." In: *Political Science: The State of the Discipline,* edited by Ira Katznelson and Helen V. Milner, pp. 693–721. New York, London: W.W. Norton & Company.

Posta, I. and Terzi, C. (2009). *Effectiveness of the International Telecommunication Union Regional Presence*. JIU/REP/2009/3. Geneva: Joint Inspection Unit of the United Nations.

PricewaterhouseCoopers SA. (2014). *WHO Financing Dialogue Evaluation: Final Report*. Geneva, available at: <http://www.who.int/about/resources_planning/financing_dialogue/FD_EvaluationFinalReport.pdf>.

Raustiala, K. and Victor, D.G. (2004). "The Regime Complex for Plant Genetic Resources." *International Organization* 58 (2): pp. 277–309.

Ravishankar, N., Gubbins, P., Cooley, R.J., Leach-Kemon, K., Michaud, C.M., Jamison, D.T., and Murray, C.J. (2009). "Financing of Global Health: Tracking Development Assistance for Health from 1990 to 2007." *The Lancet* 373 (9681): pp. 2113–24.

Rawls, J. (1999). *A Theory of Justice*. Oxford: Oxford University Press.

Rittberger, B. and Wonka, A. (2011). "Introduction: Agency Governance in the European Union." *Journal of European Public Policy* 18 (6): pp. 780–9.

Rittberger, V., Zangl, B., and Kruck, A. (2012). *International Organization*, 2nd edn. Houndmills: Palgrave Macmillan.

Rixen, T. and Viola, L. (2014). "Putting Path Dependence in its Place: Toward a Taxonomy of Institutional Change." *Journal of Theoretical Politics,* 26 (3): pp. 1–23.

Robbins, A. (1999). "Brundtland's World Health Organization: A Test Case for United Nations Management Reform." *Public Health Reports* 114 (1): pp. 30–9.

Roll Back Malaria and World Health Organization (2002). *Achieving Impact: Roll Back Malaria in the Next Phase: Final Report of the External Evaluation of Roll Back Malaria*. Geneva, available at: <http://www.rollbackmalaria.org/cmc_upload/0/000/015/905/ee_toc.htm>.

Roman-Morey, E. and Zahran, M.M. (2011). *Review of Management and Administration in the United Nations Educational, Scientific, and Cultural Organization (UNESCO)*. Geneva: Joint Inspection Unit of the United Nations.

Ruger, J.P. (2005). "The Changing Role of the World Bank in Global Health." *American Journal of Public Health* 95 (1): pp. 60–70.

Sack, K., Fink, S., Belluck, P., and Nossiter, A. (2014). How Ebola Roared Back. *The New York Times*: 29 December, <http://www.nytimes.com/2014/12/30/health/how-ebola-roared-back.html?smprod=nytcore-ipad&smid=nytcore-ipad-share>.Schäferhoff, M. (2009). "Kooperation oder Konkurrenz? Zur Kooperationsbereitschaft internationaler Verwaltungsstäbe in transnationalen öffentlich-privaten Partnerschaften." In: *Die Organisierte Welt: Internationale Beziehungen und Organisationsforschung*, edited by Klaus Dingwerth, Dieter Kerwer, and Andreas Nölke, pp. 211–31. Baden-Baden: Nomos.

Scharpf, F.W. (1988). "The Joint-Decision Trap: Lessons from German Federalism and European Integration." *Public Administration* 66: pp. 139–278.

Schein, E.H. (1985). *Organizational Culture and Leadership: A Dynamic View*. San Francisco, CA: Jossey-Bass.

Seabrook, N.R. (2010). "The Limits of Partisan Gerrymandering: Looking Ahead to the 2010 Congressional Redistricting Cycle." *The Forum* 8 (2): Article 8.

Selznick, P. (1966). *TVA and the Grassroots*. New York: Harper & Row.

Sewell, J.P. (1973). "UNESCO: Pluralism Rampant." In: *The Anatomy of Influence: Decision Making in International Organizations*, edited by Robert W. Cox and Harold K. Jacobson, pp. 139–74. New Haven: Yale University Press.

Sewell, J.P. (1975). *UNESCO and World Politics: Engaging in International Relations*. Princeton, NJ: Princeton University Press.

Sewell, W.H. (2005). *Logics of History: Social Theory and Social Transformation*. Chicago, London: University of Chicago Press.

Shanks, C., Jacobson, H.K., and Kaplan, J.K. (1996). "Inertia and Change in the Constellation of International Governmental Organizations, 1981–1992." *International Organization* 50 (4): pp. 593–627.

Sharp, W.R. (1947). "The New World Health Organization." *American Journal of International Law* 41 (3): pp. 509–30.

Sharp, W.R. (1961). *Field Administration in the United Nations System: The Conduct of International Economic and Social Programs*. New York: Praeger Publishers.

Shashikant, S. (2011). *WHO: Vague and Inadequate Reform Plans Criticised, Nothing on Financing*. TWN Info Service on Intellectual Property Issues Jul11/02. Third World Network, available at: <http://www.twnside.org.sg/title2/health.info/2011/health20111102.htm>.

Siddiqi, J. (1995). *World Health and World Politics: The World Health Organization and the UN System*. London: Hurst & Company.

Siegel, M.P. (1982). *Transcript of an oral interview with Professor Milton P. Siegel, Moderated by Mr Gino Levy, With the participation of Mr Norman Howard-Jones*. Geneva, November 15 and November 19.

Singh, J.P. (2011). *United Nations Educational, Scientific and Cultural Organization*. London, New York: Routledge.

Slaughter, A.-M. (2004). *A New World Order*. Princeton, NJ: Princeton University Press.

Slutkin, G. (2000). "Global AIDS 1981–1999: the response." *International Journal of Tuberculosis and Lung Disease* 4 (2): pp. S24–33.

Smith, R. (1995). "The WHO: Change or Die." *British Medical Journal* 310 (6979): pp. 543–4.

Soifer, H.D. (2012). "The Causal Logic of Critical Junctures." *Comparative Political Studies* 45 (12): pp. 1572–97.

Soni, A.K. (1998). *From GPA to UNAIDS: Examining the Evolution of the UN Response to AIDS*. BA Thesis, Harvard College.

Soper, F.L. (1977). *Ventures in World Health: The Memoirs of Fred Lowe Soper: Edited by John Duffy*. Washington, DC: Pan American Health Organization.

Spruyt, H. (1994). *The Sovereign State and Its Competitors: An Analysis of Systems Change*. Princeton, NJ: Princeton University Press.

Sridhar, D. and Gostin, L.O. (2011). "Reforming the World Health Organization." *JAMA: The Journal of the American Medical Association* 305 (15): pp. 1585–6.

Sridhar, D., Gostin, L.O., and Yach, D. (2012). *Healthy Governance: How the WHO Can Regain Its Relevance*. Foreign Affairs, May 24, available at: <http://www.foreignaffairs.com/articles/137662/by-devi-sridhar-lawrence-o-gostin-and-derek-yach/healthy-governance>.

Standing, G. (2010). "The International Labour Organization." *New Political Economy* 14 (2): pp. 307–18.

Staples, A.L.S. (2006). *The Birth of Development: How the World Bank, Food and Agriculture Organization, and World Health Organization Changed the World, 1945–1965*. Kent, OH: The Kent State University Press.

Stone, R.W. (2009). "Institutions, Power, and Interdependence." In: *Power, Interdependence, and Nonstate Actors in World Politics*, edited by Helen V. Milner and Andrew Moravcsik, pp. 31–49. Princeton, NJ: Princeton University Press.

Stone, R.W. (2011). *Controlling Institutions: International Organizations and the Global Economy*. Cambridge, UK: Cambridge University Press.

Strange, S. (1998). "Why Do International Organizations Never Die?" In: *Autonomous Policy Making by International Organizations*, edited by Bob Reinalda and Bertjan Verbeek, pp. 213–20. London, New York: Routledge.

Streeck, W. and Thelen, K., eds. (2005a). *Beyond Continuity: Institutional Change in Advanced Political Economies*. Oxford: Oxford University Press.

Streeck, W. and Thelen, K. (2005b). "Introduction: Institutional Change in Advanced Political Economies." In: *Beyond Continuity: Institutional Change in Advanced Political Economies*, edited by Wolfgang Streeck and Kathleen Thelen, pp. 1–39. Oxford: Oxford University Press.

The Global Fund to Fight AIDS, Tuberculosis and Malaria (2011). *By Laws*. As amended 21 November 2011. Geneva, available at: <http://www.theglobalfund.org/documents/core/bylaws/Core_GlobalFund_Bylaws_en/>.

Thelen, K. (1999). "Historical Institutionalism in Comparative Politics." *Annual Review of Political Science* 2: pp. 369–404.

Thelen, K. (2004). *How Institutions Evolve: The Political Economy of Skills in Germany, Britain, the United States, and Japan*. Cambridge, UK: Cambridge University Press.

Thomann, L. (2008). "The ILO, Tripartism, and NGOs: Do Too Many Cooks Really Spoil the Broth?" In: *Civil Society Participation in European and Global Governance: A Cure for the Democratic Deficit?*, edited by Jens Steffek, Claudia Kissling, and Patricia Nanz, pp. 71–94. Basingstoke: Palgrave Macmillan.

Thomas, C. and Weber, M. (2004). "The Politics of Global Health Governance: What-ever Happened to 'Health for All by the Year 2000'?" *Global Governance* 10: pp. 187–205.

Thompson, A. (2010). "Rational Design in Motion: Uncertainty and Flexibility in the Global Climate Regime." *European Journal of International Relations* 16 (2): pp. 269–96.

Thurner, P.W. and Binder, M. (2009). "European Union Transgovernmental Networks: The Emergence of a New Political Space Beyond the Nation-state?" *European Journal of Political Research* 48 (1): pp. 80–106.

Tollison, R.D. and Wagner, R.E. (1993). *Who Benefits from WHO? The Decline of the World Health Organization.* London: Social Affairs Unit.

UNESCO Executive Board (2004). *Report by the Director-General on the Reform Process. Part II Decentralization.* 169 EX/6 Part III. Paris: UNESCO.

United Nations (2006). *Delivering as One: Report of the Secretary-General's High-Level Panel.* New York: UN.

United Nations (2013). *A New Global Partnership: Eradicate Poverty and Transform Economies Through Sustainable Development.* New York: UN.

United Nations Educational, Scientific and Cultural Organization (1991). *In-depth Study on Decentralization.* 136 EX/SP/RAP/1. Paris: UNESCO.

United Nations Educational, Scientific and Cultural Organization (2008). *Medium-Term Strategy for 2008–2013.* Paris: UNESCO.

United Nations General Assembly (1989). *Comprehensive Triennial Policy Review of Operational Activities for Development of the United Nations System.* A/RES/44/211. New York: UN.

United Nations General Assembly (1997). *Renewing the United Nations: A Programme for Reform. Report of the Secretary-General.* UN Doc. A/51/950, 14 July 1997. New York: UN.

Urpelainen, J. (2012). "Unilateral Influence on International Bureaucrats: An International Delegation Problem." *Journal of Conflict Resolution* 56 (4): pp. 704–35.

Valderrama, F. (1995). *A History of UNESCO.* Paris: UNESCO.

Vaughan, J.P., Mogedal, S., Walt, G.K.E.-S., Lee, K., and de Wilde, K. (1996). "WHO and the Effects of Extrabudgetary Funds: Is the Organization Donor-Driven?" *Health Policy and Planning* 11 (3): pp. 253–64.

Vetterlein, A. (2007). "Economic Growth, Poverty Reduction, and the Role of Social Policies: The Evolution of the World Bank's Social Development Approach." *Global Governance* 13: pp. 513–33.

Wallander, C.A. (2000). "Institutional Assets and Adaptability: NATO After the Cold War." *International Organization* 54 (4): pp. 705–35.

Walt, G. (1993). "WHO under Stress: Implications for Health Policy." *Health Policy and Planning* 24 (2): pp. 125–44.

Weaver, C. (2008). *Hypocrisy Trap: The World Bank and the Poverty of Reform.* Princeton, NJ: Princeton University Press.

Wendt, A. (2001). "Driving with the Rearview Mirror: On the Rational Science of Institutional Design." *International Organization* 55 (4): pp. 1019–49.

Whitaker, A.P. (1954). *The Western Hemisphere Idea: Its Rise and Decline.* Ithaca, New York: Cornell University Press.

White, H. (1975a). *Metahistory: The Historical Imagination in Ninetheenth-century Europe*. Baltimore: John Hopkins University Press.

White, R.C. (1975b). "A New International Economic Order." *International and Comparative Law Quarterly* 24 (3): pp. 542–52.

Witzel, A. and Reiter, H. (2012). *The Problem-centred Interview*. London: Sage.

Wootton, D. (2007). "From Fortune to Feedback: Contingency and the Birth of Modern Political Science." In: *Political Contingency: Studying the Unexpected, the Accidental, and the Unforeseen,* edited by Ian Shapiro and Sonu Bedi, pp. 21–53. New York, NY, London: New York University Press.

World Health Organization (1947a). *Minutes of the Second Session of the Interim Commission*. Official Records of the World Health Organization, No. 4. Geneva: WHO.

World Health Organization (1947b). *Minutes of the Technical Preparatory Committee for the International Health Conference*. Official Records of the World Health Organization, No. 1. Geneva: WHO.

World Health Organization (1947c). *Minutes of the Third Session of the Interim Commission*. Official Records of the World Health Organization, No. 5. Geneva: WHO.

World Health Organization (1947d). *Proceedings and Final Acts of the International Health Conference*. Official Records of the World Health Organization, No. 2. Geneva: WHO.

World Health Organization (1948a). *First World Health Assembly*. Official Records of the World Health Organization, No. 13. Geneva: WHO.

World Health Organization (1948b). *Reports of the Executive Board First and Second Sessions*. Official Records of the World Health Organization, No. 14. Geneva: WHO.

World Health Organization (1948c). *Reports of the Interim Commission to the First World Health Assembly: Part I Activities*. Official Records of the World Health Organization, No. 9. Geneva: WHO.

World Health Organization (1949a). "Integration of Pan American Sanitary Organization with WHO." *Chronicle of the World Health Organization* 3 (6): pp. 131–2.

World Health Organization (1949b). "Second World Health Assembly." *WHO Chronicle* 3 (8-9-10): pp. 208–15.

World Health Organization (1949c). *Second World Health Assembly*. Official Records of the World Health Organization, No. 21. Geneva: WHO.

World Health Organization (1951). *Executive Board Seventh Session. Part I: Resolutions and Decisions. Annexes*. Official Records of the World Health Organization, No. 32. Geneva: WHO.

World Health Organization (1953). *Executive Board Eleventh Session. Organizational Study on Regionalization*. Official Records of the World Health Organization, No. 46, pp. 157–84. Geneva: WHO.

World Health Organization (1956). *Executive Board. Nineteenth Session. Geneva, 15–30 January 1957. Part I Resolutions Annexes*. Official Records of the World Health Organization No. 76. Geneva: WHO.

World Health Organization (1958a). *Executive Board. Twenty-second Session. Minneapolis, 16 and 17 June 1958. Resolutions Annexes*. Official Records of the World Health Organization 88. Geneva: WHO.

World Health Organization (1958b). *Executive Board. Twenty-second Session. Minutes of the Second Meeting*. EB22/Min/2 Rev.1. Geneva: WHO.

World Health Organization (1958c). *The First Ten Years of the World Health Organization.* Geneva: WHO.

World Health Organization (1959a). *Executive Board. Twenty-third Session. Minutes of the Eleventh Meeting.* Geneva: WHO.

World Health Organization (1959b). *Executive Board. Twenty-third Session. Provisional Agenda Item 8.12: Method of Appointing Regional Directors. Proposal submitted by Dr Metcalfe.* EB23/79. Geneva: WHO.

World Health Organization (1964a). *Executive Board. Thirty-third Session. Agenda Item 6.6: Procedure for the Nomination of Regional Directors (Draft Resolution proposed by Dr H. B. Turbott).* EB33/WP/10. Geneva: WHO.

World Health Organization (1964b). *Executive Board. Thirty-third Session. Minutes of the Eighteenth Meeting.* EB33/Min/18 Rev.1. Geneva: WHO.

World Health Organization (1964c). *Procedure for the Nomination of Regional Directors. Report by the Director-General. Annex 19 to Executive Board, Thirty-third Session. Geneva, 14–24 January 1964. Part I Resolutions Annexes, 89–93.* OR132/Annex19. Geneva: WHO.

World Health Organization (1968). *The Second Ten Years of the World Health Organization.* Geneva: WHO.

World Health Organization (1973). *Twenty-sixth World Health Assembly. Geneva, 7–23 May 1973. Part II: Verbatim Records of Plenary Meetings. Summary Records and Reports of Committees.* Geneva: WHO.

World Health Organization (1974). *Organizational Study on the "Interrelationships between the Central Technical Services of WHO and Programmes of Direct Assistance to Member States."* EB53/WP/1WHO. Geneva: WHO.

World Health Organization (1975a). *Organizational Study on the Interrelationships Between the Central Technical Services of WHO and Programmes of Direct Assistance to Member States.* EB/WP/3/Annex7. Geneva: WHO.

World Health Organization (1975b). *Organizational Study on the Planning for and Impact of Extrabudgetary Resources on WHO's Programmes and Policy.* EB57/25. Geneva: WHO.

World Health Organization (1975c). *Promotion of National Health Services Relating to Primary Health Care: Report by the Director-General.* Official Records of the World Health Organization No. 226. Geneva: WHO.

World Health Organization (1976a). *Report of the Programme Committee of the Executive Board.* EB59/6. Geneva: WHO.

World Health Organization (1976b). *Twenty-ninth World Health Assembly. Geneva, 3–21 May 1976. Part II: Verbatim Records of Plenary Meetings. Summary Records and Reports of Committees.* Official Records of the World Health Organization No. 234. Geneva: WHO.

World Health Organization (1978). *Organizational study on WHO's role at the country level, particularly the role of the WHO respresentative.: Official Records of the World Health Organization No. 244, Executive Board, Sixty-first session, Annex 7.* Geneva: WHO.

World Health Organization (1979a). *Programme Development Working Group. Minutes of the First Session held on 23–28 July in Geneva.* PDWG/Min/1. Geneva: WHO.

World Health Organization (1979b). *Study of the Organization's Structure in the Light of its Functions: Outline of a Possible Study of the Feasibility of Relocating WHO Headquarters. Report by the Director-General.* EB65/18 Add. 3. Geneva: WHO.

World Health Organization (1979c). *Study of WHO's Structures in the Light of its Functions: WHO's processes, Structures, and Working Relationships. Director-General's Report.* EB65/18. Geneva: WHO.

World Health Organization (1980). *The WHO You Deserve: Address by Dr H. Mahler Director-General of the World Health Organization in Presenting His Report for 1978 and 1979 to the Thirty-Third World Health Assembly.* WHA33/DIV/4. Geneva: WHO.

World Health Organization (1984). *Proposed Programme Budget for the Financial Period 1986–1987.* PB/86–87. Geneva: WHO.

World Health Organization (1985). *Handbook of Resolutions and Decisions of the World Health Assembly and the Executive Board: Volume II 1973–1984.* Geneva: WHO.

World Health Organization (1986). *Proposed Programme Budget for the Financial Period 1988–1989.* PB/88–89. Geneva: WHO.

World Health Organization (1987a). *Appointment of all Regional Directors: Note by the Director-General.* EB81/6. Geneva: WHO.

World Health Organization (1987b). *Executive Board, Seventy-ninth Session. Provisional Summary Record of the First Meeting.* EB79/SR/1. Geneva: WHO.

World Health Organization (1987c). *Executive Board: Provisional Summary Records of the Twenty-first Meeting.* EB79/SR21. Geneva: WHO.

World Health Organization (1987d). *Management of WHO's Resources.* EB81/PC/WP/2. Geneva: WHO.

World Health Organization (1987e). *Management of WHO's Resources and Review of the Organization's Structure: Consolidated Regional Committee Reports Presented by the Director-General.* EB81/7. Geneva: WHO.

World Health Organization (1987f). *Management of WHO's Resources and Review of the Organization's Structure: Report by the Programme Committee of the Executive Board.* EB81/4. Geneva: WHO.

World Health Organization (1987g). *Review of the Organization's Structure.* EB81/PC/WP/4. Geneva: WHO.

World Health Organization (1987h). *World Health for All: To Be!: Address by Dr H. Mahler, Director-General of the World Health Organization in Presenting His Report for 1986 to the Fortieth World Health Assembly.* WHA40/DIV/4. Geneva: WHO.

World Health Organization (1988). *Executive Board, Eighty-first Session: Provisional Summary Record of the Tenth Meeting.* EB81/SR/10. Geneva: WHO.

World Health Organization (1989). *Executive Board. Eighty-Third Session. Geneva, 9–20 January 1989.* EB83/1989/REC/1. Geneva: WHO.

World Health Organization (1993). *WHO Response to Global Change: Delegation of Authority (implementation of recommendations 23 and 28). Report by the Director-General.* EB93/11 Add.9. Geneva: WHO.

World Health Organization (1994). *Executive Board, Ninety-third session. Geneva 17–26 January 1994: Summary Records.* EB93/1994/REC/2. Geneva: WHO.

World Health Organization (1997). *Review of the Constitution and regional arrangements of the World Health Organization.* EB101/7. Geneva: WHO.

World Health Organization (1998a). *Amendments to the Rules of Procedure of the Executive Board: the term of office of Regional Directors: Report by the Director-General.* EB102/5. Geneva: WHO.

World Health Organization (1998b). *Dr Gro Harlem Brundtland, Director-General Elect. The World Health Organization. Speech to the Fifty-first World Health Assembly. Geneva, 13 May 1998.* A51/DIV/6. Geneva: WHO.

World Health Organization (1999a). *A Corporate Strategy for the WHO Secretariat: Report by the Director-General.* EB105/3. Geneva: WHO.

World Health Organization (1999b). *Executive Board, 103rd Session, 26 January 1999. Agenda Item 5. Proposed Budget 2000–2001: Devolution of Administrative and Management Functions to Management Support Units.* Geneva: WHO.

World Health Organization (1999c). *Executive Board, 103rd Session. Geneva, 25 January to 1 February 1999. Summary Records.* EB103/1999/REC/2. Geneva: WHO.

World Health Organization (1999d). *Human Resources: Annual Report. Report by the Secretariat.* EB105/14. Geneva: WHO.

World Health Organization (1999e). *Proposed Programme Budget 2000–2001.* Geneva: WHO.

World Health Organization (1999f). *The World Health Report 1999: Making a Difference.* Geneva: WHO.

World Health Organization (1999g). *WHO—the way ahead: Statement by the Director-General to the Executive Board at its 103rd Session. Geneva, Monday, 25 January 1999.* EB103/2. Geneva: WHO.

World Health Organization (2000a). *Executive Board, 105th Session, 26 January 2000. Provisional Summary Records of the Sixth Meeting.* EB105/SR/6. Geneva: WHO.

World Health Organization (2000b). *Implementing the Corporate Strategy: Work on the Programme Budget 2002–2003: Report by the Secretariat.* EB106/2. Geneva: WHO.

WHO Commission on Macroeconomics and Health (2001). *Macroeconomics and Health: Investing in Health for Economic Development. Report of the Commission on Macroeconomics and Health.* Geneva: WHO.

WHO Regional Office for the Western Pacific (1987). *Closing the Ranks for Health for All: Address by Dr H. Mahler Director-General of the World Health Organization.* WPR/RC38/SR/9. Geneva: WHO.

World Health Organization (2001a). *Address by Dr Gro Harlem Brundtland, Director-General, to the Fifty-Fourth World Health Assembly.* A54/3. Geneva: WHO.

World Health Organization (2001b). *Executive Board, 107th Meeting, Provisional Summary Records of the 6th Session, January 2001.* EB107/SR/5. Geneva: WHO.

World Health Organization (2001c). *Programme Budget 2002–2003.* EB107/INF.DOC./9 Annex. Geneva: WHO.

World Health Organization (2001d). *Statement by the representative of the WHO staff association on matters concerning personnel policy and conditions of service: Executive Board, 108th Session, 23 May 2001.* EB108/INF.DOC./1. Geneva: WHO.

World Health Organization (2005). *Proposed Programme Budget 2006–2007.* Geneva: WHO.

World Health Organization (2006). *Constitution of the World Health Organization.* Supplement, Forty-fifth edition of "Basic Documents." Geneva: WHO.

World Health Organization (2008a). *Primary Health Care: Now More Than Ever: The World Health Report 2008.* Geneva: WHO.

World Health Organization (2008b). *The Third Ten Years of the World Health Organization: 1968–1977.* Geneva: WHO.

World Health Organization (2009). *Medium-term Strategic Plan 2008–2013 (amended draft).* Geneva: WHO.

World Health Organization (2010). *The Future of Financing for WHO. Report of an Informal Consultation Convened by the Director-General, Geneva, Switzerland, 12–13 January 2010.* WHO/DGO/2010.1. Geneva: WHO.

World Health Organization (2011a). *Historical agreements at the Sixty-fourth World Health Assembly. Dr Margaret Chan, Director-General of the World Health Organization: Closing remarks at the Sixty-fourth World Health Assembly Geneva, Switzerland.* Geneva, available at: <http://www.who.int/dg/speeches/2011/wha_20110524/en/index.html>.

World Health Organization (2011b). *Medium-term Strategic Plan and Proposed Programme Budget 2012–2013: Proposed Programme Budget 2013.* Geneva: WHO.

World Health Organization (2011c). *Report by the Director-General to the Executive Board at its 128th session.* EB128/2. Geneva: WHO.

World Health Organization (2011d). *The Fourth Ten Years of the World Health Organization: 1978–1987.* Geneva: WHO.

World Health Organization (2011f). *Dr Margaret Chan introduces proposed reforms for WHO priorities.* Geneva, available at: <http://www.who.int/dg/speeches/2011/reform_priorities_01_11/en/>.

World Health Organization (2014a). *WHO Reform: Progress Report on Reform Implementation. Report by the Director-General.* Geneva: WHO.

World Health Organization (2014b). *Financial Report and Audited Financial Statements for the Year Ended December 2013.* Geneva: WHO.

Yamey, G. (2002a). "Faltering Steps Towards Partnerships." *British Medical Journal* 325 (7374): pp. 1236–40.

Yamey, G. (2002b). "Have the Latest Reforms Reversed WHO's Decline?" *British Medical Journal* 325 (7372): pp. 1107–12.

Yamey, G. (2002c). "WHO's Management: Struggling to Transform a 'Fossilized Bureaucracy'." *British Medical Journal* 325 (7373): pp. 1170–3.

Yamey, G. and Abbasi, K. (2003). "New Leader, New Hope for WHO: Setting an Agenda for Jong-Wook Lee." *British Medical Journal* 326 (7399): pp. 1251–2.

Zapf, D. (2004). *The Geneva Staff Association Survey of Harrassment in the Workplace: Results of the Quantitative Survey Components.* Geneva: The World Health Organization Staff Association.

Zürn, M. (2015). "Historical Institutionalism and IR: Strange Bedfellows?" In: *Explaining Institutional Change in World Politics: Historical Institutionalism and International Relations,* edited by Thomas Rixen, Lora Viola and Michael Zürn: book manuscript.

Zürn, M., Binder, M., and Ecker-Ehrhardt, M. (2012). "International Authority and Its Politicization." *International Theory* 4 (1): pp. 69–106.

Zürn, M. and Faude, B. (2013). "On Fragmentation, Differentiation, and Coordination." *Global Environmental Politics* 13 (3): pp. 119–30.

Index

Note: Page numbers followed by *f* or *t* indicate figures or tables

Rockefeller Foundation 59, 91, 103, 107 n. 13
Roll Back Malaria Partnership (RBM) 8, 106, 111

Sachs, Jeffrey 99
Scharpf, Fritz 38
sectors in UNESCO 2, 13–14, 22, 34–5, 46, 117, 129–36
Selective Primary Health Care (SPHC) 91, 99
    in comparison to Primary Health Care (PHC) 101*t*
Smallpox Eradication Programme 74 n. 3, 91
Soper, Fred 59–61
Soviet states at the WHO 56, 58, 64, 78, 82 n. 10
Soviet states at UNESCO 130
special programs of the WHO 2, 5, 8–11, 12, 22, 107–14
    historical origins of the WHO's special programs 10 n. 15
Spellman, Archbishop 47
Strange, Susan 28

Technical Preparatory Committee (TPC) 49, 55–6
    British, French, Yugoslavian and US drafts for the TPC 55
Thomas, Albert 123
trans–organizational networks 23, 146–7

United Nations Children's Fund (UNICEF) 4, 10, 51 n. 7, 59, 76–8, 96, 106
United Nations Development Group 120
United Nations Development Programme (UNDP) 81 n. 9, 84 n. 12 96–7, 136–7
United Nations Joint Inspection Unit (JIU) 8, 86–7
United States (US) government 8, 14–15, 21, 22, 29, 55, 58, 59, 65, 68–9, 97, 122 n. 4, 132, 135
    US and Guyanese centralization attempt in the WHO 88–9
    US General Accounting Office (GAO) 132–3
    US Public Health Service 54
    US Surgeon General 54

vested interests 1, 2, 24, 31, 35, 48, 65–6, 85
veto positions 13, 29, 31, 36–7, 38–9

Weaver, Catherine 20–1 n. 20, 112 n. 20
Wolfensohn, James D. 36
WHO historical development (overview) 45*f*
WHO organizational chart 52*f*
WHO–PASO Agreement 60–1, 64
World Bank 2, 4, 33, 36, 40, 74, 91, 96, 99, 141
World Health Assembly (WHA) 4, 6, 20, 51, 57, 62–3, 66, 78, 79, 80, 85, 105, 108

HARVARD UNIVERSITY

http://lib.harvard.edu

**If the item is recalled, the borrower will
be notified of the need for an earlier return.**

Thank you for helping us to preserve our collection!